Forgiven But Not Forgotten

Forgiven But Not Forgotten

The Past Is Not Past

Ambrose Mong

FOREWORD BY
George Yeo

WIPF & STOCK · Eugene, Oregon

FORGIVEN BUT NOT FORGOTTEN
The Past Is Not Past

Copyright © 2020 Ambrose Mong. All rights reserved. Except for brief quotations in critical publications or reviews, no part of this book may be reproduced in any manner without prior written permission from the publisher. Write: Permissions, Wipf and Stock Publishers, 199 W. 8th Ave., Suite 3, Eugene, OR 97401.

Wipf & Stock
An Imprint of Wipf and Stock Publishers
199 W. 8th Ave., Suite 3
Eugene, OR 97401

www.wipfandstock.com

PAPERBACK ISBN: 978-1-7252-8341-1
HARDCOVER ISBN: 978-1-7252-8340-4
EBOOK ISBN: 978-1-7252-8342-8

Cataloguing-in-Publication data:

Names: Mong, Ambrose Ih-Ren, 1959–, author. | Yeo, George, foreword writer.

Title: Forgiven but not forgotten : the past is not past / by Ambrose Mong ; foreword by George Yeo.

Description: Eugene, OR: Wipf & Stock, 2020 | Includes bibliographical references and index.

Identifiers: ISBN 978-1-7252-8341-1 (paperback) | ISBN 978-1-7252-8340-4 (hardcover) | ISBN 978-1-7252-8342-8 (ebook)

Subjects: LCSH: Forgiveness. | Reconciliation. | Forgiveness—Religious aspects—Christianity. | Reconciliation—Religious aspects—Christianity. | Forgiveness—Political aspects. | Reconciliation—Social aspects. | Postwar reconstruction.

Classification: LCC BJ1476 M66 2020 (print) | LCC BJ1476 (ebook)

Manufactured in the U.S.A. 11/23/20

For the Brothers and Novices of the Montfort Brothers
of Saint Gabriel, India (1978–1980)

In Memory of Brother Joseph John (1940–1996)

Everyone thinks forgiveness is a lovely idea until he has something to forgive.

—C.S. Lewis, *Mere Christianity*

Contents

Foreword by George Yeo | ix
Preface and Acknowledgements | xi
Introduction | xv

Chapter 1: The Sunflower: The Holocaust | 1
Chapter 2: No Future without Forgiveness: Apartheid in South Africa | 22
Chapter 3: Power of Peace: Conflict in Ireland | 45
Chapter 4: *Nunca Más*: Civil War in Guatemala | 66
Chapter 5: The Crucified People: State Oppression in El Salvador | 89
Chapter 6: From Denunciation to Dialogue: Division in the Catholic Church in China | 115
Epilogue | 143

Bibliography | 149
Index | 159

Foreword

Fr. Ambrose Mong was persuaded by a Hong Kong university professor to write this book on forgiveness and reconciliation. *Forgiven but Not Forgotten* begins and ends with Hong Kong, where Fr. Ambrose lives. Here, as a pastor, he confronts every day the passions of a divided society. Each side feels itself wronged; each insists on selective justice almost as a form of revenge for hurts and grievances. With the Covid-19 pandemic and the imposition of a national security law, there is also exhaustion and despair. Before there can be reconciliation, the past has to be confronted, like a splinter that has to be removed from a wound before it can heal.

The challenges facing Hong Kong are part of the human condition. In his book, Fr. Ambrose takes us through the trials and travails of human beings trapped in circumstances much worse than ours—the horror of the Holocaust, the inhumanity of apartheid in South Africa, sectarian divide in Northern Ireland, mass slaughter of the poor in Central America (including priests who advocated their cause), and the pain of a divided Catholic Church in China. The objective is not to preach but to reflect. In every case, there are wrenching moral dilemmas that admit of no easy solution. The problems are never completely resolved but, with reconciliation, there is hope for a better future. When others in more intractable situations can find a way out, so perhaps can we in our situation. That I read to be Fr. Ambrose's message for the people of Hong Kong.

In his Introduction, Fr. Ambrose writes that "there is no peace without justice, no justice without forgiveness." It sounds so simple, but it is so hard. It is hard enough to forgive after the offending party has been punished or has made restitution. It is almost impossible, humanly speaking, to forgive unconditionally, the way Jesus Christ did on the cross. Jesus taught us to say in the Our Father, "forgive us our trespasses, *as we forgive those who trespass against us.*" Jesus did not add "provided that . . . ." The wound in those who cannot forgive cannot heal. Forgiving is therefore self-healing. It gives us peace. Peace in the world begins with us and spread to others. This Christian insight is at the core of Fr. Ambrose's book. It is not a prescription but an admonition.

George Yeo
Singapore Foreign Minister (2004–11)

Preface and Acknowledgments

The bonds that bind society are very fragile, for the ties that unite us as people and prevent us from killing each other out of jealousy or envy can easily be broken. Therefore, among other things, a level playing field where everyone has a chance to succeed through equal opportunities in education and employment is crucial in maintaining social harmony. Hence, I would argue that the unrest in Hong Kong today is symptomatic of the unequal distribution of wealth arising from the greed of financial oligarchs and property developers colluding with senior government officials. The situation is further exacerbated by the influx of rich Chinese mainlanders who come to buy anything and everything, but especially property, which is a contributory factor to the phenomenon of many Hong Kong residents being unable to afford an apartment or raise a family without resorting to heavy mortgages or other financial encumbrances.

Thomas Hobbes, the seventeenth-century English philosopher, believed that the "state of war was the natural state of human beings and that harmony among human beings is artificial because it is based on an agreement." Hobbes advocated an absolute monarchy to counteract the fact that human beings, at their core, are selfish, brutal, and irrational. Here in Hong Kong, in the summer of 2019, we witnessed the wanton violence and mindless destruction of private and public property, which would seem to bear out Hobbes' assertion. Nowadays many people feel that the autonomy of Hong Kong guaranteed by the Basic Law has been undermined, first by the proposed Extradition Bill and more recently, by the new National Security Law that has come into effect. The government seems ineffectual while desperately appealing to the good sense of the people. The harmony of the people is under threat because the "agreement" that Hobbes refers to is seemingly being broken. The words of the Irish poet W. B. Yeats aptly describe the situation in the Fragrant Harbor:

> Turning and turning in the widening gyre
> The falcon cannot hear the falconer;
> Things fall apart; the centre cannot hold;
> Mere anarchy is loosed upon the world,
> The blood-dimmed tide is loosed, and everywhere
> The ceremony of innocence is drowned;
> The best lack all conviction, while the worst
> Are full of passionate intensity.
>
> —"The Second Coming" 1919

In view of the violent protests in 2019, Professor Lai Pan-chiu from The Chinese University of Hong Kong urged me to write about the issue of forgiveness and reconciliation in society. Ironically, it is the pandemic caused by the spread of Covid-19 that has provided us with respite from the uprisings—a brief period of anxious peace. The partial lockdown and social distancing have also given me space and time to act on Professor Lai's suggestion by researching and writing the following chapters.

Many people have assisted me with this project. Special thanks to Ellen McGill and Kenzie Lau for proofreading and editorial assistance. I would also like to thank the following, who have encouraged and supported me in my writing endeavors all these years: Denis Chang SC, George Yeo, Patrick Tierney FSC, Marie Whitcomb, Columba Cleary OP, Mary Gillis CND, Anthony Tan FMS, Wendy Wu, Teresa Au, Henry So, Ronnie Enguillo, Sylvia Lam, Garrison Qian, Teoh Chin Chin, James Boey, Josephine Chan, William Chan, Judy Chan, Charles Chu, Lothair Leung, Juliana Jie, Matthew Goldammer, K. S Goh, Esther Chu, Francis Chin, Gerard Lee, Philip Lee, Judy Lee, John Tan, George Tan, Leo Tan, Catherine Yau, Marina Kwan, Adelaide Wong, Gemma Yim, Henrietta Cheung, Abraham Shek, Vivencio Atutubo, and Emmanuel Dispo. Thanks also to the Parish Priest of St. Andrew's Church, Rev. Jacob Kwok and my colleagues, Rev. Mitch Reginio CICM and Rev. Joseph Fung, for their fellowship and care.

PREFACE AND ACKNOWLEDGMENTS

Last but not least, I owe my thanks to Robin Parry, my editor, Calvin Jaffarian, George Callihan, and the dedicated staff at Wipf & Stock Publishers for bringing this modest work into print. Any errors that remain are, of course, my own.

Ambrose Mong
All Souls' Day 2020

Introduction

The Past Is Not Past, the sub-title of this book, is adapted from William Faulkner's play, *Requiem for a Nun*: "The past is never dead; it's not even past." And according to George Santayana, "those who cannot remember the past are condemned to repeat it." Forgiveness, in politics, is not about forgetting; it is about how we remember events that have hurt us or killed our fellow brothers and sisters, so that the truth will set us free.

This work explores issues of forgiveness and reconciliation in countries that have experienced political conflicts, civil war, and even genocide. It attempts to move beyond mere abstracts by examining case studies and the initiatives taken to promote dialogue and reconciliation. In many such cases, religion can be a force for peace and play a significant role in resolving conflicts. This book also examines the relationship between justice and forgiveness, emphasizing that there can be no peace without justice and no justice without forgiveness. Human justice is fragile. Thus, respect for rights and responsibilities must include forgiveness, in order to heal and restore relationships.

At the personal level, forgiveness is understood to be a process that recognizes an injury has occurred and requires that the offence be acknowledged and the wrongdoer held accountable. By being forgiven, the wrongdoer is released from the negative psychological effects of the offence. Forgiveness begins with the will to forgive and reaches fulfilment when all feelings of resentment, anger, and hostility disappear. This normally occurs when the wrongdoer repents, suffers remorse, and apologizes sincerely. It is also possible for a person to forgive unconditionally without repentance on the part of the wrongdoer. Forgiveness lies within the power of the person who has been wronged. Reconciliation, however, requires the consent of both parties, the victim and the perpetrator.

It may seem odd to talk about forgiveness in the context of social and political struggles as we often associate it with the restoration of a relationship between two individuals. However, as we shall discuss, there is no future without forgiveness for many countries afflicted by decades of atrocities and violations of human rights. Many conflicts cannot be resolved with statecraft or political strategies. This has, therefore, created opportunities for local communities, non-governmental organizations, and truth and reconciliation commissions, backed by the United Nations, to promote forgiveness as a remedy for societies traumatized by violence. The meaning of forgiveness in this case is not confined to possessing a religious virtue but relates to how we cooperate with each other as a community.

In the political context, forgiveness involves turning from the past without forgetting or excusing the evil committed. It also does not overlook justice or merely reduce justice to punishment of the perpetrator. Forgiveness, in the context of promoting restorative justice, attempts to look upon our enemies as fellow human beings, even if they have committed hideous crimes against humanity.

The French philosopher Jacques Derrida (1930–2004) points out that forgiveness is an ambiguous word that has its roots in the Abrahamic religious traditions of Judaism, Christianity, and Islam. It has also become a common theme in law, politics, economics, and diplomacy, even in countries where the Abrahamic traditions are not dominant. In fact, seeking forgiveness or being forgiven has become a global phenomenon. The widespread incidence of repentance and forgiveness demonstrates the importance of not forgetting the past.

Since the twentieth century, grand acts of forgiveness and repentance are played out internationally. They signify a sincere desire for reconciliation and the restoration of relationships. However, "the simulacra, the automatic ritual, hypocrisy, calculation, or mimicry are often a part, and invite parasites to this ceremony of culpability."[1] In other words, forgiveness can be used to cover up injustice and exploitation. Further, Derrida thinks that if we begin to accuse ourselves and to ask for forgiveness for all the crimes against humanity we have committed collectively, there will be no innocent people left to judge or arbitrate.

---

1. Derrida, *On Cosmopolitanism and Forgiveness*, 29.

INTRODUCTION

Forgiveness has become a global concept affecting even nations with no Christian heritage. Secularization has not affected our use of such a concept. Yet forgiveness implies doing the impossible. It is because we are able to do the impossible, by the grace of God, that forgiveness is such an important, worthwhile project. Forgiveness, therefore, is not to be equated with cheap grace.

We are taught to forgive only when there is repentance on the part of the wrongdoer and at the same time we are also taught to forgive unconditionally—this, it seems, both affirms and contradicts the Abrahamic tradition. Further, do we forgive the offence, wrong, crime, or fault, or do we forgive the person who did us wrong? From whom do we seek forgiveness, the victim or God himself?

Due to its ambiguity and inherent contradiction, "forgiveness" has become a very much abused concept in the political arena. Negotiations and carefully calculated transactions are commonly linked to talk of forgiveness and national reconciliation—the whole process is actually fraught with hypocrisy, deceit, and self-interest. This kind of abuse occurred, for example, in Latin American countries where military-backed governments called for sweeping amnesties for themselves and their agents who committed crimes against humanity.

In view of the above, some thinkers treat forgiveness as a defective moral ideal that goes against justice because it shelters the wrongdoer from moral responsibility. The offender escapes punishment and does not feel remorse for the harm he or she has done to the victim. Friedrich Nietzsche (1844–1900) even regarded forgiveness as a sign of weakness. Forgiveness is morally wrong, he argued, because it refuses to denounce the wrong that has been committed. He maintains it is psychologically unhealthy because it makes people suppress their desire for revenge or retribution. Critical of Christianity, Nietzsche believed it encourages submissiveness when people allow themselves to be victimized.

Nevertheless, as a virtue, forgiveness helps us to overcome anger, indignation, or resentment that might be detrimental to our mental health. Forgiveness can help to save marriages and friendships. It does not condone offences nor withhold correct judgment from the wrongdoer. The reasons to forgive are repentance of the wrongdoer, the remorse of the wrongdoer, a sense of our shared humanity in that we ourselves also expect to be forgiven, and our relationship with the offender. It has been discovered that the mental and emotional states of people who cannot forgive are grievously affected. They are not able to overcome the feelings of anger, resentment, pain, and bitterness associated with being exploited, persecuted, harmed, or offended. On the contrary, those able to forgive find their psychological health improved.

In the Old Testament, forgiveness means forgiveness by God through the cancellation of our sins on the condition that we repent. This also applies to interpersonal forgiveness—the condition of repentance is *sine qua non*. The offended individual has the duty to forgive if the wrongdoer seeks his or her forgiveness, showing genuine remorse and repentance. Imitating divine forgiveness, the followers of Judaism and Christianity must also forgive, so that the relationship of reciprocal love can be restored. The New Testament, however, teaches that interpersonal forgiveness should be unconditional—repentance is not a necessary prerequisite for forgiveness: "be kind to one another, tender-hearted, forgiving one another, as God in Christ has forgiven you" (Eph 4:32); "And when you were dead in trespasses and the uncircumcision of your flesh, God made you alive together with him, when he forgave us all our trespasses" (Col 2:13). The idea of forgiveness is associated with reconciliation. In fact, reconciliation, the restoration of a broken relationship, should be the ultimate goal of forgiveness.

In the Gospel of Matthew, Jesus urges his followers to seek reconciliation if they have offended or sinned against another. This is the condition for divine forgiveness if the wrongdoer, in his turn, wants to be forgiven by God. "For if you forgive others their trespasses, your heavenly Father will also forgive you; but if you do not forgive others, neither will your Father forgive your trespasses" (Matt 6:14). Reconciliation cannot take place if the wrongdoer does not feel remorse or repent, though forgiveness is possible. Jesus made clear to his disciples that forgiveness must be the defining principle of their lives.

In secular literature, forgiveness includes giving up one's right to hit back or take revenge in response to an offence. Similar to a cancellation of debt, forgiveness is an active and conscious choice. It is different from pardon, which has a judicial connotation—only legal authorities can grant a pardon as a form of leniency or mercy.

By the mid-twentieth century, forgiveness was not perceived to exist exclusively within a religious context. There was a realization that there is a connection between forgiveness and psychological health. Further, forgiveness is not limited to interpersonal relationships but concerns the relations between nations, communities, and organizations as well. If individuals can forgive wrongdoing and offences, so can ethnic groups or nations.

In the aftermath of the Second World War, after the atomic bombings of Hiroshima and Nagasaki on August 6 and 9, 1945, people realized that nations needed to resolve the causes of conflict peacefully if they were not to destroy the whole planet. Reconciliation between nations is thus vital for the survival of humanity. The idea of forgiveness is now a matter of public discourse, as this book seeks to demonstrate. The underlying premise is that forgiveness and reconciliation can be a powerful tool to assist conflict resolution.

Outline and Sequence of Chapters

Chapter 1 examines Simon Wiesenthal's book, *The Sunflowers: On the Possibilities and Limits of Forgiveness*. This work is about the author's encounter with a Nazi SS soldier dying in a hospital who sought Wiesenthal's forgiveness for killing Jews, especially women and children. My opening chapter explores whether forgiveness is possible given the gravity and enormity of the crime committed by the Nazi regime against humanity. Focusing on the role of remembrance in the *Shoah* as a reminder that such crimes against humanity should not be repeated, the chapter emphasizes that forgiving is not forgetting because "the past is not past."

With reference to South Africa, a nation torn apart by racial segregation, chapter 2 discusses Archbishop Desmond Tutu's book, *No Future without Forgiveness*. While acknowledging that Christianity is a major influence in uniting the various communities in South Africa, this chapter seeks to show that the traditional African virtue of *ubuntu* or a sense of interconnectedness has also played a significant role in healing the people. This is the story of a successful integration of the African philosophy of humanity with the Christian concept of forgiveness.

Northern Ireland has a long history of conflict and sectarian violence between Protestant loyalists and Catholic nationalists. Chapter 3 examines the work of Fr. Alec Reid, who led the peace process within the Catholic nationalist community. It also discusses the success and failure of churches in promoting peace and reconciliation. Highlighting the efforts of both the Irish and British governments, this chapter seeks to show the importance of establishing socio-political structures that uphold social justice and equality.

INTRODUCTION

Guatemala, a compact Central American state, also suffered military repression from 1954 to 1985. Chapter 4 discusses the works of Rigoberta Menchú, a Quiché Maya and native Guatemalan, who has written two books, *I, Rigoberta Menchú* and *Crossing Borders*, describing the genocide committed by the army in her country. A Nobel Peace Prize winner in 1992, Menchú is an advocate for indigenous people and played a prominent role in promoting reconciliation among the various political groups, including the military, in Guatemala. The chapter also highlights the role of the Catholic Church and in particular of Bishop Juan José Gerard, who was brutally murdered for telling the truth about the atrocities committed by the army.

The civil war in nearby El Salvador lasted from 1980 to 1992 and gave rise to the killing of more than 75,000 people and the disappearance of another 8,000. These years of violence included the assassination of Archbishop Óscar Romero in 1980, the rape and murder of four American church women in the same year, and the 1989 massacre of six Jesuits, their housekeeper, and her daughter at Central American University. Chapter 5 examines the life and teaching of Archbishop Romero, who was regarded as "the voice of the voiceless," a martyr and saint even before he was beatified and canonized by the Church. Convinced that forgiveness and reconciliation can only exist in society when there is justice and truth, Romero denounced the government and the military for fraud and violation of human rights. His killing inspired the Church to expand its traditional understanding of martyrdom.

Never giving up hope in his people or even their enemies, Romero believed a better world was possible in El Salvador. Among liberation theologians inspired by Romero was the Jesuit rector of the University of Central America, Ignacio Ellacuría, who was also an outspoken critic of the Salvadoran army.

Chapter 6 discusses the Chinese Communist Party's persecution of the Catholic clergy and laity and the formation of the Catholic Patriotic Association in 1957 as a means of controlling the religious life of the people. The Communist Party has not succeeded in destroying the Catholic Church in China, but it has succeeded in dividing it. Pope Benedict XVI and Pope Francis also expressed their desire to enter into dialogue with the Chinese government, which culminated in the Provisional Agreement in 2018. It remains to be seen where this Agreement will take us. In conclusion, this work seeks to emphasize the importance of reconciliation between the demonstrators and the Hong Kong government in a city divided by economic disparity and political ideology.

— *Chapter 1* —

The Sunflower

The Holocaust

Well known for his work in identifying and locating Nazi war criminals, Simon Wiesenthal, a Jewish Austrian, authored the simple and yet gripping book, *The Sunflower: On the Possibilities and Limits of Forgiveness*. It is an account of his encounter in 1944 with Karl, a Nazi SS soldier, who was dying in the hospital and wanted to confess his crimes to a member of the Jewish community in order to seek forgiveness and be released from guilt.

In this chapter, we will examine *The Sunflower* and Wiesenthal's contributions to the complex issue of forgiveness. Given the gravity and enormity of the crimes committed by the Nazi regime against the Jewish population, forgiveness is not easy. And even if it is possible, should one forget the atrocities and heinous crimes committed during the Holocaust? Despite difficulties and impediments, could forgiveness be a healthier, more virtuous option to break the vicious cycle of hatred and revenge? This chapter discusses the role of remembrance in the *Shoah* as a reminder that such crimes against humanity should never occur again.

Simon Wiesenthal, a Jewish prisoner in a concentration camp in Poland, was sent to clean a makeshift hospital for wounded German soldiers. The building had been a technical high school where Simon had once been a pupil, and being there brought back memories of anti-Semitic propaganda from his childhood: he recalled the "day without Jews," a festival created by radical nationalists to reduce the number of

Jewish academics.[1] This is the beginning of a story about the purification of memories as the author attempts to come to terms with the realities of life in the concentration camp.

On his way to the hospital, Simon noticed a cemetery for dead German soldiers where, on each grave, a sunflower had been planted: "Each had a sunflower to connect him with the living world, and butterflies to visit his grave."[2] Simon looked back in pain and bitterness, reflecting that even in death, the Nazi murderers were treated better than the Jews, who were buried in nameless mass graves. Through the sunflowers, the deceased Germans were somehow still linked to the world of the living, whereas the Jews were consigned to oblivion. Nonetheless, Simon asked this poignant question: "Was there in fact any personal relationship between us, between the murderers and their victims?"[3] If there was a personal relationship, then there could be the possibility of forgiveness. Few are born murderers; most become one through exposure to or indoctrination in evil. Simon recognized the common humanity shared by both perpetrators of crimes and their victims.

Accompanied by a nurse, Simon arrived at the hospital and walked through the hallways into a room where he came face to face with a dying German solider, a twenty-one-year-old SS man named Karl. Wrapped in bandages that covered his eyes and head, Karl struggled to confess his horrendous crimes to Simon, the Jew. Karl was consumed with the guilt and shame of having taken part in a mass slaughtering of innocent Jewish people, especially children, women, and the aged. He was tortured by gruesome memories and images of hundreds of screaming parents and children just before they died while trying to flee from a burning building torched by the Nazis. "In that moment I saw the burning family, the father with the child and behind them the mother—and they came to meet me."[4] Karl was later mortally wounded and blinded by an exploding shell because he could not bring himself to shoot another group of Jews.

This story is also about the yearning to purify one's memories in order to obtain relief before death: "Here lay a man in bed who wished to die in peace, but he could not, because the memory of his terrible crime gave

---

1. Wiesenthal, *The Sunflower*, 19.
2. Wiesenthal, *The Sunflower*, 14.
3. Wiesenthal, *The Sunflower*, 7.
4. Wiesenthal, *The Sunflower*, 51.

him no rest."[5] "Yes, now I remembered!" As Simon recorded the bits and pieces of news or information circulated in the concentration camp and in the ghetto, the theme of remembering and forgetting was carefully woven into the narration of the story.[6]

Profoundly moved by Karl's confession, yet at the same time repelled by his horrifying story, Simon was able to see the man's repentance. Simon's thoughts kept returning to the sunflowers planted in the cemetery of the dead soldiers, reinforcing the contrasting worlds of the Germans and the Jews: the deceased German soldiers have sunflowers planted on individual graves, and the Jews were murdered and buried in mass graves.

All through Karl's narration, Simon kept still and silent. Anxious to confess and beg forgiveness, Karl seemed repentant and longed to rest in peace. Simon believed he was "a murderer who did not want to be a murderer but who had been made into a murderer by a murderous ideology."[7] As he left Karl without saying a word, he was troubled and haunted by doubts about what he had failed to do, that is, to forgive Karl's heinous crimes towards the Jews. Returning to the camp, Simon asked his fellow inmates what they would have done. Most of them felt he had done the right thing—kept silent, refused to forgive the young SS man.

After the war, Simon visited Karl's mother to find out more about his character. The mother's testimony on the goodness of her son confirmed Karl's honest narration about his family background. Karl had actually joined Hitler's army in spite of his father's strong objection. By this time, Simon had taken up the task of tracking down Nazi war criminals to bring them to justice. He was deeply disturbed by the lack of remorse in most of the Nazis who were brought to trial. As with Karl, the SS man, Simon continued to ask himself at the end of the story: "Ought I to have forgiven him?"[8] Reflecting on the many kinds of silence, he wondered if his own silence was more eloquent than words.

Convinced that only those who have suffered are entitled to forgive, Simon continued to wrestle with the issue of forgiveness. He then sought responses from his readers and other prominent people twenty-five years after the Holocaust. Below are some of the responses from famous academics, clerics, critics, survivors, and victims of attempted genocides to

5. Wiesenthal, *The Sunflower*, 54.
6. Wiesenthal, *The Sunflower*, 3.
7. Wiesenthal, *The Sunflower*, 53.
8. Wiesenthal, *The Sunflower*, 97.

Simon Wiesenthal's question: "What would I have done?"[9] What would *you* have done? While many of the respondents are from Judeo-Christian tradition, there are a few who are secular.

Possibilities of Forgiveness

Sven Alkalaj, a Bosnian diplomat, witnessed the genocide in Bosnia and Herzegovina. He asserted that only those who had lived through the Holocaust have the right to respond to the question of forgiveness. People who did not experience such mass murder of innocent people cannot understand fully the atrocities and appalling madness. Forgetting the crimes would be worse than forgiving the criminals, because such crimes insult humanity. Alkalaj insisted Simon had no right to forgive the SS man on behalf of the victims. Nonetheless, Alkalaj conceded there is a possibility of forgiveness if there is true repentance, which should lead to reconciliation.

Jean Améry, an Austrian critic and essayist, offered two aspects to deliberate: psychological and political. The psychological aspect is related to emotion or temperament. This means that Simon might have forgiven on another occasion when his sympathy and compassion could be drawn out by the pitiful state of the SS man. Politically, forgiving and not forgiving are irrelevant because forgiveness is related to the realm of guilt and atonement, a theological issue. As an atheist, Améry is indifferent to the idea of forgiveness. However, if the SS man asked for his forgiveness, he would grant it, to let him rest in peace. Yet politically, this makes no difference to him.

There is no such thing as collective guilt, claimed Smail Balić, a Bosnian-Austrian scholar, because no individual carries the sins of another. One can speak of general culpability when a society tolerates the perpetuation of crimes and wrongdoings. But rectifying an offence can be possible only between the offender and the offended. For Balić, the crimes committed during the Holocaust and other cases of genocide are so enormous that only God in his infinite mercy can forgive.

Alan L. Berger, a scholar of Holocaust Studies in the United States, also insisted that one could not, and should not, forgive on behalf of the Jews who were slaughtered. In asking for forgiveness, Karl is actually perpetuating the Nazi stereotype of Jewish people as masses or hordes, not as individuals with their own thoughts and feelings. He was purifying his own soul at the expense of a Jew. Berger maintained that Karl was

---

9. Wiesenthal, *The Sunflower*, 98.

not truly repentant and had no moral courage because he could have disobeyed orders as others did. Berger added that repentance is just a ritual that soothes the conscience of the murderer but does nothing for the victim. Critical of the Catholic Church, Berger said "forgive and forget" is "cheap grace", i.e., preaching forgiveness without requiring repentance and contrition, and should not be recommended.

Never forgive seems to be logical because forgiveness can be seen as a weakness, a sign that people can go on committing crimes and be let off. It is a moral escape route that permits evil to survive and thrive, according to Robert McAfee Brown, an American theologian. However, as a Christian, he felt rather uneasy about this logical conviction. He thought there are situations where sacrificial love, forgiving from the heart, can make a difference to human existence. For example, Nelson Mandela, a South African anti-apartheid revolutionary and political leader who was released from prison after twenty-seven years, was able to forgive his enemies. Tomás Borge, a Nicaraguan Sandinista fighter, "punished" his captors by forgiving them. These acts of compassion and forgiveness built up moral capital that we can draw on and are examples we can imitate. Hence, for Brown, *Never forgive* should be the exception rather than the rule. If he were in Simon's shoes, he would urge Karl to beg God for forgiveness, trusting in the divine mercy.

The case is not the same for Harry James Cargas, an American scholar. He maintains that forgiveness is a virtue and is necessary for spiritual wholeness. However, he reminds us that while Christians are taught to forgive, there are sins that cannot be forgiven, such as blasphemy against the Spirit and crimes such as those committed by Hitler and his followers. Thus, for him, Karl dies unforgiven. Cargas asks God to have mercy on his own soul (but not on Karl's).

Robert Coles, an American professor of psychiatry, would turn away in anger and beg the Lord to forgive Karl. He was in doubt about Karl's repentance. He had been taught by his parents to forgive, and to understand one's own mistakes so that we can also forgive ourselves. Coles admitted that it is not easy to sustain this conviction, even in his comfortable and privileged life as a medical professional in the United States. In this case, he would pray to God to forgive the Nazi Karl who claimed to be repentant.

The Dalai Lama firmly believes that one should forgive those who have committed atrocities against oneself and against others. He has witnessed how China invaded Tibet in 1949 to 1950 and caused the death of 1.2 million

Tibetans, one fifth of the nation's population, through massacre, starvation, and suicide.[10] In spite of such atrocities, Tibetans have struggled for more than four decades to be faithful to Buddha's teaching on non-violence and compassion. The Dalai Lama met with a Tibetan monk who was kept in a Chinese prison for eighteen years, and while in prison, his biggest fear was of losing his compassion for the Chinese.

As forgiveness is a cardinal principle of Judaism and Christianity, it should always be given to a sincere penitent, as Edward H. Flannery, a Roman Catholic priest, believed. Flannery pointed out that Karl, the SS man, did not ask for forgiveness for harm done to all the Jews, only for what he personally had done. It was interpersonal. Flannery stood against relativism and held firmly to this basic moral imperative to forgive. Thus, were he in Simon Wiesenthal's position, Flannery hoped he would forgive Karl. Furthermore, Flannery would pray for the repose of Karl's soul and for those of his victims.

Matthew Fox, an American theologian, pointed out that Karl expressed his repentance for only one particular crime; it was not his full story. Simon acted appropriately by giving Karl the only penance available to him at that moment—silence. Simon felt he could not have forgiven him for the millions of Jews who died in concentration camps as he had neither the right nor the power to do so. In addition, some sins are too enormous to be forgiven. Public penance is required. Since Karl did not do any public penance, he had to die in the silence of the truth. Simon was able to keep the integrity of his soul and Karl was able to unburden his soul. For Fox, it was a good situation for both of them and Simon was justified in not offering forgiveness.

By holding Karl's hand and listening to him, Simon Wiesenthal had shown compassion. There are sins that only God can forgive. Fox suggested that perhaps from this SS man Simon had received his calling to find Nazi war criminals, to bring them to justice, to allow them a deathbed conversion and confession. There was thus a strange exchange here. Simon offered a listening ear to Karl and in turn he received a calling from Karl, which later led him to set up a commission to investigate Nazi war criminals. Another act of compassion shown was when Simon visited Karl's mother to find out more about his family background. He kept the full truth from the mother so as not to hurt her. At that point, it was useless to tell the poor widow what enormous crimes her beloved son had committed. Fox stated

---

10. Wiesenthal, *The Sunflower*, 129.

that Simon listened to both mother and son and left them in silence. Both were to die with partial truth. However, at another level, Simon broke the silence by writing this book and tracking down Nazi criminals, so that the fuller truth could be made known to the whole world.

The Sunflower, like any true morality story, is still relevant for us today. Human capacity for evil and violence is not limited to certain individuals. We all participate in evil acts when we commit sins of complicity, omission, and denial. These sins are prevalent in our society when the press and social media spread lies and distorted or even fake news. As Fox emphasized, denial allows sins to take root in our society. Sins of complicity destroy our environment and the souls of our young people "as we live in denial of the prisons we are building to house young persons whose violence stems from despair."[11] Fox thus responds to Simon Wiesenthal's question as follows: non-forgiveness can be justified if there is no repentance, however, if we choose not to forgive we remain bound in resentment. In such cases of non-repentance, we would still do well to forgive, not out of altruism, but out of the need to free ourselves from the burden of the past and to move on. However, even then, like Simon, we should *not forget*, but continue to pursue justice with compassion.

Harold S. Kushner, an American rabbi, wondered if there is such a thing as forgiving another person, although he believes there is such a thing as being forgiven. To be forgiven is to feel liberated from the burden of one's past guilt and wrongdoings, to be cleansed of one's sins. To be forgiven is a gift from God. It occurs inside us when we are freed from the shame of what we have done so that we can be better persons. Had Karl, the SS man, repented earlier and not waited until his final hours on his deathbed, he could have experienced the cleansing power of repentance. Like Berger, Kushner felt that by asking a Jew, any Jew, to absolve him of his crimes is to reinforce the Nazis' perception of Jews as masses, not as individuals or, in other words, less than human. For Karl, one Jew is as good as another; they are merely interchangeable identities, not unique individuals.

We forgive people, Kushner insisted, because we do not want to continue harboring resentment, anger, and pain. By forgiving, we exorcise, as it were, the image of the offender from our consciousness. We stop being his victims. If we do not forgive, we hurt ourselves by clinging on to resentment and anger. Forgiving takes place within us, by letting go of grievances and refusing to be a victim. In the case of Simon Wiesenthal, what the SS

---

11. Wiesenthal, *The Sunflower*, 147.

man did was absolutely despicable and inhuman. But we can forgive him because we refuse to give him the power to make us his victims. We will not let hatred distort our Jewishness, Kushner stressed; we simply reject his control over us. To forgive is to be liberated.

Lawrence L. Lancer, an American academic, insisted there is no forgiveness for the mass murder of Jewish people during the Holocaust. Karl participated in this horrific genocide, and thus, cannot be forgiven. He could have defied authority, as others did, by disobeying orders to kill. A criminal cannot be forgiven for an unforgivable crime. Thus, in Lancer's opinion, Simon Wiesenthal did the right thing by not forgiving Karl. Besides, there is no way we can verify the sincerity of Karl's repentance. Lancer also pointed out that in asking for forgiveness, Karl was actually transferring his guilt to his potential victim. This reveals his failure to understand the gravity of his crime. The question we should ask, Lancer continued, is why the young man joined the Hitler Youth Movement in spite of his father's objection, and why he chose to repent only when he was dying.

The Holocaust survivor Primo Levi thought that the SS man, Karl, lacked moral integrity. He repented only when approaching death, not before. To confess to a Jew seems to be immature and presumptuous. Influenced by propaganda, he might have thought the Jews were "half-devil" or "half-miracle worker," capable of doing supernatural deeds.[12] Levi also criticized the SS man for transferring his anguish and guilt to another person, an act that revealed his ego-centrism.

Erich H. Loewy, an American scientist, called our attention to Simon Wiesenthal's compassion when he touched the SS man. Simon remained with Karl and listened to him. In this humane act, Simon was accepting the SS man into human society, from which he felt he was excluded because of his terrible crimes against innocent Jews. We can interpret this acceptance as a form of forgiveness. In fact, Loewy asserted that such acceptance is more meaningful than empty words of forgiveness. In spite of all his atrocities against the Jews, Simon was able to accept Karl as a member of one humanity: he sat beside the SS man, touched him. These simple acts convey the true measure of Simon Wiesenthal as a person and must have brought much comfort to the dying man.

Servite priest John T. Pawlikowski highlighted the difference between forgiveness and reconciliation. Deep within his heart, Simon Wiesenthal was willing to forgive Karl. He recognized a certain basic human quality

---

12. Wiesenthal, *The Sunflower*, 183.

exists in both the perpetrator and the victim: "Were we truly all made of the same stuff?"[13] For Pawlikowski, reconciliation is the public form of forgiveness. It is a complex process that takes time to mature. Reconciliation occurs in stages: "repentance, contrition, acceptance of responsibility, healing, and finally reunion."[14] In such a short time, it was not possible for Karl to reconcile with the Jewish community.

Dith Pran, a survivor of the Cambodian killing fields, said that he can forgive the Khmer Rouge soldiers, but he can never forget what they did. Hence, if placed in Simon's position, he would likewise forgive because he believes the Khmer Rouge soldiers were brainwashed. If they did not follow orders, they and their families would be killed. The key to forgiveness, he asserted, is understanding, but he cannot understand the inhuman actions of the Khmer Rouge authority. Differentiating the brainwashed from the evil masterminds, he can forgive the soldiers, but not the top leaders of this murderous regime.

The opposite of not forgiving is not cruelty, but "a way of healing and honoring our pain and grief," wrote André Stein, a psychotherapist with Holocaust survivors.[15] Stein felt that Simon's refusal to tell Karl's mother of her son's crimes was an irresponsible act. Many people have been murdered by "good sons," Stein sarcastically says. The mother needs to know the harm and atrocities her son had committed against innocent Jews instead of living with "a nasty lie."[16] This would help her to warn other parents to convince their children to avoid the influence of evil ideology. For a woman like Karl's mother to believe that her son was good and innocent is to be a collaborator in his crime, Stein insists. We need to be concerned for the welfare of the survivors and the sacred memory of the victims to prevent future genocide.

Nechama Tec, an American academic, firmly believed that Nazi criminals cannot be forgiven for the atrocities they have committed unless they take personal responsibility for their actions. Furthermore, nobody has the right to forgive crimes committed against others; only the victims have the right to forgive, Tec insisted. Critical of the SS man, Tec considered him to be self-centered and selfish; feeling sorry for himself blinded him to the needs of others. He treated Simon not as an individual but as a

---

13. Wiesenthal, *The Sunflower*, 7.
14. Wiesenthal, *The Sunflower*, 212.
15. Wiesenthal, *The Sunflower*, 239.
16. Wiesenthal, *The Sunflower*, 241.

representative of his race, implicitly defining Jews as non-humans, which is part of the Nazi ideology. Karl, the SS man, could have pleaded with other SS officers not to kill innocent Jews instead of burdening Simon with his crimes. Simon's silent response is more eloquent than words; it conveys more powerfully his compassion for the dying SS man.

Having spent nineteen years in a labor camp under Chinese Communist rule, Harry Wu said it is unthinkable that people in China would ask for forgiveness as in the story of Simon Wiesenthal. In China, the Communists, in spite of the cruelties they have committed, never feel or admit that they have done anything that is morally wrong. They have no concern for an individual's well-being, nor do they place value on human life. In order to survive, they have to numb their consciences and give up their humanity. Captain Cao, the prison guard who showed kindness to the prisoners, was an exception, an "aberration of that time."[17] Comrade Wu, who was responsible for their incarceration and punishment, was typical of a system that totally disregards human rights and dignity.

Limits of Forgiveness

Influenced by Judeo-Christian teaching, some of the respondents believe forgiveness is possible. We forgive because we want God to forgive us for our wrongdoings. Others forgive, not for altruistic reasons, but to let go of the resentment and hurt that they are harboring. Not to forgive gives power to the perpetrators by keeping those hurts and pains in our consciousness and thus continuing to make us their victims.

Eve Garrard discussed some possible reasons to forgive, such as the presence of "rational agency" in the perpetrators and the common humanity that they share with us. In fact, Simon Wiesenthal has asked if any personal relationship exists between murderers and their victims. Aren't we all members of the same humanity? When there is repentance, Tracy Govier suggests, we ought to forgive out of respect for human worth and dignity. We forgive because we recognize that humans have a capacity for moral choice and change.[18]

The majority of the respondents concur that only the victim can forgive the perpetrator and thus Simon Wiesenthal had no right to forgive the SS man. Silence was the most appropriate response, most of the

17. Wiesenthal, *The Sunflower*, 258.
18. See Garrard, "Forgiveness and the Holocaust," 147–65.

contributors agree, because it is more eloquent than words and it conveys compassion without condoning the crimes committed. Quite a few of the respondents are critical of Karl, the SS man, for transferring his guilt and sufferings to Simon, treating him only as a representative of the Jewish people, not as a unique individual. It would have been redeeming if Karl had decided to warn other German officers not to continue murdering innocent Jews. There is no forgiveness for Karl because he must face the consequences of his actions: justice must be served. He would have been a hero if he had disobeyed orders to shoot Jewish parents and their children as they fled a torched building.

To forgive easily the crimes committed by the Germans against the Jews during the Holocaust perpetuates the evil rather than alleviating it.[19] Forgiveness can trivialize human suffering and allow senseless violence, brutality, and cruelty to flourish. As mentioned earlier, the opposite of not forgiving is not cruelty, but healing and honoring our pain and grief. There are occasions when victims have forgiven their perpetrators either out of compassion or from the need to get on with their lives. But we cannot and should not forget crimes committed against humanity such as the Holocaust.

Keeping the Memory Alive

In Yad Vashem, the World Holocaust Remembrance Center in Jerusalem, there is this statement, "Remembrance is the secret of redemption." Those individuals who were mercilessly killed remind us of the appalling atrocities committed against humanity. Theodor W. Adorno says that the murdered must not "be cheated out of the single remaining thing that our powerlessness can offer them: remembrance."[20] This remembrance of the dead must serve as a deterrent to future genocides that threaten to erupt in different guises. We must do everything in our power to make sure that such terrible crimes will never occur again. The crimes of the Nazis were a big blow to the modernity that was so confident of human progress and civilization. The Holocaust reveals an evil that challenges our traditional understanding of guilt and forgiveness.

Until the end of the nineteenth century, peace treaties were based on general pardon and forgetting of past transgressions so that lives could go on. However, looking at the atrocities committed during the twentieth

---

19. Wiesenthal, *The Sunflower*, 198.
20. Adorno, "The Meaning of Working through the Past," 91.

century, a perpetual remembrance of transgressions is the only appropriate response because we are now dealing with "radical evil."[21] There are crimes that are so enormous, so beyond human comprehension, that they challenge our human capacity to forgive. In spite of that, Christians believe in the possibility of forgiveness in the light of the cross of Christ. Nonetheless, forgetting crimes and guilt will only hinder and prevent reconciliation, so we need both to remember and to forgive.

The practice of forgiveness can help us understand and remember guilt—we recognize that our debt is forgiven and we feel liberated, but we cannot disown this debt or attempt to pass it on to someone else, or we will be like Karl, the SS man, in *The Sunflower*. We remember our debt because we experienced forgiveness. Remembering our sins and guilt "is not actually the presupposition, but rather the consequence of a process of reconciliation."[22] One of the approaches for remembering is "working through the past," a concept introduced by Sigmund Freud, who helped his patients deal with traumatic experiences.

In an essay written in 1959, Theodor Adorno asserted that working through the past does not mean "seriously working upon the past, that is, through a lucid consciousness breaking its power to fascinate."[23] In fact, those who insist on forgiving and forgetting are actually the perpetrators of crimes, not the victims of injustice. The influence of National Socialism (Nazism) is very much alive, and therefore we cannot evade it, Adorno warned. We must not forget that the ghost of such monstrosity lingers on and survives in people who might still be prepared to commit such despicable crimes against humanity. There are also people who attempt to minimize the crimes of the Nazis or even deny that the Holocaust did take place. The crimes were so enormous, despicable, and inconceivable that it is easy to accuse the victims of exaggeration.

Regarding anti-Semitism, we should be wary of the so-called "facts" or what is conveyed by way of propaganda, because facts can be twisted and distorted. We must be aware of the "mechanisms that cause racial prejudice within them."[24] *Working through the past* must be understood as collective and individual self-reflection on human mechanisms that ultimately led to unimaginable crimes like those that took place in the

---

21. Beintker,"Remembering Guilt as a Social Project," 212.
22. Beintker,"Remembering Guilt as a Social Project," 213.
23. Adorno, "The Meaning of Working through the Past," 89.
24. Adorno, "The Meaning of Working through the Past," 102.

Auschwitz concentration camp. "The past will have been worked through only when the causes of what happened then have been eliminated. Only because the causes continue to exist does the captivating spell of the past remain to this day unbroken."[25] As long as prejudice exists, we must *work through the past* to discover its underlying causes, the instinctive behavior that denies the humanity in another.

After the Second World War, the defeated Germans were confronted with the enormity of their crimes, which had been tolerated among the general population. Anxious to bring about closure to this horrific chapter in their history, they sought to forget the transgression, hoping to achieve an "*overcoming* of the past."[26] But the past cannot be overcome, and certainly not the past of this evil. "This past must remain un-overcome. It must and should disturb us. It should painfully shake us from the illusion that people are disposable. In this way, it becomes a warning cry to the living."[27] We simply cannot confine this particular past to archives and history books. There is the danger that those who ignore the past are bound to repeat the same mistake again.

We Remember

Christianity, especially Catholicism, is historically responsible for the crimes committed against the Jews during the Nazi regime. Fortunately, the attitude of the Catholic Church towards Judaism and the Jews has changed for the better since the Second Vatican Council with the declaration *Nostra Aetate*. This declaration regarding the Church's relation with non-Christian religions lifted the charge of deicide, that Jewish people as a whole were responsible for the death of Jesus. John Paul II was the first pontiff to visit a synagogue in Rome on April 13, 1986. Recognizing the State of Israel in December 1993, John Paul II also issued a declaration on the Holocaust entitled, *We Remember: A Reflection on the Shoah*, in March 1998.[28]

As we approach the end of the second millennium, this declaration calls upon the Church to be conscious of the sins of its members, the times

---

25. Adorno, "The Meaning of Working through the Past," 103.
26. Beintker,"Remembering Guilt as a Social Project," 214.
27. Beintker,"Remembering Guilt as a Social Project," 214.
28. This section is summarized from *We Remember: A Reflection on the Shoah*, http://www.vatican.va/roman_curia/pontifical_councils/chrstuni/documents/rc_pc_chrstuni_doc_16031998_shoah_en.html.

when they have gravely departed from the teaching of Christ and caused "counter-witness and scandal."[29] We have witnessed during the twentieth century a most horrible crime when the Nazi regime killed almost six million Jews, men, women, children, and infants. Those who survived the Holocaust were scarred for life. This was the *Shoah*, a catastrophe, a significant historical fact that still concerns us today.

The Church cannot remain indifferent to this terrible tragedy because of its spiritual kinship with the Jewish people, unlike the relationship it shares with other faiths: "The common future of Jews and Christians demands that we remember, for 'there is no future without memory.' History itself is *memoria futuri*."[30] Because of the enormity of the crimes against the Jews, Christians have the moral obligation to ensure that such a catastrophe will never happen again. We also have the moral obligation to ensure that selfishness and hatred will never grow to a point of promoting such destruction of human lives. Furthermore, we must also ask our Jewish friends, "whose terrible fate has become a symbol of the aberrations of which man is capable when he turns against God," to hear us with open hearts.[31]

The Jewish people have suffered much throughout their history, but the *Shoah* was the worst of all sufferings. Innocent people were massacred mercilessly and cruelly for the simple reason that they were Jews. Many scholars and experts in different disciplines have tried to understand the reality of the *Shoah*, but such a reality cannot be fully understood by historical research alone. It demands "moral and religious memory," a deep reflection on its underlying causes.[32] Christians particularly have this responsibility to reflect seriously about the factors that led to the Holocaust. The fact that this atrocity took place in Europe, the cradle of Christian civilization, naturally raises the question of Christian-Jewish relations and the rise of Nazi persecution of the Jews.

---

29. *We Remember: A Reflection on the Shoah.*

30. *We Remember: A Reflection on the Shoah.*

31. *We Remember: A Reflection on the Shoah.* Regarding the Holocaust, Paul Tillich wrote of five types of guilt: i. the absolute guilt of the murderers; ii. the guilt of those who remain silent, those who did nothing to save another; iii. the guilt of those who repressed their knowledge in self deceit; vi. the guilt of those who forget the past; v. the guilt of all the Germans who think that the hurt they had suffered absolved them of "their own guilt of involvement with the concentration camps . . . ." See Friedlander, "Judaism and the Concept of Forgiving," 7.

32. *We Remember: A Reflection on the Shoah.*

Relations between Jews and Christians

Since the beginning of Christianity, relationships between Jews and Christians have been fraught with difficulties, conflicts, and misunderstandings. This was further aggravated by "erroneous and unjust interpretations of the New Testament regarding the Jewish people and their alleged culpability."[33] Jews have been made scapegoats in Europe in times of crisis, such as famine, pestilence, and social tensions, resulting in persecutions and even massacres. In spite of Christianity's teaching on love for all, including one's enemies, anti-Judaism continued in Christian communities. Capitalizing on these anti-Jewish sentiments, the Nazi regime in Germany systematically persecuted and deported Jews. Richard Rubenstein wrote:

> Given the radical demonization of the Jews in traditional Christian thought and the just-war tradition that legitimates whatever measures are necessary to combat a mortal enemy, once the Nazis succeeded in convincing a majority of Europeans that the Jews were a mortal threat to Christian civilization, it became morally acceptable for normal men and women to participate in the project of mass extermination with a good conscience and for the churches to remain silent and, in some cases, even to aid the perpetrators to escape after the war.[34]

Be that as it may, the Catholic Church had also responded by condemning racism and publishing pastoral letters denouncing National Socialism (Nazism) in 1931. Cardinal Faulhaber in 1933 rejected Nazi anti-Semitic propaganda. Pope Pius XI criticized Nazism in his Encyclical Letter *Mit brennender Sorge*, which was read publicly in German churches on Passion Sunday in 1937, resulting in Catholic clergy being attacked and punished. Condemning anti-Semitism, Pius XII, in his first encyclical, *Summi Pontificatus*, of October 20, 1939, criticized theories that denied the unity of humankind and promoted the deification of the state. He saw Nazism as the real "hour of darkness."[35]

The declaration, *We Remember*, makes a distinction between anti-Semitism, which denies the equality and dignity of all races and was rejected by the Church, and anti-Judaism, which unfortunately still exists among some

---

33. *We Remember: A Reflection on the Shoah.*

34. Rubenstein, *After Auschwitz*, 183. See also Jasper, "Retrieving a Theological Sense of Being Human," 127.

35. *We Remember: A Reflection on the Shoah.*

Christians. And not just Christians. The National Socialist ideology was atheistic and sought to wipe out the Jewish people. Deifying the state, the Nazi Party also rejected God and the Christian religion, and sought to subject the Church to its interests when it failed to destroy it. Thus, "the *Shoah* was the work of a thoroughly modern neo-pagan regime. Its anti-Semitism had its roots outside of Christianity and, in pursuing its aims, it did not hesitate to oppose the Church and persecute her members also."[36]

In particular, Nazism promoted the superiority of the Nordic-Aryan race, a secular ideology based on pseudo-scientific theories. Yet Nazi anti-Semitism would not have gotten any traction without being able to draw on centuries of hostility in Christian Europe to Jewish people. At the core of anti-Semitism in Europe, a term coined in 1879 in Vienna, is the ancient Christian condemnation of the Jew as Christ killer, a religious discrimination that became racial.[37]

Here's a question to ponder. When the Nazis brutally deported millions of Jews, did Christians offer any help to those being persecuted? Some did help to save them to the point of endangering their own lives. Pope Pius XII himself, and also through many representatives, saved hundreds of thousands of Jews. Recognizing the Catholic Church's effort in saving Jews, the State of Israel has honored many Catholic bishops, priests, religious, and laity. Nonetheless, there were also many Christians—both of the Church's hierarchy (including the pope and many bishops and priests) and the laity—who remained silent, afraid to protest against the atrocities of the Nazis against the Jews. The Church was thus, to its shame, complicit in the Nazi's demonic work. The Church deeply regrets and confesses its own culpable failure and the failure of its members to protect their Jewish brothers and sisters, or at least to protest and raise their voices against the Nazi regime. It must never happen again. The Second Vatican Council's Declaration, *Nostra Aetate*, states: "the Church, mindful of the patrimony she shares with the Jews and moved not by political reasons but by the Gospel's spiritual love, decries hatred, persecutions, displays of anti-Semitism, directed against Jews at any time and by anyone."[38] Addressing the Jewish community in Strasbourg in 1988, John Paul II emphasized: "I repeat again with you the strongest condemnation of anti-Semitism and racism, which

---

36. *We Remember: A Reflection on the Shoah.*

37. Jasper, "Retrieving a Theological Sense of Being Human," 128. See also Lewis, *Semites and Anti-Semites.*

38. *Nostra Aetate*, no. 4.

are opposed to the principles of Christianity."[39] Racist ideologies have no place in the Catholic Church.

The Catholic Church sincerely seeks to express sorrow and regret for the failure of her children through the ages. As the Church is linked to the merits and sins of its members, this sincere expression of remorse is an act of repentance (*Teshuva*). The Church remembers the *Shoah*, the sufferings of the Jews, with respect and compassion, not merely in words, but with a resounding commitment: "We would risk causing the victims of the most atrocious deaths to die again if we do not have an ardent desire for justice, if we do not commit ourselves to ensure that evil does not prevail over good as it did for millions of the children of the Jewish people. . . . Humanity cannot permit all that to happen again."[40] Forgiveness of Christians' anti-Semitic attitudes, which historically led to the Holocaust, can take place only if there is *Teshuvah*, an inner transformation in the hearts of Christians. *Teshuvah* expresses the essence of the Jewish ethical ideal.

Teshuvah: Change of Heart

Some important Jewish teaching on forgiveness and repentance is found in the Hebrew Bible. To forgive in the rabbinical and biblical sense involves the cleansing of the individual by God followed by the person performing penance such as weeping, fasting, and rending clothes (2 Sam 12: 16). The penitent must be contrite and perform acts of repentance, demonstrate an inner turning away from sins towards purity of heart. God can forgive a person only if he or she cleanses him- or herself of past misdeeds. This involves *Teshuvah*, repentance: a change of heart. This teaching is a development of monotheistic faiths that put emphasis on a personal relationship with God, a relationship that is ethical in nature, and that is considered as a covenant between God and his people, two parties involved in "bringing the world to perfection."[41]

Sin violates the covenant between God and the person; *Teshuvah* is the process by which this rupture is mended and the covenant renewed. Judaism views the following of God's commandments as a means to renew the covenant, and returning to God means returning to his covenantal teaching. Rabbi Leon Klenicki says the *Teshuvah* is "at once restorative and utopian

---

39. *We Remember: A Reflection on the Shoah.*
40. *We Remember: A Reflection on the Shoah.*
41. Klenicki, "Can Jews Forgive after the Holocaust?" 162.

in character."⁴² This means that an ideal state existed in the past, before sin entered into humankind. *Teshuvah* is an attempt to reach a perfect future that is different from any reality that currently exists. Since the beginning of time, every religious renewal is a *Teshuval movement* in Judaism.

Biblical sources teach that *Teshuvah* requires the penitent to confess his or her sins and to seek forgiveness. This requires a recognition of trespasses with remorse and a determination to live a new life.

> Let the wicked forsake their way, and the unrighteous their thoughts; let them return to the LORD, that he may have mercy on them, and to our God, for he will abundantly pardon. (Isa 55:7)
>
> For after I had turned away I repented; and after I was discovered, I struck my thigh; I was ashamed, and I was dismayed because I bore the disgrace of my youth. (Jer 31:19)
>
> Take words with you and return to the LORD; say to him, Take away all guilt; accept that which is good, and we will offer the fruit of our lips. (Hos 14:2).

Forgiveness in the Jewish tradition is thus a two-fold process whereby a person forgives and the sinner undergoes a profound change in his personal life. It is an inner transformation in which the sinner returns to God after confessing his sins. Consequently, forgiveness occurs only when the sinner has undergone such a transformation. Forgiveness without a corresponding change of heart is merely forgetting the crime and the criminal Klenicki says, "I personally will forgive a real repentant but will never forget the crimes against my people or humanity."⁴³

The Catholic Church desires to forge a good relationship with the Jewish people, to build a new future where there will be mutual respect between two people who claim God as their creator and Abraham as their father in faith. Inviting all people of goodwill to reflect deeply on the significance of the *Shoah,* the Catholic Church warns us not to forget the terrible sufferings of the Jews so that the "spoiled seeds" of anti-Judaism and anti-Semitism will never again take root in human hearts.⁴⁴ Clearly, the Church wants fellow Christians to remember the crimes committed in the past just as we remember the merits gained by the saints, by acts of repentance, and by a commitment to justice and peace.

42. Klenicki, "Can Jews Forgive after the Holocaust?" 162.
43. Klenicki, "Can Jews Forgive after the Holocaust?" 164.
44. *We Remember: A Reflection on the Shoah.*

Religious Virtue

Evil begets evil, but forgiveness can break this vicious cycle. Forgiveness tells us not to follow our instinct to take revenge; it answers hate with compassion, hostility with generosity. To forgive means not to allow past grievances to have a grip on us in the present. It is the ability to live freely, not burdened by harbouring hatred and bringing resentments of the past into the present. A sense of grievance weighs us down and thus forgiveness represents human freedom. Through forgiveness, we can "change course, reframe the narrative of the past and create a new set of possibilities for the future."[45] The ability to forgive is a gift that helps us to live in the present without resentments and with hope for a better future.

As mentioned, forgiveness is a religious virtue that has its origin in Judaism and that, of course, has great influence on Christianity. It applies to human beings and their relationships with one another and with God. The laws of nature are inevitable and unforgiving—we cannot blame crocodiles, tigers, volcanoes, and earthquakes, etc., for killing human beings. Animals and natural calamities do not require forgiveness.

As a religious virtue, forgiveness has its origin in God's love for us. "Love distinguishes between the person and the deed."[46] A person may commit an evil deed, but they are not totally identified with that act. Most wrongdoing can be rectified if the wrongdoer expresses remorse and repentance. Forgiveness means a person is no longer defined by what he has done.

God teaches us to forgive motivated by his willingness to forgive us our trespasses. The psalmist writes: "Happy are those whose transgression is forgiven, whose sin is remitted. Happy are those to whom the LORD imputes no iniquity, and in whose spirit there is no deceit" (Ps 32:1–2). Forgiveness, thus, is a gift from God that allows his children to survive, even before the world was created, according to some strands of Jewish tradition. Some, for instance, interpret Psalm 90 as concerning repentance. "Before the mountains were brought forth, or ever you had formed the earth and the world, from everlasting to everlasting you are God. You *turn us back* to dust, and say, *'Turn back,* you mortals'" (Ps 90:2–3). This turning back—in Hebrew, *shuv*—is related to the word for repentance, *teshuvah*.[47]

---

45. Dobkowski, "Forgiveness and Repentance in Judaism after the Shoah," 96.
46. Dobkowski, "Forgiveness and Repentance in Judaism after the Shoah," 96.
47. Dobkowski, "Forgiveness and Repentance in Judaism after the Shoah," 97.

In *The Sunflowers*, the majority of the respondents seem to spurn forgiveness because they insisted that only the victims can forgive. Doubting the sincerity of Karl's repentance, many of the respondents were indignant that Karl just wants any Jew to hear his graphic confession to unburden himself of guilt before he dies. He treated Jews as if they are all the same, not as individuals. As a Catholic, Karl could have asked for a priest.

In spite of its difficulties, I would maintain that forgiveness is the healthier option for both the perpetrator and the victims, because, as mentioned, it breaks the vicious cycle of hate and revenge. Simon's silent presence and touch can be interpreted as compassion for the dying SS soldier. Silence is not just an absence of sound, but a "complex phenomenon," a kind of "rhetoric" that forces the practitioner and the listener to consider what ought to be said and what not. Silence is not merely a "passive response," but rather "an active attitude."[48] Simon's silence reveals his shock at Karl's appalling crimes and his struggle to be there for him. His silence also symbolizes his solidarity with a dying man in need of mercy and forgiveness.

Forgiveness may be unfair or illogical, but it halts the overwhelming power of retributive "justice." Commenting on the Sermon on the Mount, Catholic theologian Romano Guardini says, "As long as you cling to 'justice' you will never be guiltless of injustice. As long as you are tangled in wrong and revenge, blow and counterblow, aggression and defense, you will be constantly drawn into fresh wrong. . . . He who takes it upon himself to avenge trampled justice never restores justice. . . . In reality, insistence on justice is servitude. Only forgiveness frees us from the injustice of others."[49] If we follow the maxim of "an eye for an eye," that is, the principle of retributive justice, the whole world would go blind.[50]

Finally, forgiveness is not so much what you do for another person, but what actually happens inside, as Rabbi Kushner says. Forgiveness helps us to let go of the grievances that are toxic to our human constitution. We acknowledge that what the SS soldier did to Jews was totally despicable and unjustifiable, but we will not be held captive by hatred. I believe healing had taken place in Simon's heart when he decided to write *The Sunflower*. He broke his silence so that we can respond to his dilemma regarding forgiveness. "To save the dead from the second death of oblivion, and thus to

---

48. Finn, "Truth without Reconciliation?" 311.

49. Quoted in Yancey, "Holocaust & Ethnic Cleansing," 27.

50. This idea is frequently attributed to M. K. Gandhi, although there is no evidence that the Indian leader had said it.

remain faithful to them, was for almost all the survivors the predominant motivation for breaking the walls of silence."[51] Simon becomes the sunflower that links the living to the dead.

---

51. Tück, "Unforgivable Forgiveness?" 523.

— Chapter 2 —

No Future without Forgiveness

Apartheid in South Africa

In this chapter we approach the theme of forgiveness from another context—the South African experience of apartheid, which caused so much suffering and death not only to black people but also to white people because of the vicious cycle of revenge and reprisal. According to the Anglican Archbishop Desmond Tutu,[1] author of *No Future without Forgiveness*, a racist ideology such as apartheid victimizes both victims and perpetrators. On April 27, 1994, when South Africa was transformed from a despotic to a democratic nation, ending forty-six years of apartheid, it was a miraculously peaceful transition, avoiding the bloodshed and revenge some had expected. Tutu regarded the election on that day, when Nelson Mandela became President, as not just a political event but as a spiritual experience. During those long hours of waiting to vote, people discovered their shared humanity. They realized that race, ethnicity, and skin color were not the most fundamental aspects of our humanity.

This chapter discusses the role of the apartheid policy in the drive towards forgiveness and reconciliation undertaken by the Truth and Reconciliation Commission (TRC) chaired by Archbishop Tutu. The TRC examined the different approaches to forgiveness found among the survivors

---

1. For a more detailed account of Desmond Tutu's life and his philosophical and theological outlook, see Maluleke, "Desmond Tutu's Earliest Notions and Visions of Church, Humanity, and Society," 572–90. Some material in this chapter appeared as an article in Ambrose Mong, "Inculturation and Reconciliation: Uniting Forgiveness and Ubuntu in Post-Apartheid South Africa," *Ecumenical Trends*, vol. 49, no. 4, July/August 2020 (12–20).

and victims of apartheid and Nazi regimes. While Christian influence facilitated the healing process, this chapter argues that the non-violent transition in South Africa to universal suffrage was aided also by concepts of virtue in African traditional religion, especially *ubuntu* or a sense of interconnectedness; *ubuntu* informs the theological outlook of Tutu and other participants. This is a story of a successful integration of the African philosophy of humanity with the Christian virtue of forgiveness.

Compared to South Africa's relatively smooth transition from despotism to democracy, Latin American nations did not fare as well, in spite of their Christian heritage. The mechanism of apartheid systematically segregates people along racial lines, promoting inequality and injustice that can only result in deep-seated hatred and resentment. Given this background, the South African success seems all the more miraculous. Still, apartheid was such a deeply entrenched racial ideology that it took the nation a long time to remove it.

Apartheid: One Country, Two Nations

The British occupied Cape Colony in 1806 and abolished slavery in 1833. The early Dutch settlers, unhappy with British domination, moved into the interior of the colony, which was rich in natural resources. In 1910, the South Africa Act was passed in Britain; it granted dominion to the white minority over native Africans and people of mixed race. This Act brought together Cape Colony, Natal, Transvaal, and the Orange Free State into the Union of South Africa. With the white minority monopolizing political and economic power, a legal system was established to segregate those people categorized as white from those categorized as black and mixed-race. It was a system that involved political and economic discrimination against non-white people in a policy known as "separate development."[2]

The Population Registration Act of 1950 classed all South African people as either "Bantu" (Blacks), "Colored" (mixed race), or "White." A fourth category— "Indians"—was later added; its members were mostly from India and Pakistan. Legally sanctioned racial segregation was widely practiced in South Africa before 1948. The National Party, which gained office in 1948, fine-tuned this segregation policy and called it *apartheid* (Afrikaans: "apartness"). This Party went further in dividing the races by creating the Group

---

2. "Apartheid," in *Encyclopædia Britannica*. See also Tutu, Mothobi, and Webster, *Hope and Suffering*, 89–98.

Area Act of 1950, which allotted specific areas where white people and black people were to live and work separately in residential and business sections. The Land Acts adopted in 1913 and 1936 had already resulted in white people occupying 80 percent of South Africa's land.[3]

To further strengthen the segregation of races, "Black" and "Colored" people were not allowed to enter freely into white domains; they also had to carry documents if they entered into such restricted areas. Mixed marriages between races were made illegal. There were separate and typically superior public facilities such as schools and hospitals for white people. Non-white people were restricted to certain types of employment, which were meant to keep them as servants and laborers. The education system for the Bantu was especially designed to teach them simple skills to perform menial tasks. Hendrik Verwoerd, the system's architect, said:

> There is no place for him [the black student] in the European community above the level of certain forms of labor. . . . For that reason, it is of no avail for him to receive a training which has as its aim absorption in the European community. . . . Until now he has been subject to a school system which drew him away from his own community and misled him by showing him the green pastures of European society in which he is not allowed to graze.[4]

With an inferior education system, non-white people were perpetually unemployed or underemployed. They were also excluded from political involvement and from formulating policies for the nation. The Bantu Homelands Citizenship Act of 1970 forced all those categorized as "Black" and "Colored" to live in the ten territories, or settlement camps, created especially for them.[5] Condemned to ghettos, black and other non-white people lived in squalid conditions with neither clean water nor adequate shelter.

Apartheid was more than a set of legally sanctioned rules and policies: it was a sophisticated system of racial and economic discrimination and domination adopted from the West to regulate and control the lives and work of millions of non-white people.[6] It determined the worth and value of a person by a biological trait, and so incentivized viewing interracial disunity and enmity as matters of natural law. In practice, apartheid promoted

---

3. "Apartheid," in *Encyclopædia Britannica*.
4. Quoted in Haws, "Suffering, Hope and Forgiveness," 480.
5. "Apartheid," in *Encyclopædia Britannica*.
6. Haws, "Suffering, Hope and Forgiveness," 479.

injustice, oppression, and exploitation, which affected the lives of the black people as well as the white people in the most negative ways.

Referring to the colonized countries of Africa, Frantz Fanon made the acute observation in his seminal work, *The Wretched of the Earth*, that the zones where natives live are not "complementary" to the zones where settlers dwell. In South Africa, the settlers would be the white people. The two zones are opposed, but not for the sake of a higher unity; rather, the zones followed the "principle of reciprocal exclusivity."[7] The settlers' town was well built, clean, with good facilities for white people; the natives' place was a "hungry town, starved of bread, of meat, of shoes, of coal, of light."[8]

Anglican Archbishop Desmond Tutu had actually witnessed people starving in settlement camps because of this segregation policy.[9] Obviously the natives looked towards the settlers' zone with great envy and hoped to be able to live there at some time. The settlers understood this very well and would do anything to protect their privileged lifestyle.

Fanon attributed this immense inequality in living conditions to division in the colonized world based on race. "The economic substructure is also a superstructure. The cause is the consequence; you are rich because you are white, you are white because you are rich."[10] Like most places in Africa occupied by white settlers, South Africa is actually "a motionless Manicheistic world," compartmentalized into black and white.[11] Thabo Mbeki, who succeeded Nelson Mandela as president, said:

> South Africa is a country of two nations. . . . One is white, relatively prosperous, regardless of gender or geographic dispersal. It has ready access to a developed economic, physical, educational, communication and other, infrastructure. The second and larger nation of Africa is black and poor. . . . This nation lives under conditions of a grossly underdeveloped economic, physical, educational, communication and other infrastructure. It has virtually no possibility to exercise what in reality amounts to a theoretic right to equality.[12]

---

7. Fanon, *The Wretched of the Earth*, 38–39.
8. Fanon, *The Wretched of the Earth*, 39.
9. Tutu, Mothobi, and Webster, *Hope and Suffering*, 97.
10. Fanon, *The Wretched of the Earth*, 40.
11. Fanon, *The Wretched of the Earth*, 50.
12. Quoted in Vorster, "Reformed Theology and 'Decolonised' Identity," 1.

Apartheid is a type of compartmentalization where the native person is forced by the white government to keep in his or her assigned place with regard to both dwelling and occupation, with no hope for social and economic advancement. In such a difficult and complex situation, it is possible for some to be both victims and perpetrators.

For example, the young white people who joined the army and police force were subjected to so much brainwashing and propaganda from their superiors and politicians that they were convinced they were defending the nation against communism and terrorism. In carrying out their duties, especially as the situation became worse, their consciences deteriorated and were gradually deadened, leading them to commit the worst kind of atrocities. The majority of the white politicians and their followers considered non-white people as "inferior" or even "subhuman,"[13] and thus they had no qualms about torturing and killing them.

Brutally treated by white people, black people learned to retaliate with the same appalling atrocities.

The Tragedy and Madness of Apartheid

P.W. Botha, leader of the National Party, and Winnie Madikizela-Mandela, the second wife of Nelson *Mandela* and regarded as the Mother of the Nation, represent the tragedy and madness of apartheid in South Africa. Though they were from very different social and political backgrounds, both were caught up in this tragic phase in the history of the nation.

Botha became the Prime Minister of South Africa on September 28, 1978. The fact that he continued as Defence Minister while serving as Prime Minister reveals his war-like and power-hungry character. Botha developed the "Total Strategy," a linking of political, economic, and military forces to combat resistance to apartheid.[14]

Botha was a true believer in the apartheid policy, and critical of the Truth and Reconciliation Commission (TRC). He refused to cooperate with TRC's investigations. He was accused of giving orders to bomb the Khotso House, the headquarters of the South African Council of Churches, in 1988. There was a considerable amount of evidence that Botha had been guilty of

---

13. Boraine, *A Country Unmasked* 128–29. Ordinary people, even youth, could be perpetrators of atrocities because apartheid is inherently immoral: "the banality of evil" (Quoted in Tutu, *No Future without Forgiveness*, 144).

14. Boraine, *A Country Unmasked*, 184.

human rights violations, both directly and indirectly, especially when he was chairperson of the State Security Council. Yet he refused to seek amnesty, believing that he had nothing to apologise for.

The TRC published a report stating that Botha, as Prime Minister (1978–84) and as Executive President (1984–89), had committed the following crimes: deliberate unlawful killing and attempted killing of persons opposed to government policies; torture and abduction of persons in neighboring countries; and acts of arson and sabotage against organizations and persons opposed to the government.[15] Refusing to testify at the TRC, Botha remained stubborn and defiant until the end. Steeped in Afrikaner nationalism, he believed white people were chosen by God to rule South Africa and apartheid was essential to maintain that domination.

Winnie Madikezela, born in Bizana, Pondoland, on September 26, 1934, was the first African medical social worker at Baragwanath Hospital, Soweto. Married to Nelson Mandela in 1957, she became a prominent member of the African National Congress (ANC). Winnie was known "as a fighter for justice" and "the mother of the struggle." After her husband was sent to prison, Winnie was subjected to many years of political persecution by security forces. Detained under the Terrorism Act in 1969, she was held in solitary confinement for seventeen months. Winnie was jailed again in 1974 for six months for defying a restriction order.[16] She was united with Nelson Mandela when he was released from prison on February 11, 1990. They were divorced in 1996, but Winnie continued to be influential in ANC's National Executive Committee and ANC Women's League.[17]

In spite of repeated harassment and arrest, Winnie Mandela was able to help establish the Black Women's Federation and the Black Parents' Association, with the aim of giving legal and medical assistance to those who got into trouble with the police. In addition to her involvement in politics, she raised the two daughters she had had with Nelson Mandela.[18] Yet something went terribly wrong in her fight against apartheid.

Winnie Mandela had started the Mandela United Football Club to assist youth who were victims of apartheid and of conflicts in the townships. The TRC found that the Mandela United Football Club was involved in a number of criminal activities, such as killing, torture, and assault in

---

15. Boraine, *A Country Unmasked*, 218.
16. Boraine, *A Country Unmasked*, 224.
17. Boraine, *A Country Unmasked*, 225.
18. Boraine, *A Country Unmasked*, 224.

the community. Winnie Mandela was aware of these criminal activities; in fact, she not only had knowledge of but also participated in these atrocities. Those who were opposed to her and her football club were branded as informers and killed brutally. Winnie was convicted and the Appeal Court found her guilty of kidnapping and of gross violations of human rights.[19] Nonetheless, Winnie Mandela, like P. W. Botha, refused to admit that she had done anything wrong and did not apply for amnesty.

After listening to so many horrendous stories, Archbishop Tutu, as Chairman of TRC, realized that everyone has the capacity for evil when subjected to the same negative influence and conditioning such as found in apartheid. Winnie Mandela was both victim and perpetrator. A powerful and charming woman, her passion for justice and fierce anti-apartheid attitude was transformed into a vengeful campaign that shocked both friends and foes. Bishop Storey expressed this tragic figure well:

> The primary cancer may be, and was, and will always be, the apartheid oppression, but secondary infections have touched many of apartheid's opponents and eroded their knowledge of good and evil. One of the tragedies of life is that it is possible to become like that which we hate most.[20]

A member of the TRC, Alex Boraine, deeply regretted that Winnie Mandela did not apply for amnesty. An admission of guilt and accountability on the part of Winnie Mandela and P. W. Botha would have gone a long way in the healing of the nation. In spite of their differences in race, culture, and gender, they are brought together as key players in this South African tragedy.

Bound Together

It is unthinkable today that some people could enjoy so many privileges and benefits while others were deprived of the basic necessities of life because of an accident of birth or skin color. The abolition of apartheid rule liberated not only the black people but the white people as well. Tutu remarked that South African white people could not be truly free until the black people were also free. Black and white in South Africa are like two convicts chained together.

---

19. Boraine, *A Country Unmasked*, 226.
20. Quoted in Boraine, *A Country Unmasked*, 222.

If they fell into a ditch with slippery slopes, the only way to get out is for both to strive together because one is chained to the other.

While white people doubtless benefitted in numerous material ways from apartheid rule, in another sense they were also victims of such a vicious system. Since humanity is intertwined, in the process of dehumanizing another, the perpetrators dehumanized themselves. All must liberate themselves from a racist mentality: "Unless we learn to live together as brothers and sisters we will die as fools."[21] None of the people of South Africa can make it on their own; they are bound together by God.

According to Tutu, the reason why South Africa experienced this veritable miracle of non-violent changeover and transfer of power, in spite of so many years of cruel exploitation and oppression, is the willingness to forgive. To continue the process of national healing and reconciliation, Nelson Mandela set up the Truth and Reconciliation Commission to deal with the nation's tragic past of oppression, carnage, torture, and gruesome killings.

The African Approach

The post-apartheid reconciliation process in South Africa is often compared to what followed the Holocaust. The Nuremberg model, which brought Nazi war criminals to trial for crimes against humanity, was rejected by Bishop Tutu and his co-workers because it was a kind of "victor justice" in which the accused had no say. In South Africa, there was no victor since there was a military stalemate.[22] The security forces of the apartheid government would never enter into such a negotiation, knowing that they would be judged without mercy as alleged perpetrators. The TRC was a better way to obtain the truth, especially the "truth of wounded memories" as part of a process of healing the nation.[23]

A general amnesty along the lines of the Chilean approach was also rejected. In other words, there was no automatic pardon; individuals had to apply for amnesty before an independent panel. General amnesty would really be a kind of amnesia: "Let bygones be bygones." Like the anti-Semitism of the Nazi government, the apartheid rule in South Africa cannot be forgotten. It will continue to haunt the people like a phantom, and thus the horrific past must be dealt with seriously: "Unless we look the beast in

---

21. Quoted in Tutu, *No Future without Forgiveness*, 8.
22. Tutu, *No Future without Forgiveness*, 20.
23. Tutu, *No Future without Forgiveness*, 26.

the eye we find it has an uncanny habit of returning to hold us hostages," Tutu wrote.[24] The philosopher George Santayana said, "Those who forget the past are doomed to repeat it."[25]

South African mediators opted for a "third way," which is a compromise between the two extreme models of upholding justice represented by Nuremberg and Chile. This third way was to grant amnesty to individuals in exchange for full disclosure of the crimes they had committed—"possible freedom in exchange for truth."[26] This third way, implemented by the Truth and Reconciliation Commission, forgave and released perpetrators of crimes through confession and apology.

In 1982, Tutu visited Yad Vashem, the Holocaust museum in Jerusalem, and when interviewed by the media, he spoke about forgiveness, pointing out the fact that Jesus was also a Jew. Tutu also criticized the Israelis regarding their unjust treatment of the Palestinians, which he believed was contrary to prophetic and rabbinical teachings. Charged with anti-Semitism, Tutu was branded by some as a "black Nazi pig."[27] Such a vehement racist outburst reveals the (understandable) sensitivities surrounding suggestions that Israel should offer forgiveness to the perpetrators of crimes committed against the Jewish people. Judaism has a venerable tradition of treating neighbors and even enemies with compassion and mercy, but in the absence of repentance and in the face of such colossal crimes many Jewish people find it hard to forgive (see chapter 1).

At a meeting in Jerusalem in 1999, Tutu attempted to convince the Israelis that true security cannot be won through arms but through the restoration of justice, human rights, and dignity. The peaceful transition in South Africa had given Tutu the credibility to speak about forgiveness and reconciliation. Israeli leaders and politicians, such as Shimon Peres, a Nobel Peace Laureate, witnessed the success of South Africa in restoring peace and justice after abolishing apartheid rule.

In the Jewish context, as described in the previous chapter, forgiveness can only be granted if there is repentance and remorse. Tutu, looking at the example of Jesus dying on the cross, believed that one should not wait for the perpetrator to repent or even to ask for forgiveness. One can forgive preemptively as a refusal to be locked into the wrongdoer's whim.

---

24. Tutu, *No Future without Forgiveness*, 28.
25. Quoted in Tutu, *No Future without Forgiveness*, 29.
26. Tutu, *No Future without Forgiveness*, 30.
27. Tutu, *No Future without Forgiveness*, 268.

Of course, acknowledgement by the wrongdoer is very important indeed, but not absolutely indispensable.[28]

Further, not only can the dead not forgive, but survivors of the Holocaust also believed they cannot forgive on behalf of their loved ones who died as its victims. Tutu, however, took a different approach as a Christian and the chairperson of South African's Truth and Reconciliation Commission.

From a Christian perspective, it is possible to forgive on behalf of those who have suffered and died from atrocities, such as those committed by the Afrikaners and members of the Dutch Reformed Church, who sought theological justification for apartheid rule. For Tutu, the nature of Christian community is not atomistic—there is a historical continuity between the past and present. If we can celebrate and share the glory and past achievements of the saints, should we not also share the guilt and shame of the sinners?[29] Tutu reminded us that the failures of the past are also part of us as members of the church, whether we like it or not. It is clear in the Gospels that Jesus taught his disciples to forgive when someone asks to be forgiven.

Willie Jonker, a prominent theologian, apologized and sought forgiveness on behalf of the Dutch Reformed Church (DRC) for supporting apartheid rule in the past. Many people in the DRC and the Afrikaner community questioned Jonker's authority for making a confession on their behalf. Tutu, on the other hand, wholeheartedly accepted Jonker's confession and granted forgiveness on behalf of millions of apartheid victims, including those who had died. Many black people likewise questioned Tutu's right and authority to forgive on their behalf,[30] but for Tutu, it was important to forgive if the nation were to move on and not be locked in the prison of hatred and conflict:

> If the present generation could not legitimately speak on behalf of those who are no more, then we could not offer forgiveness for the sins of South Africa's racist past. . . . The process of healing our land would be subverted. . . . True forgiveness deals with the past, all of the past, to make the future possible. We cannot go on nursing grudges even vicariously for those who cannot speak for

---

28. Tutu, *No Future without Forgiveness*, 270, 272.
29. Tutu, *No Future without Forgiveness*, 276.
30. Vosloo, "Difficult Forgiveness?" 361–62.

themselves any longer. We have to accept that what we do, we do for generations past, present, and yet to come.[31]

Tutu believed that God wanted to show us there is life after conflict and there is a future because we forgive. Jews accepted reparations, that is, substantial financial compensations from European institutions for their role in the Holocaust, but did not forgive. He argued that if those who did not suffer directly cannot forgive on behalf of those who have died, then they should not be accepting reparation either. The Jewish refusal to forgive, he said, is a great hindrance to normalizing the relationship between the victims and perpetrators: "There will always be this albatross hanging around the neck of the erstwhile perpetrators."[32]

Given our shared humanity, the burden still exists within the communities in spite of efforts to reconcile. New relationships will always be vulnerable if there is no forgiveness, and hence no future. Tutu hoped that the Jewish community, which is very influential in global affairs, would eventually take a different approach—to forgive for the sake of world peace. As understood by Tutu, this willingness to forgive personally and on behalf of others, has its roots in the traditional Bantu philosophy known as *ubuntu*.

Ubuntu

Ubuntu offers a unifying vision of society built upon compassion and respect for one another, and thus serves as a rule of conduct, a social ethic, and a moral and spiritual foundation of existence.[33] The concept of *ubuntu* was recognized in the epilogue to the interim Constitution (Constitution of the Republic of South Africa Act 200 of 1993). An important source of law, *ubuntu* assists in the healing of broken relationships. Since it is not easy to understand fully the essence of *ubuntu* if one is not familiar with African traditional religion and philosophy, the following list is a useful guide.

Ubuntu is a term that:

1. is to be contrasted with vengeance;
2. dictates that a high value be placed on the life of a human being;

---

31. Tutu, *No Future without Forgiveness*, 279.
32. Tutu, *No Future without Forgiveness*, 278.
33. "Reflections on Judicial Views Of *Ubuntu*."

3. is inextricably linked to the values of and which [*sic*] places a high premium on dignity, compassion, humaneness, and respect for the humanity of another;

4. dictates a shift from confrontation to mediation and conciliation;

5. dictates good attitudes and shared concern;

6. favors the re-establishment of harmony in the relationship between parties and emphasizes that such harmony should restore the dignity of the plaintiff without ruining the defendant;

7. favors restorative rather than retributive justice;

8. operates in a direction favoring reconciliation rather than estrangement of disputants;

9. works towards sensitizing a disputant or a defendant in litigation to the hurtful impact of his actions to the other party and towards changing such conduct rather than merely punishing the disputant;

10. promotes mutual understanding rather than punishment;

11. favors face-to-face encounters of disputants with a view to facilitating differences being resolved rather than conflict and victory for the most powerful;

12. favors civility and civilized dialogue premised on mutual tolerance.[34]

People who acknowledge *ubuntu* are open and available to others; they affirm others. They are self-assured and confident, hence not threatened by others who are better than they are. They understand themselves as belonging to a community or a group. More importantly, a person committed to *ubuntu* is magnanimous and ready to forgive, and possesses qualities such as compassion, hospitality, and generosity. *Ubuntu* refers to the essence of being human, the sharing of what I have with another. Being aware that I belong to the same human family, I can say: "My humanity is caught up, is inextricably bound up, in yours."[35] I become a person through other persons; I am human because I belong; I participate and share with other human beings. Bound up in a network of interdependency, "a person is a person through other persons."[36]

---

34. "Afri-Forum and Another v Malema and Others."
35. Tutu, *No Future without Forgiveness*, 31.
36. Tutu, *No Future without Forgiveness*, 35.

A good example of an African's sense of interdependency is the case of an ordinary woman, Cynthia Ngewu, whose son, Christopher Piet, was killed during the apartheid era. At the TRC hearings, Cynthia was asked about forgiveness and she responded:

> This thing called reconciliation . . . if I am understanding it correctly . . . if it means this perpetrator, this man who has killed Christopher Piet, if it means he becomes human again, this man, so that I, so that all of us, get our humanity back . . . then I agree, then I support it all.[37]

Cynthia Ngewu actually believed that the killer of her son had lost his humanity when he committed the crime. If there is a possibility that the killer would regain his humanity through a profound transformation, then she was willing to forgive. She also understood that the loss of her son affected her own humanity. If the perpetrator could regain his humanity through her forgiveness, Cynthia believed that she would also regain her own full humanity. In accordance with traditional *ubuntu* philosophy, Cynthia viewed all people as interconnected with one another: a being is an "embedded being."[38]

Hence, as Tutu emphasized, social harmony is the greatest good and therefore must be protected at all costs. We must not let rage, resentment, and revenge threaten the common good, or the good of any person who is corrupted by such emotions. To forgive, according to Tutu, is not just altruistic; it is for our own good. Forgiveness strengthens people and helps them to survive, even in a system that seeks to dehumanize them. To dehumanize another is also to dehumanize oneself. It is to our benefit to forgive since anger and resentment destroy the common good, which is crucial for our growth as persons. Even though *ubuntu* is part of African culture, it does not occur automatically, Tutu warned. Only confident, compassionate, and self-denying persons possess *ubuntu*: South Africa is blessed with exceptional people such as Nelson Mandela who are willing to make sacrifices for the sake of the nation.

---

37. Krog, "The Young Wind Once Was a Man," 379.
38. Krog, "The Young Wind Once Was a Man," 379.

De Klerk and Mandela

Among the remarkable people in South Africa, Tutu first mentioned F. W. de Klerk, an Afrikaner who helped Nelson Mandela to dismantle apartheid and establish universal suffrage. Without de Klerk's skillful negotiation, South Africa would have experienced much more bloodshed and violence. De Klerk had the courage and skills to persuade the white community to give up their exclusive political control for the sake of peace. By advocating power-sharing, de Klerk actually placed his political career in great danger had he not succeeded.[39] Tutu wrote, "Nothing will ever take away from F. W. de Klerk the enormous credit that belongs to him for what he said and did then . . . whatever our assessment of what he did subsequently, we should salute him for what he did in 1990."[40] He had the courage to pursue unpopular policies for lasting peace.

South Africa was blessed to have a white leader like de Klerk at that critical point in the nation's history. But all the good will and efforts of de Klerk would have been useless if he did not have a counterpart who was able to measure up to the challenge of the time—Nelson Mandela, a saintly person, who would emerge from prison, not hell-bent on seeking revenge but rather as a visionary of reconciliation.

Mandela had spent twenty-seven years in prison by the time he was released on February 11, 1990. He suffered much in prison, doing hard labor on Robben Island. Much was done deliberately to break his spirit and morale, and his eyesight was ruined through long exposure to sunlight as he labored in the lime quarry. Yet these decades of suffering transformed Mandela into a compassionate and magnanimous person. The hardship he endured on behalf of others gave him authority and credibility to rule the nation.[41] When Mandela was released, he was determined to reconcile, to bind the wounds of the nation, and to engender trust and confidence: "Mandela was reconciliation and reconciliation was Mandela."[42] He returned to politics not for self-glorification but to serve his fellow men and women, irrespective and inclusive of their race. He did so, first, by setting up the Truth and Reconciliation Commission.

---

39. Tutu, *No Future without Forgiveness*, 37–38.
40. Tutu, *No Future without Forgiveness*, 37.
41. Tutu, *No Future without Forgiveness*, 39.
42. Klerk, "Nelson Mandela and Desmond Tutu," 323, 325.

Question of Justice

There was a fear that the TRC process would encourage impunity: people getting away scot free in spite of committing gruesome atrocities. In this reconciliation system, perpetrators had only to confess and disclose their crimes; they were not required to show remorse or repentance. Tutu was convinced that granting amnesty would not encourage impunity because amnesty was granted only to those who pleaded guilty and who accepted responsibility for what they had done. This created a new atmosphere where human rights were respected and people were accountable for their actions.

This amnesty provision was an *ad hoc* arrangement specifically for this transitional period and not to be regarded as a permanent feature in the South African judicial system. It was not "retributive justice," whose chief goal is to punish wrong doers, but "restorative justice," whose chief concern is the "healing of breaches" in the spirit of *ubuntu*.[43] Restorative justice mends broken relationships, reconciling both the victim and the perpetrator and reintegrating the perpetrator into the community, which has itself been offended. But the community's well-being comes at a cost. Once amnesty is given to a perpetrator, he cannot be sued for civil damages—it is as if the crime has never taken place. Thus, Tutu reminds us, victims paid a very high price for the peace and stability that South Africans enjoy.

In spite of the spirit of *ubuntu* and the generosity of the victims, the process of reconciliation was hindered by social and economic inequalities, which formed the core framework of apartheid rule. Systematic racial disparities in income have caused social unrest and conflict in society everywhere. In South Africa, this huge economic gap meant that white people enjoyed a luxurious and privileged lifestyle, supported and maintained by racist policies, while others often lacked even basic necessities such as decent housing, healthcare, education, and employment. Without a more equal distribution of income, there would not be any *true* reconciliation. South Africa faced the task of nation-building by uplifting the poor and the downtrodden through just social and economic policies aimed at alleviating poverty.

---

43. Tutu, *No Future without Forgiveness*, 54. For an account of the shortcomings of the TRC, namely the insufficiency of restorative justice in its effort to seek reconciliation in the nation, see Lephakga, "Radical Reconciliation," E1–E10. See also Dixon, "The Words Get in the Way," 3–9.

Sin, Sinner, and Self

The appointment of an Anglican Archbishop by President Nelson Mandela to be chairperson of the TRC emblematized the spiritual approach that the Commission would undertake with the healing process, emphasizing confession, forgiveness, and reconciliation. Retreats and prayers were organized to invoke God's help in this challenging task of uniting the nation. The whole work of the Commission was to be sustained by love, prayers, and thanksgiving from people throughout the world. Christian theological and spiritual perspectives guided by psychological and medical insights informed much of the Commission's policies regarding reparation and rehabilitation.

Tutu reminds us that, *in spite of a perpetrator's diabolical deeds*, we must not turn the person into a demon. Rather we need to distinguish the sin from the sinner, not confuse the two as one.[44] Forgiveness is about understanding that each of us has the capacity for good and evil. There is always a possibility for repentance. As Martin Luther King, Jr. articulated:

> Love, even for enemies, is the key to the solution of the problems of the world. . . . Let us be practical and ask the question, "How do we love our enemies?" . . . We must recognize that . . . an element of goodness may be found even in our worst enemy. . . . This means that there is some good in the worst of us and some evil in the best of us. When we discover this, we are less prone to hate our enemies. When we look beneath the surface, beneath the impulsive evil deed, we see within our enemy-neighbor a measure of goodness and know that the viciousness and evil of his acts are not quite representative of all that he is.[45]

To distinguish between the sin and the sinner, we need to be conscious that we are opposing the sin in the perpetrator on behalf of those he has hurt, and also on behalf of the sinner himself. Tutu said if we reduce those who harm us to monsters, then we cannot hold them accountable for what they did; monsters act monstrously—it is their nature.[46] In the real world, those who act monstrously are human beings; thus we should not reduce human beings to the sins they have committed, as they possess a fuller humanity and are accountable for what they have done.

---

44. Tutu, *No Future without Forgiveness*, 83.
45. Quoted in Makransky, "Confronting the 'Sin' Out of Love for the 'Sinner,'" 88.
46. Tutu, *No Future without Forgiveness*, 83.

When we go on a crusade of condemning crimes and injustices, pointing fingers at others, there is a danger that we ourselves end up imitating the evil we condemned: "we tend to propagate evil in the name of fighting evil."[47] When we view perpetrators as purely monsters, not human beings like ourselves, "in the most essential way, we have joined them, for that is how they have viewed other persons. Every time we identify with the inner pattern of misperception operative in evil action, we have joined evil at its root, even in the name of fighting evil."[48] This could be what happened to Winnie Mandela, "Mother of the Nation," yet also guilty of gross violations of human rights.

To prevent ourselves from falling into this vicious trap, we need to connect with the humanity and dignity of others, including that of our so-called enemies. Instead of just fighting for the black people against the white people in the name of justice, we need to learn how to support the humanity of each person so that all people can live together as one people. Desmond Tutu and Nelson Mandela are shining examples of this approach in their peace effort. For them, solidarity did not mean solidarity with some against others, but rather recognition of and support for the humanity of all people in South Africa.

Christian theology imbued the TRC with the sense that we live in a moral universe where good and evil exist, but good will eventually triumph. The paschal mystery of the death and resurrection of Jesus is proof that love is stronger than hate, life stronger than death. On the basis of this theological perspective, Tutu reiterated that the vicious cycle of reprisal and revenge can only be broken by going past retributive justice to restorative justice. This is no less true for countries like Rwanda, Nigeria, Angola, and Ethiopia, all of which have suffered from genocide and all kinds of atrocities. Tutu reiterated that the vicious cycle of reprisal and revenge can only be broken by going past retributive justice to restorative justice because there is no future without forgiveness. Tutu also emphasized that it was God's intention that we should live in peace and harmony as narrated in the biblical story of the Garden of Eden. This primordial harmony was disrupted when human beings started blaming one another and became alienated from their Creator. The story in the Bible, narrated in such an imaginative and symbolic way, reveals a profound existential truth concerning our human existence. In addition to alienation, disharmony, conflict, and hatred,

---

47. Makransky, "Confronting the 'Sin' out of Love for the 'Sinner,'" 90.
48. Makransky, "Confronting the 'Sin' out of Love for the 'Sinner,'" 90.

all of which exist in our society, our environment has also been exploited and destroyed for the advantage of a few.[49] Those of us with faith in God know a better world is possible if we are united in a spirit of forgiveness, compassion, and *ubuntu* or selfhood in community.

The South African Truth and Reconciliation Commission was very much influenced by the Bantu concept of selfhood, according to South African poet Antjie Krog. The TRC individualized amnesty while perpetrators in most countries received general or blanket amnesty through their own commissions. The usual practice was that all testimonies were heard privately, behind closed doors, but the TRC allowed the victims to testify in public. Victims from both sides of the conflict were allowed to testify during the same trial.[50]

While Christianity had a clear influence on TRC's approach and overall orientation, Krog believes that the African philosophy of *ubuntu* had a stronger direct impact. The TRC would have failed without this "communitarian logic," which "forms a kind of pervasive and fundamental concept in African socio-ethical thought that animates other intellectual activities and behaviour, which provides continuity, resilience, nourishment and meaning to life."[51] This native wisdom helped people of South Africa to reinterpret Judeo-Christian concepts such as justice, forgiveness, and reconciliation in a way that is acceptable and meaningful. Christian virtues become infused and energized with African philosophy, as they have long been fused and energized with Greek philosophy. Christianity is not simply added on to *ubuntu* or held to be compatible with it, but rather it finds new self-understanding and expression through deep engagement with the local socio-ethical philosophy: this is inculturation at its best.

The Theology of Tutu

Archbishop Tutu's theology emphasizes liberation from sins through repentance and confession. Jesus forgave his enemies, those who nailed him to the cross, without their confession or request for forgiveness. He even gave them an excuse: "Father, forgive them, for they do not know what they are doing" (Luke 23:34). We should not wait for the perpetrator to show remorse and

---

49. Tutu, *No Future without Forgiveness*, 263–64.
50. Krog, "The Young Wind Once Was a Man," 380.
51. Krog, "The Young Wind Once Was a Man," 380.

repentance, says Tutu; otherwise we will be "locked into victimhood."[52] In forgiving, Tutu wrote, we are proclaiming our faith in the future for a better relationship, with the hope that the wrongdoer will repent. Without forgiveness, there would be no future in South Africa, no chance to make a new beginning. Further, we must follow the example of Jesus to forgive seventy times seven, which means an infinite number of times.

Tutu never considered the white people as his enemies, in spite of the fact that they tried to demonize him. He wanted only to abolish the apartheid system, which he believed was a heresy and inherently evil.[53] As a churchman and chairman of the TRC who cared for his flock and for people belonging to other faiths, he hoped to unite the people of South Africa. Tutu criticized the complicity of the white South African church with the ruling regime. In fact, the Dutch Reformed Church (DRC) of South Africa established by Jan van Riebeeck in 1652 supported the apartheid system with spurious biblical justification.[54] The Bible was used by this church to serve the ideology of the white regime in South Africa, which was to control the black people.[55]

Christianity, established by western missionaries in Latin America, Asia, and Africa, was justly associated with colonialism in these places. Tutu spoke jokingly about that fact this way:

> When the white man first came here he had the Bible and we had the land. Then the white man said to us, come let us kneel and pray together. So we knelt and closed our eyes and prayed, and when we opened our eyes again, lo!—we had the Bible and he had the land.[56]

In such sentiments as these, Tutu was partially in agreement with critics like Frantz Fanon, who argued that the church in the colonies is a white man's church, a foreigner's church. The church does not, Fanon believed, teach the natives the ways of God but the way of the white man, the oppressor, the

---

52. Tutu, *No Future without Forgiveness*, 272.

53. Tutu, *Hope and Suffering*, 158 and 166.

54. Tutu, *Hope and Suffering*, 37and 87. John De Gruchy wrote that the churches that were committed to the anti-apartheid movement—such as the Anglican, Roman Catholic, Methodist, Congregational, and Presbyterian churches—were the first to admit their failures, but the Dutch Reformed Church's confession was rather disappointing. This reflects the struggle within the churches between supporters and critics of the apartheid policy. See De Gruchy, "Giving Account," 1180–82.

55. See Lephakga, "Radical Reconciliation," 1.

56. Quoted in Battle, "The Effects of Christian Mission on Political Change in South Africa," 471.

master.[57] And yet, Tutu continued to speak boldly and frankly about Christian theology and mission—when properly understood—as legitimate and necessary for the reconciliation process in South Africa:

> You whites brought us the Bible; now we blacks are taking it seriously. We are involved with God to set us free from all that enslaves us and makes us less than what He intended us to be. . . . I will demonstrate that apartheid, separate development, or whatever it is called, is evil, totally and without remainder, that it is unchristian and unbiblical. If anyone were to show me otherwise, I would burn my Bible and cease to be a Christian.[58]

For Tutu, the Christian message is a call to action, a promise of liberation from slavery and injustice. Tutu believed that God is always on the side of the oppressed, but also that when God liberates the oppressed, the oppressor is liberated as well. Only when black people are liberated, therefore, will white people be truly free—restored to the fullness of their own human dignity, free of the stain of their complicity in others' oppression.

In spite of the church's colonial ties, African American theologian Michael Battle believed that it was a great promoter of the non-violent transition from despotism to democracy in South Africa. Through moral assertion on behalf of respect in the rule of law, human rights, and dignity, great leaders such as Desmond Tutu, Nelson Mandela, and others had "envisioned a symbiotic relationship between Christian and political leadership."[59]

Proclaiming that the mission of Jesus was to effect reconciliation between God and his people, and between human beings, Tutu condemned segregation and oppression. He maintained that if one part of the body suffers, the whole body suffers. His vision for South Africa was multi-racial, uniting black people and white people, with freedom for all. In the true meaning of shared humanity, if the black people are not free, the white people will not be free either: "Freedom is indivisible."[60] If freedom is indivisible there is no excuse for discrimination.

Tutu was critical of western nations, especially the United States, for keeping silence, for being impartial, in the face of so much injustice

---

57. Fanon, *The Wretched of the Earth*, 42.

58. Quoted in Battle, "The Effects of Christian Mission on Political Change in South Africa," 479.

59. Battle, "The Effects of Christian Mission on Political Change in South Africa," 468.

60. Tutu, *Hope and Suffering*, 45.

and exploitation. For Tutu, being "impartial" to atrocities is to condone them.[61] God is not neutral; he takes the side of the slaves and the oppressed. Christians cannot be indifferent to the sufferings and cries of others. Influenced by Archbishop William Temple, Tutu asserted that Christianity is the "most materialistic of the major religions"—the criteria for entry into the kingdom of God is to feed the hungry, clothe the naked, and visit the sick and the imprisoned, those whom Christ called the least among the brethren (Matt 25:31–46).[62] In fact, Christianity became a secular faith when the Word became Flesh and lived among us (John 1:14). The theology of Tutu is essentially a theology of liberation based on praxis in the context of South Africa.

Reflection

Ubuntu is a test case of shared humanity and restorative justice. It shows that one can make God's love visible by offering forgiveness and reaching out for reconciliation, difficult as these actions might be.

Forgiveness is only the first step taken by the victim as part of the healing process. It is given in the hope that the perpetrator will respond with repentance; this acknowledgement by the perpetrator is important but not absolutely vital.[63] Forgiveness has its own intrinsic moral value.

Reconciliation is an outcome of forgiveness, but it does not happen automatically. The grace of God is needed. In addition, Tutu also highlighted the importance of remembrance, of not forgetting, and of confessing the truth of what actually happened irrespective of how ghastly the deeds were. In fact, the perpetrators' experience of guilt and the ordeal of confessing their crimes may be a punishment in itself.

Genuine forgiveness and reconciliation do not ignore wrongdoing. In fact, they expose abuse, pain, and degradation, and reveal the truth, which eventually brings about healing. Remembering helps in "drawing out the sting in the memory that threatens to poison our entire existence."[64] This is regarded as the purification and healing of memory. The work of the TRC has been characterized as a "cathartic process" of

---

61. Tutu, *Hope and Suffering*, 51, 115.

62. Tutu, *Hope and Suffering*, 59. For a more detailed account of the theology of Desmond Tutu, see Klerk, "Nelson Mandela and Desmond Tutu," 322–34.

63. Tutu, *No Future without Forgiveness*, 270.

64. Tutu, *No Future without Forgiveness*, 271.

self-cleansing, where anger, grief, and sadness are allowed to surface and the dead are laid to rest.[65]

Recalling the pain and anguish the black people of South Africa suffered marks the beginning of the healing process—they are recognized by the nation and heard in their pain when they testify at the TRC. The accounts of their sufferings have been recorded and received into "the memories of the nation."[66] Perpetrators and torturers who were untouchable in the past were made to confess and were held responsible for the crimes they had committed. This is restorative justice.

Forgiveness is about personally letting go of resentment and anger; reconciliation is about mutual commitment to restoring the relationship. In the light of the philosophical understanding of *ubuntu*—that self, forgiveness, and reconciliation cannot be separated—we see that they are dependent on one another. The TRC testimonies revealed the significance of this view of interconnectedness and wholeness, while forgiveness and reconciliation allowed the victims and perpetrators to grow together and in view of one another into a "fuller personhood."[67]

The call for forgiveness and reconciliation has been characterized as religious and therapeutic. But the right of the victims not to forgive should also be respected. Some critics commented that moral anger and resentment can be used for resistance against evil, oppression, and the tragic drama of racial segregation. In fact, in his research on the South African TRC, Thomas Brudholm argued that resentment can also be "a virtue and a necessary position in a reconciliation process."[68] There is thus a place for resentment as a resistance against evil, and the right of the victim to express his or her anger towards the perpetrator who is caught up in the tragic drama of racial segregation.

Unlike most Jewish survivors of the Holocaust, who felt they have no right to forgive on behalf of the deceased victims, Tutu accepted the right of a third party to forgive. Tutu believed this moral imperative was the only way for the nation to move forward. Without forgiveness, South Africa would be doomed again. Retributive justice involves satisfying the individual victims through punishment of the offender or through reparation. The TRC gave only token compensation to the victims. The purpose was not really to

---

65. Battle, "A Theology of Community," 180.
66. Battle, "A Theology of Community," 181.
67. Krog, "The Young Wind Once Was a Man," 381.
68. Leer-Salvesen, "Reconciliation without Violence," 169.

compensate the individuals but to restore integrity to a just community and to unite the nation as a whole. This restoration of justice to the community is, then, the hallmark of the South African approach to forgiveness, manifesting the fruits of inculturation in the political order and yielding real hope for a better future in a once-divided society.

— *Chapter 3* —

Power of Peace

Conflict in Ireland

> I still hold two truths with equal and fundamental certainty. One: the British did terrible things to the Irish. Two: the Irish, had they the power, would have done equally terrible things to the British. And so also for any other paired adversaries I can imagine. The difficulty is to hold on to both truths with equal intensity, not let either one negate the other, and know when to emphasize one without forgetting the other. Our humanity is probably lost and gained in the necessary tension between them both.
>
> —JOHN DOMINIC CROSSAN

The creation of Northern Ireland in 1921 resulted in division and conflict between the Protestant community (also called loyalists or unionists), a majority of whom regarded themselves as British, and the Catholic minority (republicans or nationalists), who regarded themselves as Irish. These ethnic, political, and religious differences led to much tension, discrimination, and bloodshed. Inspired by Martin Luther King, Jr's 1960s civil rights movement in the United Sates, Catholics, who saw themselves being discriminated against by Northern Ireland's Protestant-dominated government, began to stage protests and peaceful marches. Unfortunately, with the involvement of paramilitary groups, this sparked off violence on both sides, and led to the arrival of the British Army in 1969.

This chapter first examines the spiritual impulse that led the late Redemptorist, Fr. Alec Reid, to direct the peace process in Northern Ireland within the nationalist community. It discusses the success and failure of the churches in promoting peace and highlights the efforts of the Irish and British governments and their supporters in establishing a political framework that would lead not only to peace and equality, but also to forgiveness and reconciliation. To understand the conflicts and troubles in Northern Ireland, where memories of past injustice and humiliation are so firmly embedded in the collective consciousness, we need to go back in history.

A Historical Sketch

From the fourteenth century onward, the English occupiers of Ireland treated the local people unjustly. There were laws prohibiting private warfare and regulating trade to protect English interests. As time passed, more prohibitions were imposed, notably—after England became Protestant—that of making the practice of the Catholic faith illegal, despite the fact that the great majority of the population was Catholic. Also prohibited was the use of the Irish language, names, laws, and dress. At the individual level, intermarriage was restricted between the communities. Further, local Irish people were excluded from administering the cathedrals and religious houses.[1] These policies of discrimination and bigotry revealed the prejudice of the English, bent upon suppressing Irish identity and traditions.

During the fifteenth century, the Irish legislature was made subservient to the English and, needless to say, this law was fiercely opposed by the Irish. After Elizabeth I became Queen of England and Ireland in 1558, she imposed the new Protestant (Anglican) religion on Ireland, but it was never accepted by the majority of the people. Elizabeth further enraged the Irish by her policy of plantation, confiscating land from the Irish and giving it to Protestants brought in from England while Presbyterians from Scotland were given land in the north of the country. By 1660 Ireland had three Christian denominations: Catholic, Anglican, and Protestant Dissenters.[2] In spite of the Gospels' teaching of forgiveness and love, conflicts, distrust, and rivalries were rife among them.

To make Ireland's economy dependent upon England, there was a deliberate attempt to keep the Irish poor and subservient. Irish wool and

---

1. Wells, *People Behind the Peace*, 11. Some material in this chapter appeared as an article in Ambrose Mong, "Power of Peace; Forgiveness and Reconciliation in Northern Ireland," *Dialogue & Alliance*, vol. 34, no. 1, Summer 2020 (85–104).

2. Wells, *People Behind the Peace*, 14–17.

cattle industries were regulated and Irish trade with the American colonies was restricted. Acts were passed to exclude Catholics from the Irish Parliament, and to restrict their right to acquire land, and in 1801 Ireland's Parliament was dissolved and incorporated into the British Parliament. To add insult to injury, Catholics had to pay tithes to the (Anglican) Church of Ireland. Catholic nobility and leaders were suppressed and so the people turned to the clergy, which enhanced the power of the Catholic Church.[3] The governmental power that was meant to reduce the influence of the Catholic Church ironically strengthened its base.

The Catholic Emancipation Act of 1829, giving Catholics freedom to practice their religion, brought some relief to Catholics; it meant also that Catholics could be elected to Parliament, and throughout the nineteenth century Irish members of the British Parliament, led initially by Charles S. Parnell, consistently demanded that Ireland be made a free state, a self-governing Republic, independent of Britain.

The unjust and oppressive policies of England towards Ireland served only to produce profound feelings of resentment and hatred among the native Irish towards the settlers. This deep-seated animosity led to uprisings, cruelly suppressed by the British military, and culminated during the twentieth century in what is known as the Troubles—a carnage that lasted for thirty years.

The Troubles

At the risk of over-simplification of a complex history, here is a sketch of the Troubles, which lasted from 1968 to 1998. The crucial issue was whether the northern part of Ireland should be part of the United Kingdom or part of the Republic of Ireland. Unionists wished for the former and nationalists, the latter.[4] "Republicans" are a minority of nationalists who supported armed struggle, usually waged by the Irish Republican Army (IRA)

---

3. Wells, *People Behind the Peace*, 18

4. Ulster Protestants, a political minority in Ireland, strongly opposed home rule because they feared that they would be oppressed by the Catholic majority. This strong opposition was symbolized by the signing of the so-called Ulster Covenant of 1912. This agreement pledged to use "all means which may be found necessary to defeat the present conspiracy to set up Home Rule Parliament in Ireland." This was a religious-political pledge by the Protestants to resist the political self-determination of the Irish. Amstutz, *The Healing of Nations*, 167.

to gain Irish independence.[5] In a similar manner, "loyalists" are a minority of unionists who resorted to violence, often with the connivance of the police and state, leading to a vicious cycle of vengeance. Approximately 3,288 people died in this conflict.[6]

A split among the unionists, with the radical side headed by Rev. Ian Paisley and his Democratic Unionist Party (DUP) founded in 1971, further aggravated the volatile situation in Northern Ireland. Among republicans, there was also a split between the "Official" and "Provisional" IRA and their political representatives *Sinn Féin* (Gaelic for "Ourselves Alone"), whose aims were the unification of Ireland and an end to British rule in Northern Ireland.[7] It is within the complex and changing circumstances of Irish politics that Fr. Alec Reid started his work in the peace ministry. His mission was further complicated by the sheer number of political parties, which made consensus among them almost impossible.

As a member of the Redemptorist community[8] in Clonard, West Belfast, Fr. Reid saw himself as a servant of Christ led by the Holy Spirit to reach out to those caught in the vicious cycle of violence and vengeance. His interest in the peace ministry was not political but pastoral. He believed that a priest, as a representative of the Church, should not be involved in nationalist/republican party politics. However, because he was a priest, he felt he must respond to the human and moral dimensions of the situation, especially when it involved people suffering and dying. Fr. Reid aimed to help people who might be killed or imprisoned if the conflict continued. In his letter to John Hume, a founding member of the SDLP,[9] Fr. Reid revealed that it was the death of

---

5. Created in 1919, Irish Republican Army (IRA), was a paramilitary organization that sought to end British rule in Northern Ireland and attain the reunification of Ireland. Its purpose was to use armed force against the British to achieve its objective. The IRA operated independently of political control, but in some periods its membership has overlapped with that of Sinn Féin, the Irish nationalist party. "Irish Republican Army," *Encyclopaedia Britannica*.

6. Biggar, "Forgiving Enemies in Ireland," 565.

7. McKeever, C.Ss.R., *One Man, One God*, 15–17.

8. The Redemptorists are members of the Congregation of the Most Holy Redeemer (C.SS.R.), a community of Catholic priests and brothers founded by St. Alphonsus Liguori in 1732 at Scala in Italy. Their main work is preaching the gospel to the poor, giving parish missions, and retreats. Besides administering shrines, they also promote scholarship in the field of moral theology.

9. Founded in August 1970, the SDLP (Social Democratic and Labour Party) is an Irish nationalist political party in Northern Ireland. As a civil rights party, the SDLP works for an Ireland that is free from poverty, prejudice, and injustice. It wants an Ireland

a man from the Ulster Defense Regiment (a predominantly Protestant and Unionist branch of the British Army) that prompted him and his colleagues to end this violent situation and work for peace in Northern Ireland. He regarded his peace ministry as a divine calling.

Led by the Spirit

In the midst of conflict, Fr. Reid saw himself as an agent of the Holy Spirit, a witness to the moral dimensions of human actions. He insisted the motives for conflict and confrontation are always human, with all the moral dimensions, good and evil, that human nature entails. It is the role of the Christian to identify these dimensions with the guidance of the Holy Spirit. Fr. Reid stressed that peacemakers must know the conflict "from within" rather than "from without," and with this knowledge and the help of the Spirit, they could grasp the moral issues and resolve the conflict in a Christian way.[10] Like the Anglican Archbishop Desmond Tutu, Fr. Reid adhered to an incarnational theology that emphasizes the healing presence of Christ in the world.

Convinced that he could resolve the conflict in Northern Ireland only with the help of the Holy Spirit, Fr. Reid also believed that it was the Spirit that enabled him to face with courage the many setbacks, deadlocks, mistakes, and failures he experienced in his peace ministry. The Holy Spirit guided him to discern all the moral issues and give direction in a reasonable and compassionate way. It is only through faith in the "dynamic presence of the Holy Spirit" that a Christian can learn how to face adversity and move forward.[11]

This reliance on the power of the Holy Spirit is cultivated through constant prayer and meditation. Fr. Reid reminded us that Jesus himself was also caught up in the human dimensions of good and evil. Jesus fell victim to the moral and physical violence that are so prevalent in human conflicts. Fr. Reid emphasized that the "companionship" between God and us that Jesus established is one that exists in the Trinity.[12] It is witnessed in the Gospels, where we see Jesus eating and drinking with sinners and tax-collectors. This

that is peaceful and united and free from violence. See their website, The Social Democratic and Labour Party (SDLP) https://www.sdlp.ie, for more information.

10. McKeever, C.Ss.R., *One Man, One God*, 139.
11. McKeever, C.Ss.R., *One Man, One God*, 141.
12. McKeever, C.Ss.R., *One Man, One God*, 141.

companionship involves the sharing of food, drink, and conversation, which enhances friendship and builds community.

Following Christ, Fr. Reid held that Christians in the midst of conflict must always seek to communicate with people, especially with those one does not like. In other words, there must be dialogue with all the participants in an attempt to resolve conflict in a Christian manner. This was crucial in Northern Ireland, where people had experienced centuries of prejudice against the "other" due to historical and political circumstances. As the pastoral leader of the peace ministry, Fr. Reid's impetus was to discern the moral issues pertaining to the conflict in order to give proper direction for its resolution. He spelt out the following guidelines:

i. The first step would be to list all the participants in the conflict and to grade them according to their significance for its resolution.

ii. Next would be to meet authoritative representatives of all the participants with a view to explaining the role of the Christian ministry to resolve the conflict and urge cooperation.

iii. Finally, to set up a programme for pursuing the strategy of the ministry in an organized, dynamic and, therefore, effective way.[13]

Fr. Reid's peace ministry was essentially a ministry of communication characterized by a spirit of Christian dialogue. The most important thing in the ministry of conflict resolution is to listen with compassion and discernment. In practical terms, it means to listen to the viewpoints of all the parties involved; to understand their political positions; and to discern elements of moral truth and justice, thus bringing about a common ground from which to resolve conflicts. Fr. Reid wrote, "The way to peace is to be found within the conflict itself."[14] He was essentially following the scriptural teaching that sees Jesus as present in the world; especially when he looked at the suffering and death of so many people in Northern Ireland.

Once the elements of moral truth and justice in the various party positions were identified, Fr. Reid would write down the reasons for accepting or not accepting them. This written response would be the basis for dialogue, and the participants would focus on areas of disagreement in order to resolve them. The parties would be informed of the elements of moral truth and justice, which the reconciliation ministry would support.

---

13. McKeever, C.Ss.R., *One Man, One God*, 144.
14. McKeever, C.Ss.R., *One Man, One God*, 144.

In turn, the parties would have to give an authoritative response. He stressed that the faithful in their congregations be informed and given leadership roles so that the peace process would have the spiritual and moral support of the people. Fr. Reid believed there are representatives in all the Christian traditions in Ireland, both lay and clerical, who are gifted by God to undertake this demanding mission of reconciliation. It was an ecumenical effort that involved Catholics and Protestants.

A Rational and Christian Approach

Fr. Reid's underlying principles regarding the peace process were based not just on his Christian faith, but common sense as well. He took an informed and rational approach toward the Troubles, while at the same time being open to the guidance of the Holy Spirit. He believed that the most Christian way to achieve reconciliation between people is through dialogue carried out in an atmosphere of mutual respect and compassion.

As we know now, it was faith and dialogue that eventually ended the armed struggle and opened the nation to lasting peace. Fr. Reid had witnessed how his peace ministry had initiated and advanced the process of healing and reconciliation within the nationalist/republican communities, and also between the nationalist and unionist communities. While putting his faith in the Lord in the peace ministry, Fr. Reid also utilized his knowledge and experience in dealing with strong characters in both communities. He sought the advice of nationalists and unionists whose judgment he could trust because of their insights regarding the political situation of their respective communities. He asked them how the Church could help in their quest for peace.

Generally, both nationalists and unionists agreed that the churches could be instrumental in the peace process because of their resources, influence, independence, and authority. The churches could initiate dialogue between parties and groups who were deadlocked in conflicts and rivalries. Sinn Féin members, who were involved in armed conflict, also believed the Church could play an important role in the pursuit of peace, in addition to finding solutions to end the "armed struggle."[15] In fact, most people in Northern Ireland (at that time) believed the Church was in a unique position to help in peaceful negotiations among the various parties.

---

15. McKeever, C.Ss.R., *One Man, One God*, 115

Many people remembered Pope John Paul II's speech at Drogheda, in the Republic of Ireland, on the need to end violence. John Paul also reminded the political leaders about the need to use peaceful means to overcome injustices, rather than taking up arms. It was the lack of justice that led some people to consider the use of violence as justified. The Pope said:

> *Christianity does not command us to close our eyes to difficult human problems.* It does not permit us to neglect and refuse to see unjust social or international situations. What Christianity does forbid is to seek solutions to these situations by the ways of hatred, by the murdering of defenceless people, by the methods of terrorism. . . . Christianity understands and recognizes the noble and just struggle for justice.[16]

Prompted by the Pope's speech, Irish leaders understood that the only way to persuade the IRA to end their violent campaign was to convince them that it was no longer necessary to use force to achieve justice for the nationalist community. There were other peaceful means to achieve a more equitable society. Listening to the representatives of Sinn Féin, church leaders understood that the only way to end the armed struggle was through dialogue where "an alternative method" could be formulated and proposed to the IRA as feasible.[17]

The proposal for an alternate method emphasized the importance of unity among the nationalist parties, to be achieved through dialogue. The aim was to formulate a common nationalist policy with regard to objectives and approaches to resolve conflicts and achieve lasting peace. The establishment of a powerful nationalist united front would encourage the IRA to lay down arms as a first step in the peace process. Fr. Reid believed this proposal would end the violence and the tragedies that afflicted the nation. A "broad nationalist consensus" that was just and rational would gain the support of the Church, as well as respect and sympathy from the international community.[18] Such a common nationalist policy would also hopefully gain the support of the unionist community because it would end the use of violence as a strategy for change.

---

16. John Paul II, Apostolic Journey to Ireland, *Holy Mass in Drogheda*, no. 5.
17. McKeever, C.Ss.R., *One Man, One God*, 115
18. McKeever, C.Ss.R., *One Man, One God*, 116.

Question of Violence

A number of theories were put forward regarding political violence in Northern Ireland. The first view, held by Irish nationalists, especially Sinn Féin, believed political conflict in Northern Ireland was the result of colonialism, i.e., the British occupation of Ireland. The only way to resolution was for Britain to withdraw completely from Ireland. When nationalists demanded a separate Gaelic nation-state, they meant that the establishment of the Irish Republic in 1921 was only a partial fulfillment of their national aspiration.

The second view stressed the socially, economically, and politically discriminatory policies of the Protestant government that promoted inequalities and injustice, which in turn victimized and oppressed Catholics.[19]

The third view maintained that the violence was due to intense political sectarianism between nationalists and loyalists. There was a lack of a universal and rational norm that could enable the two communities to be more inclusive.

A fourth view was the "ethnonationalist perspective," in which the Ulster Unionists, who were usually Protestants, regarded themselves as British, and Irish nationalists, who were typically Catholics, regarded themselves as Irish.[20] Here, religion serves as a fundamental cause of the conflict: Protestantism versus Catholicism. Most scholars would agree that all these explanations contributed in various ways to the conflict in Northern Ireland.

On an optimistic note, Fr. Reid believed such violence would not have erupted if the situation had been handled properly in time, and that the armed struggle could have been stopped within six months if there had been skillful mediation by competent people. In fact, centuries of political conflict between Irish nationalists and British unionists could be ended within a reasonable time if both parties could base their negotiations on the principles of democracy, justice, and charity.

---

19. According to Mark Amstutz, discrimination and inequalities in Northern Ireland were a result of political conflicts and deep psychological distrust between nationalists and unionists. Protestant leaders in local and regional government in Ulster gave preferential treatment to their fellow believers and the Catholic republicans did likewise when in power. Protestant favoritism was more prevalent because they had more political power and opportunities to be corrupt. See Amstutz, *The Healing of Nations*, 170, 172–73.

20. Amstutz, *The Healing of Nations*, 173–74. For a detailed account of the conflicts in Northern Ireland, see also McGarry and O'Leary, *Explaining Northern Ireland*.

Speaking on behalf of the nationalist tradition, Fr. Reid understood that a majority of nationalists had long ago rejected violence as a means to end British rule in Northern Ireland. They preferred to use peaceful, political, and diplomatic means to achieve their goal. But there was a nationalist tradition that goes back to the French Revolution, called Irish republicanism, the proponents of which believed that they had the right to use military force to gain Irish Independence. Thus, they held that armed struggle was justifiable because British presence in the country was a violation of their rights.[21] In spite of condemnations by many nationalists and by the Church, the republican movement, represented by the Irish Republican Army (IRA) and Sinn Féin, continued their armed struggle. However, they too believed that military force alone could not achieve Irish independence; political negotiations were eventually also necessary.

The use of armed force was perceived by the republican movement as an effective tactic to pressure the British to negotiate with them. Fr. Reid believed republican violence was used as a means to an end. In fact, the republican movement and its military leaders were willing to search for an alternative to armed struggle for achieving Irish independence. But this must be handled with great diplomatic skill and patience because the republicans have a strong military tradition that counted their slain fighters as some of the greatest heroes in Irish history.[22] This armed tradition has been handed down from generation to generation, quite like their Catholic faith. Fr. Reid was convinced that many Irish Catholics would lay down their lives for their faith as quickly as they would for their nation.

Even though many republicans were devout Catholics, they continued to ignore the Church's warning against the use of violence. Through their long experience of suffering and persecution, they knew that bishops and priests were not infallible in matters of politics. They preferred to use their own judgment and discretion when it came to deciding their political future: "the democratic principles of republicanism have taught them to think for themselves and to be independent of mind in matters of personal conscience."[23] Priests who served the nationalist flock were advised by Fr. Reid that they must keep this in mind and refrain from criticizing the proponents of violence in public, even as they continued to guide them on moral issues.

21. McKeever, C.Ss.R., *One Man, One God*, 134.
22. McKeever, C.Ss.R., *One Man, One God*, 135.
23. McKeever, C.Ss.R., *One Man, One God*, 136.

Only through direct communication would the republicans be persuaded to lay down their arms and to negotiate peacefully. The republicans would join forces with nationalist political parties only if there was a strong strategy and a viable political option to achieve Irish nationalist/republican objectives. The nationalist parties involved insisted that the republican movement stop the armed struggle before they would come to the table to talk. Since the parties (nationalist and republican) heretofore had refused to communicate, the republican movement continued its armed campaign. It was at this critical juncture that Fr. Reid's influence came into play. He intervened to facilitate channels of communication and dialogue. He was convinced that only the Church had the moral authority and resources to provide a sanctuary where all parties were willing to give peace a chance.

Most unionists would also respect a powerful but peaceful and united nationalist front. Fr. Reid believed that there were more realistic, wise, influential, and compassionate people among the unionists than there were hard-liners. In fact, these were the ones who were open to the political options and responded positively towards a common nationalist policy. More important, Reid emphasized, was the necessity to have ongoing open-ended dialogue among the various parties concerned, initiated and coordinated by the Church.

Role of the Church

Although the Church's role is purely pastoral, Fr. Reid believed that in a situation like Northern Ireland, it should be involved in helping political parties to find a way to end violence and avoid tragic consequences. In fact, the division between pastoral and political responsibility is not clearly demarcated, given the complex circumstances of Ireland.[24]

Since 1969, there had been a breakdown in law and order, as well as trust and communication, in Northern Ireland. Without the Church's intervention, Fr. Reid believed, the situation would get worse and then only the police and soldiers could "contain" the conflict by means of armed force. The Church thus had a pastoral responsibility to create a neutral and supportive setting where different political groups could communicate. In spite of repeated condemnation by the Church regarding the use of violence to achieve political aims, many Catholics were involved in the armed struggle because the situation had not improved. Following John

24. McKeever, C.Ss.R., *One Man, One God*, 118.

Paul II's call for justice and peace at Drogheda, the Church felt it must support political parties to find peaceful means to secure a just peace, if not outright Irish independence.

Fr. Reid held the conviction that the Church should be involved in politics if it meant being responsible for the common good of the people, not just their spiritual good alone. If politics is part and parcel of human life, then it is the duty of the Church to communicate with all political schools.[25] The presence of the Church in peaceful negotiation was crucial because Sinn Féin and the IRA in particular trusted its impartiality and concern for the common good. They would not even consider any ceasefire unless the British had actually declared their intention to withdraw from Irish affairs. The involvement of the Church in searching for alternative methods would give the negotiations a moral and pastoral stature.

While Fr. Reid personally stood on the Catholic and nationalist side, he understood the longings and concerns of the unionist community, nurtured in them through historical circumstances. Their political fears and constraints had crippled their best instincts. They could not be liberated from their fear as individuals and as a community if they were under constant attack from the IRA. Wishing to protect their own traditions, the unionist community thus withdrew deeper behind "emotional and political barriers" they had built up through the years against the nationalist community.[26] Fr. Reid, however, believed a political reconciliation between nationalists and unionists was possible and when that happened, both communities would be able to flourish and preserve their own unique traditions. A time of healing and seeking forgiveness from both sides was urgently needed to rebuild Northern Ireland. No one was in a better position to represent the churches in seeking forgiveness than the two primates in the United Kingdom and Ireland: Archbishop George Carey and Cardinal Cahal Daly.

Primates Seeking Pardon

In 1994, the Archbishop of Canterbury, Dr. George Carey, went to Christ Church Cathedral, Dublin, and preached on the scandal of the religious conflicts in Northern Ireland, and the urgent need for forgiveness and reconciliation. He said, "I am aware of just how much we English need to ask forgiveness for our often-brutal domination and crass insensitivity

---

25. McKeever, C.Ss.R., *One Man, One God*, 121.
26. McKeever, C.Ss.R., *One Man, One God*, 128.

in the eight hundred years of history of relationships with Ireland. . . . [To recognize] the follies, the evils and the atrocities committed in the name of whatever ideals we follow, is to begin to build the bridge."[27] These words coming from the Anglican primate contributed greatly to the healing process.

The Roman Catholic Cardinal Cahal Daly, Primate of Ireland, reciprocated when he apologized for the wrongs inflicted by the Irish on the British, especially during the Troubles. The Cardinal recalled the atrocities committed by Catholics against Protestants such as those that happened in Whitecross, Darkley, the Shankill Road, and Enniskillen. He pleaded for forgiveness on behalf of the perpetrators, who had been warned by their bishops to refrain from violence. In his homily in Canterbury Cathedral on January 22, 1995, Cardinal Daly said:

> I wish to ask forgiveness from the people of this land for the wrongs and hurts inflicted by Irish people on the people of this country on many occasions during our shared history, and particularly in the past twenty-five years. I believe that this reciprocal recognition of the need to forgive and to be forgiven is a necessary condition for proper Christian and human and indeed political relationships between our two islands in the future.[28]

In spite of skepticism expressed by both sides, unionists and nationalists, the church leaders' request for forgiveness was taken seriously. An example was when the Catholic and Presbyterian Churches issued a joint statement to condemn republican strong-arm tactics as well as unionist marches that led to violence. Later, twenty-five Presbyterian clergy sought forgiveness from God and Catholics because of their involvement in "communal sin."[29] Such specific and personal acts of asking for forgiveness, of expressing remorse, go a long way in healing relationships.

Archbishop Brady, the Catholic Primate of Armagh, on September 1, 2004, lauded the risks taken by Protestant clergy in communicating with republicans to achieve an early ceasefire and to break the political impasse. Likewise, Archbishop Eames, the Anglican Primate, called on people to renew their trust, and to take risks by crossing boundaries.[30] Churches in

27. Quoted in Wells, *People Behind the Peace*, 46.
28. Quoted in Amstutz, *The Healing of Nations*, 181.
29. Wells, *People Behind the Peace*, 47. Regarding communal and individual forgiving, see Lennon, SJ, "Forgiving: A Doubting Thomas," 27–28.
30. Smyth, OP, "Respecting Boundaries and Bonds," 153.

Ireland have played a role in "boundary-crossing," especially in the worst times of violence, thus promoting peace and reconciliation. Be that as it may, there are skeptics who still believe the churches were the original source of the Irish Troubles.

The Failure of Churches

Christianity preaches forgiveness, repentance, compassion, and contrition. Nonetheless, the presence of churches, Roman Catholic and Protestant, has been part of the Irish problem historically. Even though the two churches share many common theological tenets, their cultural and political differences were deeply embedded in their segregated communities, each establishing their own schools, places of worship, and political organizations. Sectarianism thrived when there was segregation and mutual distrust. In Northern Ireland, religion has often served to divide rather than unite people.[31] Besides, the raison d'être of Protestantism was to protest against some of the practices of Catholicism, as Steve Bruce, a professor of sociology, put it succinctly:

> Protestantism and Catholicism were not any two different religions. They stood in opposition to each other. The former began as a "protest" against features of the latter and, after they separated, each developed those elements which most clearly distinguished it from the other. They were thus fundamentally irreconcilable.[32]

By emphasizing denominational identity, churches unwittingly promoted sectarianism and conflict. Dominican theologian Sister Geraldine Smyth acknowledges there were times when churches in Ireland clung strongly to their denominational identities and kept to themselves. Constrained by political circumstances, the churches sought to protect their own doctrines and way of worship.[33]

---

31. Amstutz, *The Healing of Nations*, 183. "Sectarianism is a complex of attitudes, beliefs, behaviors and structures in which religion is a significant component, and which (i) directly, or indirectly, infringes the rights of individuals or groups, and/or (ii) influences or causes situations of destructive conflict." Quoted in Falconer, "Healing the Violence," 164.

32. Quoted in Elliott, "Religion and Sectarianism in Ulster," 96. Bruce also argues that unionist politicians were mostly interested in promoting their Protestant beliefs and values, rather seeking national identity.

33. Smyth, OP, "Respecting Boundaries and Bonds," 153.

In spite of their good works, many churches were guilty of reinforcing sectarianism and cultural division in Northern Ireland. The lack of social interaction and different curriculums, especially in the teaching of history, between Catholic and Protestant schools did exacerbate the Troubles. Church leaders who selectively condemned violence or showed ambivalence with regard to sectarian conflict were seen to give tacit approval for acts of atrocity committed on their behalf: "religion in the concrete church forms it takes on in Ireland bears significant direct responsibility for social division and indirect responsibility for violence."[34] Religions often upheld social boundaries through prohibiting mixed marriages and encouraging segregated schooling.

Duncan Morrow, Chief Executive Officer of the Northern Ireland Community Relations Council, held that churches, both Catholic and Protestant, failed to admit their shortcomings and to provide a channel of communication to facilitate the debate regarding the hostilities in Northern Ireland. Although the Troubles were not a purely religious issue, the churches' "fingers [were] all over the conflict." The churches also maintained a self-righteous position, which did not help in alleviating the situation. Further, they tried to absolve themselves of the conflict and now they "look like institutions that do not know how to repent and forgive."[35]

In spite of their failures, we cannot ignore the good influence of churches, as seen in the 1998 Good Friday Agreement. This accord is probably one of the most powerful examples of how churches can use their authority to promote peace and reconciliation. Efforts in promoting peace made by religious leaders on both sides were initially ignored by their own respective militant groups bent upon taking revenge. Ultimately, it was the joint efforts of Irish political leaders, the British government, the United States, working with the critical support of the churches on both sides of the divide, that led to the successful conclusion of the Good Friday Agreement.

The Good Friday Agreement

The Good Friday Agreement (GFA) of 1998 provided a political framework for power-sharing between unionists and nationalists in Northern Ireland. It was signed by the British and Irish governments together with four major political parties: Sinn Féin, the Ulster Unionist Party, the Social Democratic

---

34. Quoted in Elliott, "Religion and Sectarianism in Ulster," 97.
35. "The Possibility of Forgiveness," 263.

and Labour Party, and the Alliance Party. The GFA confirmed that Northern Ireland was part of the United Kingdom. It also specified that Ireland could be united if the majority of people in both Northern Ireland and the Republic of Ireland so decided through a ballot. The GFA also called for a transfer of authority over certain policy areas from the Parliament of the United Kingdom to the newly created Assembly in Belfast. This led to the disarmament of paramilitary groups, which drastically reduced incidents of violence in the region.[36]

A ministerial council was established to promote socio-economic co-operation between the Irish Republic and Northern Ireland. Bilateral co-operation between Britain and Ireland was to be promoted in areas regarding transport, agriculture, health, environment, and education. The GFA also called for an early release of prisoners from groups who promised to give up the armed struggle. An independent committee was set up for decommissioning to ensure the disarmament of all paramilitary groups. Approved by an overwhelming majority, the Good Friday Agreement led to the establishment of a power-sharing government.[37]

The GFA provided a new political framework that would stop violence and guarantee constitutional order to protect the rights of the people. The goal was to create a power-sharing political framework where the various parties could pursue their political objectives without violence. This was to establish an environment where Catholics and Protestants learn "to live in disagreement but in dialogue with each other."[38] The GFA required the multi-party government of Northern Ireland to pursue policies that promoted democratic decision-making, tolerance, and trust. The main aim of the GFA was to establish peace among the various conflicting groups, an initial "agreement to disagree," but with the hope that it would eventually lead to healing, forgiveness, and reconciliation in the nation.

Two individuals from differing sides of the divide contributed to the success of this peace process: David Trimble of the Ulster Unionist Party and John Hume of the Social Democratic and Labour Party (Nationalist) jointly shared the Nobel Peace Prize in 1998. Trimble was courageous and skillful in marginalizing the more extreme attitudes of Ian Paisley and his party. Hume's genius lay in his ability to keep up the momentum of the peace talks and to invite Gerry Adams of Sinn Féin to take part in the

---

36. Council on Foreign Relations, "The Northern Ireland Peace Process."
37. Amstutz, *The Healing of Nations*, 176–77.
38. Amstutz, *The Healing of Nations*, 177.

political negotiations. But the truly great heroes are the vast majority of the Irish people who wanted to give peace a chance, who wanted to forgive and to reconcile with their adversaries.

Political Forgiveness

Forgiveness is a central tenet in Christianity. Since religion is deeply embedded among the people of Northern Ireland, forgiveness and reconciliation were part and parcel of their efforts to negotiate for peace at the personal and institutional levels. Forgiveness in religion is often interpreted at the personal level, but history shows that with conflicts such as those that took place in Bosnia, South Africa, and Rwanda there is an urgent need for political forgiveness and reconciliation. Hannah Arendt, a Jewish scholar, emphasizes the political importance of forgiveness. She argues that in our modern world where conflicts and oppression are prevalent, asking for forgiveness and being forgiven, as well as making promises, are important for the survival of the nation. Arendt writes:

> The possible redemption from the predicament of irreversibility—of being unable to undo what one has done though one did not, and could not, have known what he was doing—is the faculty of forgiving. The remedy for unpredictability, for the chaotic uncertainty of the future, is contained in the faculty to make and keep promises.[39]

Donald Shriver, an American theologian, says that we are all "stuck here for a while," and whether we can stay together without killing each other is fundamentally a political and ethical question. Do we have to live with people we don't like? Aware of the vulnerability of their people, some politicians stir up hostility that leads to genocide and even mass murder. Other leaders understand that we cannot afford to live in isolation, and seek a different kind of political loyalty: "sober acceptance of the fact that people do not have to like each other in order to become politically settled into ongoing relationships."[40]

Political forgiveness is necessary if we want to heal and purify the memory of the harms we have inflicted upon each other. Memories can imprison a community and contribute to division within a society, but memories can

---

39. Arendt, *The Human Condition*, 237.
40. Shriver, Jr., *An Ethic for Enemies*, 6

also be liberating: a "reconciling memory" allows communities to enter into a more positive relationship.[41] Without forgiveness and repentance, "political humans remember the crimes of ancestors only to entertain the idea of repeating them."[42] Forgetting, however, is not a solution, for, as we know very well, those who forget the past are doomed to repeat it.

Forgiveness at the personal level normally starts with the victim forgiving the perpetrator, but in politics, it goes both ways, as Shriver asserts. Forgiveness in politics does not mean that we refrain from punishing the perpetrator, but it does require us to stop vengeance. It is thus a question of forbearance and patience, and of restraining ourselves from self-justification, which often engenders new enmities. Shriver also suggests that forgiveness is possible if we possess empathy for our enemy's humanity. This means we try to sympathize with our enemies' cause and their methods of pursuing it. Empathizing with the humanity of the enemy is a step, albeit hard, towards accepting them and the possibility of living with them as fellow human beings, even in the midst of war.

Human relationships are renewed with forgiveness when people are prepared to live with their enemies at some level of "positive mutual affirmation."[43] This implies some kind of peaceful co-existence and civil relationships between strangers. Political forgiveness thus involves forbearance, empathy, and a determination to repair fractured relationships between the parties. It neither forsakes justice nor seeks revenge. Political forgiveness focuses on the humanity of the enemies even when they have been guilty of acts against humanity. It is more about restorative justice than retributive justice; a justice that restores community rather than one that destroys.[44]

The salvation of souls and the welfare of society go hand in hand—political forgiveness must be expressed in a personal way to be effective. Those who have offered apologies and repented must live lives that are worthy to be called Christian. They should work actively to promote peace and help their communities to be more compassionate and forgiving towards their enemies. Getting rid of rage and revenge is related to spiritual salvation as well as to the "survival of democracy."[45]

---

41. Falconer, "Healing the Violence," 164.
42. Shriver, Jr., *An Ethic for Enemies*, 6.
43. Shriver, Jr., *An Ethic for Enemies*, 8.
44. Shriver, Jr., *An Ethic for Enemies*, 9.
45. Wells, *People Behind the Peace*, 49.

Forgiveness in a political context has to start at the personal level, the saying of "I am sorry." Fortunately, in Northern Ireland, there were noble souls who were willing to forgive without being asked. In 1971, Patrick McGurk, whose wife and daughter were killed in the bombing of the family bar in Belfast, offered forgiveness in the hope of stopping the violence. Forgiveness was also expressed by Gordon Wilson, whose daughter Marie was killed in the Remembrance Sunday bombing in Enniskillen in November 1987. Michael McGoldrick, whose son Michael was shot dead in July 1996, likewise forgave the killer.[46] The idea of forgiveness is not new in political reconciliation but political leaders and church members in Northern Ireland found ways and means to enhance this virtue.

A Shared Future

Nigel Biggar speaks of forgiveness first as compassion when the victim allows his or her feelings to be tempered by sympathy for the perpetrator. He or she accepts the fact that we all have done wrong. The truth is that we have people who are capable of doing immense good and also of doing immense evil. However, we are committed to reconcile rather than to take revenge. In the context of Northern Ireland, interlocutors stressed political forgiveness, a desire to co-exist in the same neighborhood, even on the same street. Vengeance does more harm than good because it only multiplies atrocities. After compassion, the second moment of forgiveness is absolution—when the victim addresses the perpetrator to express forgiveness. This offer of forgiveness, according to Biggar, is not to be given unconditionally; there must be genuine signs of repentance and remorse in the perpetrator.[47]

In the context of Northern Ireland, "a shared future" has to be built by people with different views and judgments regarding the Troubles.[48] Reconciliation and peace happened when those with opposing understandings of Northern Ireland's political past moved on so that they can at least co-exist without killing each other. In the Good Friday Agreement of 1998, the various paramilitary groups agreed to decommission their arms. Nigel Biggar also calls upon the state to honor and uphold the dignity of the victims by punishing the perpetrators for the crimes they have committed through court trials, convictions, and appropriate sentencing.

46. McLernon, et al., "Views on Forgiveness in Northern Ireland," 285.
47. Biggar, "Forgiving Enemies in Ireland," 561–63.
48. Biggar, "Forgiving Enemies in Ireland," 566.

In response to Biggar's two moments of forgiveness—compassion and absolution—David Tombs suggests that the Protestant understanding of forgiveness tends to see it as a single act rather than a process that takes time. However, the experience of the Troubles in Northern Ireland has shown us that it may take years or decades for forgiveness and repentance to take place.[49] In other words, Protestant understanding is overly optimistic or unrealistic. The Gospels teach us to forgive unconditionally, but this does not mean that we offer it immediately. We need time and space to allow moments of forgiveness to take place—the healing of memories and hurts is not immediate. Churches preach forgiveness, but it should not be forced; otherwise, it would be abusive and counter-productive. Like Biggar, Tombs also acknowledges that being able to forgive and to let go of bitterness and resentment is beneficial to the victims in the long run. As the people of Northern Ireland regard themselves as Christians, whether Catholics and Protestants, Tombs believes unilateral forgiveness is possible, although repentance by the perpetrator is welcomed. Forgiveness can be offered unconditionally, but we need to repent to receive it.

There is no peace without justice. A combination of criminal proceedings as well as a Truth Commission might help to promote the peace process. Ronald Wells, an American scholar familiar with the Troubles, writes that a full-blown Truth and Reconciliation Commission like the South African model might not be necessary. In the first place, the British government and the IRA would never agree to have such a commission. Secondly, the civil institutions in Northern Ireland are strong enough to handle personal, social, and cultural healing. There are also a number of Christian communities like Corrymeela in Ballycastle, Christian Renewal Centre in Rostrevor, and Clonard Monastery in West Belfast that can help people to tell their personal stories as part of the healing process.[50]

Justice meted out will help to console the victims, enabling them to have the courage and grace to forgive their perpetrators. In that way, they might be willing to co-exist with each other, to have a shared future. Northern Ireland has enjoyed relative peace, thanks to the Good Friday Agreement that ensured the decommissioning of arms. We can call it a shared future or co-existence; but forgiveness and reconciliation will take time and must first occur at the personal level.

49. Tombs, "The Offer of Forgiveness," 589.
50. For a moving story on forgiveness in Northern Ireland see Wells, "Facing Truth," 27–30.

It is hard to say "I'm sorry." It is also hard to forgive those who sin against us. But if we believe that we are all children of the same Father, sharing the same humanity, seeing ourselves as creatures conditioned by biological and social forces, then we can allow ourselves to move beyond the wrongdoings of others, of those who have hurt us. Compassion can help us understand and accept those who have sinned against us and eventually help us forgive our enemies, who after all are also living on this planet where we are stuck together for the time being.

Forgiveness in the context of the Northern Ireland conflict can be defined as releasing anger, giving up the right to revenge, overcoming resentment or denying our right to be resentful. Be that as it may, many people find it difficult or even impossible to forgive. McLernon suggests that victims from the Protestant community tend to see forgiveness as resulting from a healing process, which takes time, and varies from individual to individual. Catholics in Ireland tend to reject talk of "forgiveness" and prefer to use the word "acceptance."[51] Thus, we need to approach the concept of forgiveness carefully because it means different things to different people. We must avoid trivializing others' suffering or exacerbating their hurt, especially when church leaders casually preach about "forgiving and forgetting." Groups that have experienced atrocities from another group often prefer to forget (though as we saw in chapter 1, this is not a healthy option), but individuals need to go through a personal peace process. The recent conflicts in Northern Ireland lasted for thirty years; forgiveness (without forgetting) is the only choice if its people want to move towards a better future.

---

51. McLernon et al., "Views on Forgiveness in Northern Ireland," 286.

— Chapter 4 —

Nunca Más

Civil War in Guatemala

Having gained independence from Spain in 1821, Guatemala witnessed a long history of authoritarian rule and military regimes until it achieved democratic government in 1985. From 1954 the dictatorial government was faced with strong guerrilla opposition which sparked a civil war that lasted for thirty-six years, until peace agreements were signed in 1996. The details of the conflicts, the brutality of the various regimes, the suffering and death of the people during this period, are revealed in the writings of Rigoberta Menchú, a Quiché Maya, and an advocate for indigenous people. She has written two books: *I, Rigoberta Menchú* and *Crossing Borders*. For her relentless efforts in alleviating the plight of indigenous people, fighting for the rights of women, and advocating peace and reconciliation among the various political groups including the military in Guatemala, Rigoberta Menchú was awarded the Nobel Peace Prize in 1992.

This chapter first highlights Rigoberta Menchú's efforts to promote peace and reconciliation in her beloved but embattled homeland. Further, this chapter argues that in spite of its shortcomings and checkered past, the Catholic Church has contributed much to the reconciliation and healing of the nation. The clergy and laity have worked relentlessly in the peace process to ensure that the unspeakable atrocities and violence that the Guatemalans had suffered for the past thirty-six years will never happen again—*nunca más* (never again). The brutal murder of Bishop Juan José Gerardi, a "martyr for truth," reveals not only the crimes of the military, but also the resolute commitment of the Church in the peace process. A brief discussion of the history and people of Guatemala will help us understand the difficulties and challenges that Rigoberta Menchú and the Church had to face in their peace and reconciliation ministry.

Background

Located in Central America, Guatemala boasts an ancient civilization, the Mayan, which was highly developed and sophisticated. With their great construction skills, the Mayans built the majority of the cities in the country during the classic period dating from 300 to 900 CE. Due to a combination of climate change and tribal warfare, the cities declined and were abandoned, and their civilization collapsed. Thus, when the Spanish conquerors arrived in 1524, they found it easy to subdue the natives, even though there were still isolated Mayan resistance movements.[1]

During the colonial period (1524–1821), the region was influenced by many aspects of Spanish culture, and the old city and the other major towns were developed and achieved great magnificence. Sadly, an earthquake in 1773 destroyed the old city and the capital was moved by royal order to the present site of Guatemala City. Unfortunately, being without many mineral resources, Guatemala was not as prosperous as neighboring countries like Mexico and Peru. It subsisted on the cultivation of cocoa, beans, indigo, and other agricultural staples, and the production of cochineal, an insect that makes a red dye. As good transportation and an efficient port were lacking, commerce was not well-developed in Guatemala. In spite of these shortcomings, Guatemala City became the administrative and religious center of the entire region between Mexico and Panama. The High Court and Archbishop's residence were established in this city. In fact, the Spaniards administered the other parts of Central America like El Salvador, Honduras, Nicaragua, Costa Rica, and Chiapas, Mexico, from Guatemala.

The population of Guatemala consists of two main ethnic groups, Ladinos and Maya, who form the vast majority of the people in the country. The Ladinos (mestizos) are those of mixed Hispanic-Mayan blood and make up approximately 60 percent of the entire population in the country, while the Maya make up about 40 percent. The Ladinos, who live mostly in the urban areas, speak Spanish, are more prosperous, and are

---

1. This section is summarised from "Guatemala," *Encyclopædia Britannica*. For an excellent account of race relationships in Guatemala, see Gotkowitz, *Histories of Race and Racism*.

politically influential. There are also some minorities of mixed African and Caribbean descent.

Roman Catholicism is the dominant religion in Guatemala. It is infused with Mayan popular piety and is often called "folk Catholicism." During the mid-twentieth century, evangelical Protestantism became widespread among the poor. Today Protestants make up about two-fifths of the population, one of the highest proportions of non-Catholic Christianity in Latin America.

After achieving independence from Spain in 1821, the liberal government in Guatemala implemented policies to deprive the Catholic Church of its privileges and promoted anti-clericalism. In the 1820s and 1830s, monasteries were closed, religious orders expelled, and church properties confiscated. In the nineteenth century, the government had proclaimed religious tolerance and Protestants were invited to weaken the hold of the Catholic Church. However, during the second half of the twentieth century, the Catholic Church regained its influence and power, and became one of the key players in Guatemala as well as in Central America. The arrival of foreign missionaries, and economic resources from the United States and Europe, allowed the Catholic Church to assert its presence among the people.[2]

Clerics and lay people began to play important roles in finding solutions to the country's social and economic problems in the aftermath of the Second Vatican Council (1962–65). In addition, lay movements such as Catholic Action worked with Mayan communities in the Western Highlands and contributed much to their well-being and development through charitable works. One of the most significant achievements of the Catholic Church was the establishment of the Recuperation of Historical Memory (REMHI), and the publication of *Nunca Más* (1998) to assist in the implementation of the Peace Accords and to start the healing process in the nation. For, as we shall see later, this was a nation in desperate need of healing after a protracted, violent, and bloody civil war (1960–96), with an estimated 200,000 killed or "disappeared."

---

2. Hernández Sandoval, "Reforming Catholicism," 255–56 and *Guatemala's Catholic Revolution*. For a detailed discussion of church-state relations in the nineteenth century, see Miller, "Conservative and Liberal Concordats in Nineteenth-Century Guatemala: Who Won?" 115–30.

Women's Power

The transition from despotic to democratic rule was not smooth in Guatemala, as one can imagine. Elections were held regularly following the Peace Accords in 1996 when various guerrilla groups disarmed themselves and entered into the political process. But there were many political parties competing for power and consensus was hard to achieve. Among the voters, there was also the fear that the military might return if there was continued social and political unrest. In this tense period, women in Guatemala played an important role in the healing of the nation.[3]

With the encouragement and backing of international organizations, women's support groups began to emerge and their voice strengthened over time. They were instrumental in gathering and documenting information regarding the disappearance and killings of Guatemalans during the civil war. Having spent time in refugee camps during these horrific periods, these women learned to read and write, and also equipped themselves with other skills. Empowered, they returned home and started teaching and sharing their experiences with other Guatemalan women who had not left their homes. The emergence of women as a political force was influenced and inspired by Rigoberta Menchú, an indigenous human rights activist who won the Nobel Peace Prize in 1992. In many exceptional ways, her life involves crossing multiple borders—geographical, cultural, and spiritual.

Crossing Borders

In *I, Rigoberta Menchú: An Indian Woman in Guatemala* (1984), the author gives testimony to her family's struggle with the Ladinos, whom she portrays as greedy for possession of land. In *Crossing Borders*, a sequel to *I, Rigoberta Menchú*, she also narrates how her two brothers, mother, and father were violently murdered by the military: "Inhuman are their soldiers, cruel their fierce mastiffs";[4] "[m]y mother said that when a woman sees her son tortured, and burnt alive, she is incapable of forgiving, incapable of getting rid of her hate."[5] Working as a maid for a wealthy Ladino family

---

3. Regarding the role of market women in supporting the Catholic Church against Guatemala's democratically elected revolutionary governments, see Harms, "'God Doesn't Like the Revolution,'" 111–39, 170.

4. Menchú, *Crossing Borders*, 150

5. Menchú, *Crossing Borders*, 172.

in the city, Rigoberta describes the mistreatment she had to endure: "I was incapable of disobedience. And those employers exploited my obedience. They took advantage of my innocence."[6] In narrating the story of her life, she contrasts idyllic accounts of her indigenous Mayan cultural practices in the mountains to the materialistic lifestyle of the city: "When I went to the city for the first time, I saw it as a monster, something alien, different."[7] Much bitterness, anger, hatred, and violence is expressed dramatically and graphically in Menchú's first book.

In *Crossing Borders,* we find a transition towards a more accommodating account of the Ladinos, and an acceptance of herself as a recipient of the Nobel Peace Prize, one who commands respect and admiration, not just in Guatemala but also in the international community. Literally and symbolically, she has crossed borders towards embracing a more pluralistic and multi-ethnic society in Guatemala. Instead of conflict and criticism, her narrative is filled with hope and goodwill in working for peace and reconciliation in her divided nation.

As a sequel to *I, Rigoberta Menchú, Crossing Borders* is part memoir, part political reflection testimony. When her parents were murdered by the Guatemalan right-wing military regime in 1980, Rigoberta Menchú went into exile in Mexico, where she established a movement to fight for the rights of indigenous peoples. Although Guatemala had made some progress in becoming a more pluralistic society, Menchú was still critical of the landowners and the army who oppressed the native people and deprived them of their fundamental rights.[8] In *Crossing Borders,* she discusses with pride the Mayan culture and its myths, with its cosmovision rooted in reverence for Mother Earth, in stark contrast to present-day exploitation and abuse of the environment. She also writes, with great affection and admiration, about her mother, a peasant leader, midwife, and healer, who was tortured and killed by the army.

The Maya, one of the twenty-one language groups found in Guatemala, represents between 40 and 50 percent of the total population in the country. In spite of their majority status, they were excluded from political power even when Guatemala became independent from Spanish

---

6. Menchú, *Crossing Borders,* 91.

7. Menchú, *Crossing Borders,* 28. For a critical and controversial review of this work, see Stoll, *Rigoberta Menchú and the Story of All Poor Guatemalans.*

8. For a detailed analysis of the military's actions in the highlands of Guatemala against the indigenous communities, see Handy, "Anxiety and Dread," 43–65.

colonial rule in 1821. Affected by economic disparity and social discrimination, the indigenous population has the lowest standard of living in the American continent. A Maya Movement has emerged demanding that political culture become more pluralistic or multi-racial.[9] As a human rights activist, Rigoberta Menchú has contributed much in publicizing issues of abuses and violations in Guatemala and the Americas: she gives voice to the voiceless, especially women.

Lobbying at the United Nations for twelve years, Menchú wanted non-governmental organizations to have a greater voice in representing indigenous and native people who were dispossessed. Advocating equitable land distribution, she also fought against racism and bigotry. Lamenting the plight of indigenous people, Menchú is critical of self-serving and corrupt politicians, Western environmentalists, academics and writers who plagiarize, and artists who "have stolen these concepts from us and not given us credit."[10]

Menchú admits that there was opposition from politicians, even from her own people, when she was nominated for the Nobel Peace Prize. Eventually the Mayans came to regard the prize as an important symbol legitimizing their struggle for justice and peace. Her victory started a healing process, uniting people of diverse backgrounds and political ideologies in Guatemalan society.

In the final chapter of *Crossing Borders*, Menchú pleads for ethnic and religious tolerance. Her parents were an example of religious tolerance and accommodation: her mother was steeped in Mayan animistic spirituality while her father was a devout Catholic. Yet, they never quarreled because "they were showing humility towards something greater than themselves."[11] While religion can be manipulated by politicians, the rich, and the powerful to advance their ambitions, it can also be an instrument for reconciliation. Menchú argues that genuine religion satisfies the spiritual hunger of the people, and various religious traditions can be complementary and enhance the welfare of the believers.

In Mayan memory, there exists a sign of balance in the sense that good and evil are two sides of a single reality—"negative aspects are offset

---

9. Regarding the lack of Mayan political representation in the national government of Guatemala, see Pallister, "Why No Mayan Party?" 117–38.

10. Menchú, *Crossing Borders*, 170.

11. Menchú, *Crossing Borders*, 89.

by good ones."[12] This suggests that the Nobel Prize or any prestigious award will not change or get rid of the problem, as it exists in humanity. Our human weaknesses such as greed or jealousy are exemplified in her account of the fake kidnapping conspired in by her own relatives, and the 1995 massacre of eleven refugees who had resettled in Xamán. Menchú was resigned to the fact that there was a plot to destroy her and she needed to be vigilant. Further, after the incident that involved her family members, she had a better understanding of the pain of those whose children were kidnapped. Through her efforts, the perpetrators of the massacre were brought to court and the military suffered a blow.

Like her father, Menchú worked for the Committee for Peasant Unity (CUC) where she learned "to be generous with life and with our people's history."[13] This meant helping people to establish what they believe to be an ideal existence, a utopia, which gives them hope for the future. Their slogan was "Clear Head, Caring Heart, Fighting Fist of Rural Workers."[14] Menchú was able to combine Mayan mysticism with practical knowledge in her work to uplift poor peasants. Like Fr. Alec Reid, she emphasizes companionship, compassion and tolerance. A *compañero* (companion) sees the pain of another as her own and does not abandon her friends in good times or in bad times. It was in CUC that Menchú learned to fight as a woman for human rights, especially women's rights, justice, and democracy.

After receiving the Nobel Prize, Menchú started an independent foundation to support a new peace mission and to challenge conventional ideas about development, which had not been working for the benefit of the poor. She wishes to represent not only the poor of Guatemala, but also the poor throughout the world. The Nobel Prize of Peace that Menchú won does not belong to her, but to all who work for lasting peace, as she proclaims: "Let there be lots of parties, let the Evangelicals light their fireworks and the Catholics ring their church bells. Let the wait for the Nobel Prize be a vigil for the peace everybody in Guatemala craves. Let it be a joyous occasion for everybody."[15] For Menchú, being chosen as Nobel Peace Prize winner became a celebration of the dignity of the continent.

Organizing a reception to celebrate the award of the Noble Prize for Peace, Menchú had the idea of inviting the army and the URNG

12. Menchú, *Crossing Borders*, 22.
13. Menchú, *Crossing Borders*, 107.
14. Menchú, *Crossing Borders*, 107.
15. Menchú, *Crossing Borders*, 12.

(Guatemalan National Revolutionary Unity, the political arm of the Guatemalan People's Army) with the hope that both sides would reach a peaceful settlement since they were in the middle of a civil war—"the party should be a symbol of dialogue."[16] She wanted the reception to reflect national unity between indigenous people and Ladinos, and also unity between various political movements and opposition groups: it was a time for celebration not confrontation, she insisted. In spite of civil wars and conflicts in the country, Menchú believes in a multi-ethnic, multi-lingual, plural society where the natives and Ladrinos can live in peace and harmony.

Like the American civil rights activist Martin Luther King, Jr., Menchú also has a dream: "My dream is that one day this place [Kaminal Juyú] will be declared a Centre of National Unity and Peace in Guatemala."[17] Kaminal Juyú, an important ceremonial and political center for the ancient Mayans, which was to be the venue to celebrate the winning of the Nobel Peace Prize. She said: we are all *chapines*, fellow Guatemalans, whether we are Ladinos or natives. No one is a stranger in Guatemala.

As a winner of the Nobel Prize for Peace, Menchú is conscious that she should not be seen as siding with one particular political party, however much she shares its beliefs and principles. Focused on justice and peace, she writes: "The solution may lie in educating people differently, or in strengthening the judicial system by giving heavy sentences so that people who commit crimes do not get away with them. It may lie in creating a culture of peace, a lasting peace that stems from a system of values, not one that is simply the aftermath of war."[18] There is certainly no peace without justice.

The issues that Rigoberta Menchú raises in her work concerning the environment, racism, violations of human rights, exploitation of women, and sexual discrimination are more relevant than ever. "Crossing borders" may refer to her travel to different countries to explain the plight of indigenous people and to advocate human rights, justice, and peace in developing nations. It may also refer to the efforts Menchú takes to reach out to her critics such as the Ladinos, politicians, and military personnel.

---

16. Menchú, *Crossing Borders*, 16.
17. Menchú, *Crossing Borders*, 20.
18. Menchú, *Crossing Borders*, 225.

Theological Reflections

The idea of crossing borders is present in the Gospels where we see Jesus visiting both the Jews and the Samaritans. In fact, the New Testament frequently dramatizes Jesus crossing boundaries between Jews and gentiles. Of particular significance is Jesus crossing the lake, moving from his own place to alien territory on the other side.[19] It was the Samaritans, rather than his own people, that recognized him as the one who could heal and save them. In his hometown, we are told, Jesus "could do no deed of power there, except that he laid his hands on a few sick people and cured them. And he was amazed at their unbelief" (Mark 6:5–6). In fact, his own people "took offence" at the wisdom of his teaching, resenting the fact that such wisdom came from a carpenter's son.

Likewise, Rigoberta Menchú faced resistance from her own people when her name was put forward as a candidate to receive the Nobel Peace Prize. She writes, "Many indigenous brothers and sisters did not agree with my candidacy. They said, 'Who does she represent?' 'Who made her a leader?' 'Who elected her?'"[20] They wanted to put her in her place; they refused to let her cross boundaries, as it were. Nonetheless, she won the Nobel Prize and inspired people with her message of peace and tolerance, which is no small feat in a country where the people, especially the indigenous population, have suffered racism and witnessed systematic killings for so many years.

La Violencia

The Irish had their Troubles, and the Guatemalans faced violence daily in their lives, especially in the 1980s, the ten-year period that the people simply called *La Violencia*.[21] In fact, the Maya people had always experienced violent suppression and persecution ever since colonial days began some 450 years ago, when Spanish conquerors brutally destroyed Mayan traditional culture and religion, in the name of God. In the seventeenth

---

19. See Matt 8:18; 9:1; Mark 4:35; 5:21; 8:13; Luke 8:22; John 6:17, etc.
20. Menchú, *Crossing Borders*, 2.
21. See Reilly, *Peace-building and Development in Guatemala and Northern Ireland*. This book compares and contrasts lessons learned from the implementation of the peace accords in Guatemala (1996) and Northern Ireland (1998). Both countries are deeply divided along class or ethnic differences, exhibit power asymmetries, and are also heavily influenced by foreigners and their own diaspora.

century, conquistador Pedro de Alvarado, citing the authority of the Spanish monarch and the Church, killed the Quiche kings and nobles. He wrote to King Carlos V that it was for the benefit of this country that he burned their rulers and ordered their city to be razed to the ground. Hence, what happened in the 1980s was in fact a continuation of a racist ideology that had continued from the era of the conquistadors, who regarded indigenous people as sub-human and, because of their populous numbers, a threat to their power.[22] Like most developing countries in Latin America, Guatemala is afflicted by unequal distribution of wealth, by racism and by military rule, factors that lead to systematic violations of human rights.

Guatemala's civil war (1960–96) involved the army fighting against counter-insurgent guerrilla forces, which led to the victimization of the indigenous population, who were caught in the crossfire. Between 1978 to 1982, approximately 70,000 native people were killed, 40,000 disappeared, and over a million were displaced. In 1984, motivated by fear of communism, the United States supported a coup to overthrow the democratically elected government of President Jacobo Arbenz. His government implemented a land distribution that adversely affected the United Fruit Company, a US-based corporation and Guatemala's biggest landowner. After the coup, the government became more militarized. This despotic rule led to increasing opposition in the form of counterinsurgent guerrilla forces influenced by Marxism and liberation theology.[23]

Originally made up of Ladinos, this guerrilla force began to recruit Mayans into their ranks. The Mayans began to clamor for land rights and democracy. The government and the military retaliated with brutality, resulting in large-scale massacres and systematic violations of human rights through a scorched earth policy aimed at annihilating the indigenous communities. Pressured by the international community and the desire to receive aid, civilian rule began to assert itself while the military were granted amnesty and impunity. As a result, crimes and violations of human rights went unpunished.[24]

---

22. Wee, "The Role of the Lutheran World Federation in the Guatemala Peace Process," 49.

23. O'Neill, "Writing Guatemala's Genocide," 333. For a detailed description of economic developments in Guatemala, characterized as militarized-state-capitalism, and the suppression of the Indian communities, see Smith, "The Militarization of Civil Society in Guatemala," 8–41. Regarding some testimonies, see Olson, "Waging Peace," 343–59. See also Preti, "Guatemala: Violence in Peacetime," 99–119.

24. O'Neill, "Writing Guatemala's Genocide," 333.

The government and the military were determined to maintain the status quo and did not hesitate to use all their power to eliminate any opposition: "The apparatus of state power was to be used against anyone who sought to undermine the legacy of those who came to Latin America under the Spanish flag with a mission to expand their superior civilization and faith. In return they expected gratitude as well as the labor and the wealth of their subjects."[25] Any resolution of the conflict would have to involve substantial change in its economic, social, and political policies, as well as moving towards democratic reforms.

Guatemala had actually enjoyed a short period of peace, free elections, and economic re-distribution of wealth known as the "Revolutionary Spring" in 1944 when the dictator Jorge Ubico was ousted through popular uprisings and strikes.[26] Regrettably, this peaceful era was brief, ending in 1954 when President Arbenz was replaced by military officer Carlos Castilla Armas, who banned labor unions and land reforms that might threaten the banana industry. His government was the first of a series of repressive military regimes that continued to oppress the native people with widespread torture and slaughter of those who opposed them. Supported by the United States, the military regime relentlessly sought to eliminate not just the Marxists but any opposition, which included the unions, universities, churches, and peasant-cooperatives throughout the 1960s and 1970s.[27]

Inspired by Fidel Castro's revolution in Cuba and materially supported by the Soviet Union, opposition parties began to wage war on the government in 1960. The first phase of the war started on the eastern side of the country inhabited by the Ladinos. Defeated by the army, the guerrillas retreated to reorganize themselves and re-entered the country in 1970. They waged war on the western highlands, inhabited by indigenous people who supported the guerrillas against the military government. The army retaliated with a brutal

25. Wee, "The Role of the Lutheran World Federation in the Guatemala Peace Process," 50.

26. Weld, "Dignifying the Guerrillero, Not the Assassin," 39.

27. Weld, "Dignifying the Guerrillero, Not the Assassin," 40. Through violent and oppressive measures, the leadership, assumed by the military, attempted to impose "order" on a nation divided by various warring factions from the right and left of the political spectrum. For a detailed analysis of the conflict in Guatemala, see Frundt, "Guatemala in Search of Democracy," 25–74. According to Carol Smith, the Guatemalan army can no longer depend on the support of the United States because since 1978 it had refused to subject itself to President Carter's human rights standards. The military has thus pursued its own course of action, which is different from that of the US and the elite class of Guatemala. Smith, "The Militarization of Civil Society in Guatemala," 35.

"scorched-earth" campaign that left between 100,000 to 150,000 people dead or disappeared between 1981 and 1983 alone.[28] Quite a few prominent foreigners were killed, but most victims were Guatemalans. These victims were common people—students and local political leaders. It was reported that during the first nine months of 1990, there had been 276 political murders and 145 disappearances in Guatemala.[29]

Dialogue and Peace Accords

In 1982, four of these opposition groups united themselves to form the Guatemalan National Revolutionary Unity (URNG).[30] The URNG realized that military victory was impossible without heavy casualties on both sides and decided to enter into dialogue and seek a peaceful settlement with the elected civilian government in 1986. Further, five Central American presidents signed the Esquipulas II accords in August 1987. The aim of the accords was to begin dialogue and provide a framework for peace negotiation in a region ravaged by conflicts and arm struggles. President Vinicio Cerezo of Guatemala implemented these agreements and conducted talks with the guerillas in Madrid in October 1987. Supported by the majority of the people, but boycotted by the army, the government, and the private sector, the National Reconciliation Commission sponsored a National Dialogue in 1989.[31] Yet powerful conservative elements in Guatemalan society were determined to crush any opposition that threatened their status quo.

Meetings resumed in Oslo, Norway, in March 1990, when the Guatemalan army was persuaded by an international ecumenical peace delegation to allow talks between the National Commission of Reconciliation (CNR) and

---

28. Jonas, "Can Peace Bring Democracy or Social Justice?" 42. For a detailed description of the unspeakable crimes of the army, see Hatcher, "Truth and Forgetting in Guatemala," 139–60

29. Millett, "Limited Hopes and Fears in Guatemala," 127. The *Christian Science Monitor* reported police were killing street children and soldiers killed thirteen Zutuhil Indians and seriously wounded another nineteen in the town of Santiago Atitlan in December 1990. Millett, "Limited Hopes and Fears in Guatemala," 127. See also Millett, "Guatemala's Painful Progress," 413.

30. They were the Guerrilla Army of the Poor (EGP), the Revolutionary Organization of Armed People (ORPA), the Rebel Armed Forces (FAR), and the Guatemalan Labor Party (PGT). "Guatemalan National Revolutionary Unity (URNG)," *Global Security*.

31. Calder, "The Role of the Catholic Church and Other Religious Institutions in the Guatemalan Peace Process, 1980–1996," 776.

the URNG. This breakthrough led to the signing of "The Basic Agreement on the Search for Peace by Political Means."[32] The aim of this agreement was to solve national problems and initiate democratic reforms in Guatemala. The situation in Guatemala in 1990 was rather precarious, although there was hope that the economy would improve and human rights would be protected with a democratic government. Guatemalans believe having limited hope is better than having no hope at all,[33] and hope begins when people are willing to dialogue in spite of all that has taken place.

Beyond the scope of formal meetings, dialogue opens up "spaces within a repressive context" for various groups to discuss issues, which was unthinkable thirty years ago. These spaces eventually became avenues for democratic reforms in Guatemala. A breakthrough occurred in 1991 when the government of Jorge Serrano and the military held peace talks without demanding disarmament from the URNG. This led to partial agreement on human rights issues and principles of democratization. Unfortunately, these talks were derailed in May 1993 when Serrano attempted to seize total control with the aid of the military. With the exception of the military and the private sector, this attempt was condemned by all sectors of the society as well as by the international community.[34]

From 1991 to 1993, Guatemala's peace negotiation was moderated by Msgr. Rodolfo Ignacio Quezada Toruño of the Catholic Bishops' Conference, with the United Nations as an observer.[35] In 1994, a Framework Accord was established that formalized a role for the Assembly of Civil Society (ASC), which included nearly all sectors of society, as well as women's organizations, which had played an important role in the peace process. Pluralistic and inclusive, the ASC helped build consensus among groups with divergent views.[36] It gave opportunities for people from various sectors to participate actively in the political process, which was crucial for the democratization of Guatemala. Dealing with issues regarding a definitive ceasefire, constitutional and electoral reforms, the integration

---

32. Calder, "The Role of the Catholic Church and Other Religious Institutions in the Guatemalan Peace Process, 1980–1996," 776.

33. Millett, "Limited Hopes and Fears in Guatemala," 128.

34. Jonas, "Can Peace Bring Democracy or Social Justice?" 43. Regarding problems facing Serrano, see Millett, "Limited Hopes and Fears in Guatemala," 126–27.

35. The United Nations has played an important role in mediating the Guatemala Peace Accord of 1996, which includes its promotion of human rights and democratic institutions. See Burgerman, "Building the Peace by Mandating Reform," 63–87.

36. Jonas, "Can Peace Bring Democracy or Social Justice?" 44.

of URNG, amnesty for both URNG and the military, and a timetable to fulfill all the agreements, the Peace Accords was signed, finally, on December 29, 1996 at the Guatemala National Palace amidst great celebration both inside and outside the country.

Role of the Church

Church authorities and lay movements played a decisive role in the peace process in Guatemala between 1980 and 1996. Denouncing violence, the Catholic Church after Vatican II was deeply committed to justice and peace issues, which include the rights of indigenous people, the plight of refugees, and economic inequality. The peace movement was also an ecumenical joint venture in which Catholic, Protestant, and Jewish communities participated actively. These religious communities also worked hand in hand with secular Mayan organizations. This cooperation resulted in a kind of "synergy" within the peace process, which enabled them to participate actively in Guatemalan society.[37]

Support from the international community was also vital for the peace process to be successful. Catholic bishops were among the key participants in the Esquipulas-mandated National Commission of Reconciliation (CNR), together with the government, opposition parties, and other important representatives. By establishing the National Dialogue in 1989, the CNR provided a platform for different sectors of Guatemalan society to enter into dialogue and to seek solutions to their problems. Thus, people were trained to be responsible citizens would take an active role in Guatemala's emerging civil society.

Another international community is the Lutheran World Federation (LWF). They mediated a breakthrough during a dialogue session between the Guatemala military, the government and the URNG, held in Oslo, Norway in 1990. Jorge Rosal, a member of the URNG, did not criticize the government or the military for their atrocities, but spoke about himself and the intense sufferings that the people had gone through in spite of his good intentions. The irony of the whole situation was that Guatemalans on both sides of the conflict, including those at the meeting, had actually grown up together and wanted peace and prosperity for the nation. Jorge

---

37. Calder, "The Role of the Catholic Church and Other Religious Institutions in the Guatemalan Peace Process, 1980–1996," 774. Regarding Protestants' contribution towards democratic transition in Guatemala, see Samson, "From War to Reconciliation," 63–93.

Rosal laid the blame on himself, not on his "enemies." Likewise, Mario Permuth, a member of the National Reconciliation Commission, committed to working for peace in Guatemala, blamed himself for the atrocities and destruction in the country.[38]

In the light of these confessions, they were able to draft a document known as "The Basic Agreement on the Search for Peace by Political Means." This document, which became the framework for a series of subsequent meetings, eventually led to United Nations-sponsored negotiations between the Guatemalan government and the URNG, which culminated in the signing of the Peace Accords on December 29, 1996. The confessions initiated the movement towards national reconciliation. Paul Wee, a delegate of the LWF who was involved with the mediation, wrote:

> The transforming dynamic that was at work is clearly not a possession of the church, nor does religion or even Christianity have a corner on it. Rather, it is a reality available to all as a gift, a potential waiting to be activated when the time (*kairos*) is right. It is the one dynamic that is able to break the vicious circle of pretention and arrogant self-justification. Christianity does not own the power; it simply tells the story of how it takes on flesh and blood in the human community.[39]

The ability to confess and admit one's mistakes is a sign of strength and sincerity. Jorge Rosal blamed himself for the sufferings his people had endured. His confession revealed his humility and willingness to change. He might not have thought of this consciously as a Christian, but it is clearly a sign of grace in theological terms, as Wee remarks. Healing can only be achieved with the help of divine grace and human initiative.

The Quintessential Healing Process

Fundamental to the peace process is the healing of broken relationships, which involves truth-telling, the need for perpetrators to confess their crimes, and a way for victims to share their traumas. This usually occurs within the framework of truth commissions where both perpetrators and victims have the opportunity to share their thoughts and feelings in a formal setting. Though

---

38. Wee, "The Role of the Lutheran World Federation in the Guatemala Peace Process," 52.

39. Wee, "The Role of the Lutheran World Federation in the Guatemala Peace Process," 53.

it cannot be forced, mercy, in the form of forgiveness for wrongdoings, is necessary for both parties to move on. Justice in the form of reparation, restitution, and financial or other types of assistance is equally needed for the peace process and healing to take place. For peace to be long-lasting, perpetrators and victims must have hope for a better future, for themselves and future generations. In other words, different parties envision a new society where there is justice and peace. This process takes about twenty years, according to John Paul Lederach, an American professor of International Peace-building at the University of Notre Dame in Indiana.[40]

This peace-building process begins with a ceasefire agreement, followed by crisis intervention for the first five years after the conflict. When there is some level of social stability, perpetrators and victims are brought together to begin dialogue about the future. Participants in the meeting explore ways and means to facilitate the healing process by first identifying the root causes of past conflicts, and then finding ways to avoid them in the future. Once this envisioning is done, structures and processes must be in place to unify the nation. Workshops must be organized within three to five years after the civil war in order to make it possible for grassroots leaders to acquire professional training in conflict transformation and trauma healing.[41]

Trauma Healing Project

When the Peace Accords was signed in 1996, the Catholic Church in Guatemala responded by providing professional rehabilitation services for victims of torture and violence in the seven dioceses most affected by the civil war. Services included formation of self-help groups, exhumation, and individual counselling. Trained volunteers were made available to promote mental health in the villages.

In 2003, 344 self-help groups were established, and reached out to some 10,680 people over a period of four years. Furthermore, twenty-one groups were formed to help in exhumation of mass graves, identification of dead relatives, and provision of proper burial, according to their respective cultural and religious traditions. Mental health was also a somber issue

---

40. Hart, "Grassroots Peacebuilding in Post-Civil War Guatemala," 3.
41. Hart, "Grassroots Peacebuilding in Post-Civil War Guatemala," 3.

as many of the victims suffered from depression, paralyzing fear, extreme anxiety, and heart palpitations, among other illnesses.[42]

Due to lack of professional workers, volunteers who were not well-trained assisted in facilitating the trauma healing process. In fact, these non-professionals had an advantage because Mayan people tend to be more open to helpers from within their own communities who speak their language. More people were able to receive help through non-professional helpers. Survivors and victims came together to share their stories with the volunteers, and that in itself contributed to the healing process because they came to know that they were not alone in their trauma. Unfortunately, only 10,000 victims could avail themselves of the help provided by the Catholic Church due to lack of resources and personnel.[43]

Truth Commissions

To implement the Peace Accords, the Guatemalan government and the URNG agreed to establish a Commission for Historical Clarification (CEH) in order to reveal the atrocities and sufferings of the people during the previous thirty-six years of civil war. In spite of adverse political pressure, CEH reported that acts of genocide had been committed against indigenous groups in Guatemala, as well as other crimes against humanity. The army was the biggest perpetrator of violations of human rights, while the elite (oligarchy) of the country gave material support to the military to protect their own interests. The fact that the commission was not able to name the individual violators gave the commission the freedom to investigate more thoroughly with minimum risk.[44] The Catholic Church was the first to start the peace process by establishing the Recuperation of Historical Memory (REMHI). The CEH and REMHI published two reports respectively: *Memoria del Silencio* (1999) and *Nunca Más* (1998). Through testimonies given by the victims and perpetrators, these two commissions hoped to promote reconciliation and forgiveness among the people.

Reconciliation involves a series of moral issues: recognition of wrongdoing, contribution on the part of the offender and forgiveness on the part of the victim, and a commitment to co-exist peacefully in the future. It is

---

42. Hart, "Grassroots Peacebuilding in Post-Civil War Guatemala," 4.

43. Hart, "Grassroots Peacebuilding in Post-Civil War Guatemala," 5.

44. For a study of the CEH and history of truth finding in Guatemala, see Oettler, "Encounters with History," 3–19.

not easy and at times reconciliation is impossible, especially if the crimes are atrocious, beyond the pale of human decency. Paul Seils, legal director of the Centre for Human Rights Legal Action in Guatemala from 1997 to 2001, laments that the burden of reconciliation always falls on the victims themselves. Regarded as vengeful if they seek justice, the victims feel obliged to forgive.[45] Seils insists that in a transition society like Guatemala, contrition on the part of the perpetrators is a prerequisite to reconciliation. One must not confuse reconciliation with forgiveness. Reconciliation is the restoration of the fundamental bonds of trust and confidence between the state and citizens, a bond that had been torn apart by conflicts and violence. Thus, the Catholic bishops spoke of social reconstruction as reconciliation.

Kevin O'Neill, an academic, maintains that *Nunca Más* (Never Again) has been edited or modified until it conforms to the teaching of the Church. In fact, the document embodies a "Catholic analogical imagination."[46] The Church links the suffering of Guatemalans in the genocide with the suffering body of Jesus Christ. The report aims to denounce the atrocities of the military as well as to announce the hope for a better future, "the memory and image of Christ crucified anew."[47] Representing a Catholic understanding of genocide, *Nunca Más* emphasizes the pain and sufferings of Guatemalans as a community, the body of Christ crucified, the face of God speaking to us.

Likewise, *Memoria del Silencio* (Memory of Silence) uses Christian concepts, images, and rhetoric to represent Guatemala's genocide. However, unlike the Catholic emphasis on the communal experience (that is, analogical imagination), *Memoria del Silencio* puts the emphasis on the individual who facilitated the process of reconciliation by telling the truth of what had happened. O'Neill considers this focus on the individual a Protestant view, one that makes use of a "dialectical Christian imagination" to articulate what is considered a secular report sponsored by the United

---

45. Seils, "Reconciliation in Guatemala," 46–47.

46. O'Neill, "Writing Guatemala's Genocide," 335. According to David Tracy, Christian theology has two conceptual imaginations: analogical and dialectical. Roman Catholic theology favours an analogical imagination, which emphasizes the sacramental relationship between God and humans. Protestants, on the other hand, prefers dialectical imagination and stresses the distinction between divine and human natures through a negative dialectic. This dialectical imagination places the individual above the community because "human communities are always, potentially, an idolatrous source of oppressive power and overweening pride that must be resisted" (quoted in O'Neill, "Writing Guatemala's Genocide," 332. See also Tracy, *The Analogical Imagination*, 431).

47. O'Neill, "Writing Guatemala's Genocide," 337.

Nations.⁴⁸ Protestant emphasis on the individual has influenced human rights reports in modern times. Whatever their differences, the main aim of these two reports, *Nunca Más* and *Memoria del Silencio*, is to encourage forgiveness and reconciliation in Guatemala.

According to Canadian researcher Rachel Hatcher, truth commissions assume that knowing the truth will lead to healing, forgiveness, and reconciliation. However, this is not always the case. While the truth sets us free from denial of the past, it does not naturally set the victims and survivors in Guatemala free from the harm and damage that they experienced. The truth helps them in terms of moral recognition, but it is not automatically followed by contrition. Hatcher accuses the commissions of selective listening and reporting in order to promote reconciliation and to forgive. But she admits that the reports were on the whole successful, "a victory" in helping Guatemalans to come to terms with what had happened and to hope for a better future.⁴⁹

This author holds that forgiveness can take place only when individuals let go of the pain and bitterness at a personal level, yet this process is often not fully documented. Although we can witness the fruits of reconciliation in society, forgiveness, if it happens, takes place only in the interiority of one's own conscience. Of course, there will always be victims who cannot forgive, who demand reparation and revenge. This is perfectly understandable when we read about the immense cruelty and unspeakable violence inflicted on the indigenous population in Guatemala. This was the predicament of Rigoberta Menchú's family; her mother simply could not forgive those who kidnapped her son and burnt him alive. But there are others who, through the grace of God, were able to forgive and move forward, and others who, like Gerardi, died for the sake of truth so that their people might have a better future.

Bishop Gerardi: A Martyr for Truth

Reports and testimonies collected by CEH and REMHI give voice to those who were suppressed and silenced. They create space for a more open discussion of what had actually taken place in the society, so that Guatemalans can assimilate and come to terms with it. Such documentation inevitably

---

48. O'Neill, "Writing Guatemala's Genocide," 340.

49. Hatcher, "Truth and Forgetting in Guatemala," 134. See also Oglesby, "Educating Citizens in Postwar Guatemala," 79.

involved editing and narrowing of narratives to facilitate forgiveness and reconciliation. It was a very risky affair as church members who came forward to testify against the atrocities of the army exposed themselves to military reprisals. For example, Bishop Gerardi, who was in charge of collecting testimonies, was bludgeoned to death two days after he announced the release of the report on victims and perpetrators of Guatemala's genocide.

A strong critic of the army, Juan José Gerardi Conedera was appointed Auxiliary Bishop of the Archdiocese of Guatemala in 1984. As Director of the Human Rights Office of the Archbishop of Guatemala (ODHAG) in 1989, he was also involved in the Recovery of Historical Memory project (REMHI). Gerardi was determined to expose the truth of what happened during the armed conflict that killed so many people in Guatemala, so that such tragedy would never happen again. He and his colleagues conducted hundreds of interviews from all over the country, during which they heard and recorded the experiences of the victims and the identities of the perpetrators.[50]

On April 24, 1998, Gerardi published the findings of the REMHI in a document entitled *Nunca Más* (Never Again). This report exposed the atrocities of the Guatemalan military. The army was responsible for 85 percent of the violations of human rights during the thirty-six years of internal conflict, while the guerrillas were responsible for 9 percent. Later investigation by the CEH showed that the percentage of violations committed by the military was even higher: 93 percent, with only 3 percent committed by the guerrillas. This big difference in percentage, however, does not lessen the seriousness of the violations of human rights committed by the guerillas. The report by Gerardi was particularly damaging for the army as it identified those who committed crimes against humanity by name.[51]

On April 26, Gerardi was brutally murdered in Guatemala City. Obviously, the military did not want the Church to implicate them in violations of human rights or crimes against humanity. Gerardi's assassination revealed the strong and demonic determination to obstruct the work of REMHI: If there is no protection or justice for a bishop, who can expect to be safe in Guatemala?

Eventually, on June 8, 2001, three former military soldiers were tried and convicted of killing Gerardi: Col. Byron Disrael Lima Estrada, his son, Capt. Byron Lima Oliva, and José Obdulio Villanueva. What a victory for justice! This was the first time high-ranking military officers

50. Guatemala Human Rights Commission, *Assassination of Bishop Gerardi*.
51. Guatemala Human Rights Commission, *Assassination of Bishop Gerardi*.

had been tried since 1966.⁵² Unfortunately, the mastermind behind this murder was never found.

The Reports of CEH and REMHI reveal without doubt that the military had committed violent crimes characteristic of genocide, such as forced disappearance, rape, torture, and massacres.⁵³ The reports also refuted the army's claims of threats of communism and of insurgency.

Nunca Más was not only a denunciation of military atrocities, but also an affirmation of life, of "the resurrection of the martyred people" in Guatemala.⁵⁴ The reports reveal that the guerrillas were also involved in kidnapping and killings. In fact, with the exception of children, the elderly, and most women, no one was totally innocent. The civil war in Guatemala involved the political and economic elite, civil society, and the Church.

The Canadian historian Rachel Hatcher holds that few testimonies given suggest that the victims were able to forgive and to be reconciled with the perpetrators because they had experienced too much pain and grief. She writes, "The commission interpreted the testimonies in an attempt to make people remember differently, in ways that were contrary to the victims' and survivors' memories, contrary to their emotions, and contrary to their understanding and experience of the war."⁵⁵ Thus, while the victims and survivors supported the Church's call for social reconstruction, forgiveness was not possible for many who had experienced unspeakable violence and suffering. The victims were still full of anger and hatred against the military.

Victims and survivors did not come and tell their gruesome experiences in order to forgive the perpetrators, says Hatcher. Rather they gave their testimonies so that the perpetrators would be punished. They were seeking justice, even revenge. The victims also wanted to find out what had happened to their loved ones, those who had disappeared, whether they were dead or alive.

---

52. Guatemala Human Rights Commission, *Assassination of Bishop Gerardi*. See also Brett, "Peace without Social Reconciliation?" 285–303.

53. Through interviews and archival research, Manolo Castañeda has made a study of the perpetrators of genocide and their willingness to kill. He believes it is the training and the philosophy behind that turned them into murderers: "These acts raise the question of how young and mostly indigenous and illiterate soldiers, with a low level of indoctrination, were transformed into genocidal perpetrators, committing massacres against indigenous peoples and non-indigenous communities alike." Vela Castañeda, "Perpetrators: Specialization, Willingness, Group Pressure and Incentives," 226.

54. Quoted in Hatcher, "Truth and Forgetting in Guatemala," 145.

55. Hatcher, "Truth and Forgetting in Guatemala," 147.

Be that as it may, the purpose of the reports was to prevent violence in the future and to heal divisions in Guatemalan society. The reports published by the commissions give recommendations on how to come to peace and harmony, which include facilitating reconciliation between victims and perpetrators. The Church's mission was to help the victims and survivors to achieve closure through forgiveness. They can choose to move on with their lives—there is no future without forgiveness.

Supported by ecclesiastical authorities, both the CEH and REMHI promoted the teaching of the Church on how to establish peace "from below and from within."[56] The REMHI had the advantage in gathering testimonies from remote villages through the Church's evangelization network and parishes. The Church desired a peace cemented in truth, justice, forgiveness, and reconciliation. Following Christ, the Church truly believes that by giving testimony, the victims can be liberated from their suffering and the pain that has afflicted them for so many years: "the truth will set you free" (John 8:32). The reports are meant to break the silence the victims had kept for so long. Bishop Gerardi believed that by allowing the victims to tell their stories, they could be relieved of the burden and be healed eventually. The Church in its relentless search for the truth did not end with the publication of the testimonies, but continued to use the document as a tool for rebuilding Guatemalan society. Bishop Gerardi proclaimed:

> the Church has a mission to accomplish in terms of constructing the social order.... [The REMHI Project] is an alternative aimed at finding new ways for human beings to live with one another.... This is a pastoral approach. It is working with the light of faith to discover the face of God, the presence of the Lord. In all these events it is God who is speaking to us. We are called to reconciliation. Christ's mission is one of reconciliation. His presence calls us to be agents of reconciliation in this broken society and to try to place the victims and perpetrators within the framework of justice.[57]

This move towards reconciliation promoted by the Church in its REMHI Report included the issues regarding demilitarization, exhumations, forced recruitment of soldiers, and distribution of land.[58] In pursuing social

---

56. Quoted in Hatcher, "Truth and Forgetting in Guatemala," 150.

57. Quoted in Hatcher, "Truth and Forgetting in Guatemal," 151.

58. Jennifer Schirmer maintains that while the military proclaims that it will comply with the peace accords, it plays on the civilian government's fear of unrest to justify its continued control of internal security in the country. One of the major challenges for the attainment of true democracy in Guatemala is to make the military subject to civilian rule. Schirmer, "The Guatemalan Politico-Military Project," 93.

reconstruction and peaceful co-existence, the Church hoped that Guatemalans would come to terms with the past and move forward towards a brighter future. Forgiveness is an integral part of the Church's teaching and is found in the scriptures. No one is so perverse and evil that they cannot be forgiven, but the Church understands that it cannot force people to forgive. Forgiveness has to be a voluntary act that comes with knowing the truth and experiencing justice, as acknowledged in the REMHI Report.

The testimonies reveal that the victims wanted not just an end to the violence, corruption, and impunity, but justice and changes for a better future. They wanted their dead to be given a proper burial and land to be distributed to the poor. Evidently, the Church fully supported these demands in the REMHI Report. The main aim of the report, however, was to advocate forgiveness as a recipe for peace and social reconstruction. It may not be easy or even possible for some victims, but what are the alternatives? There is an urgent need to break the vicious cycle of retaliation and revenge. The Church was not asking people to forget the violence they had experienced, but to seek for a way to forgive. Attempting to give meaning to suffering and death, the Church sought to heal the wounds of the past so that victims and survivors could look forward to a brighter future.[59]

Perhaps it may be easier for the victims to forgive if they understand the motives and fears of the perpetrators, who are often their own neighbors and even relatives. *Nunca Más* attempts to explain why some Guatemalans became soldiers and took part in the torture and massacre of their own people. Some were forced to join the military and ordered by their superiors to kill without mercy. During this period of internal conflict, victims and perpetrators both suffered a great deal. The testimonies showed that some of the perpetrators were remorseful. Hatcher accuses the REMHI of trying to make victims out of the perpetrators. Be that as it may, one must also remember that the perpetrators shared the same humanity as their victims; many even shared the same ethnic and cultural identities. Thus, it could not be just racism that turned them into merciless butchers. The perpetrators were also victims of a perverse political and military ideology.

If Guatemalans insist that this violence of the past is never to be repeated, *nunca más*, perhaps the only way is to ensure this is for promotion of forgiveness and reconciliation to become part of the social reconstruction process—a process desired by both victims and survivors.

---

59. Hatcher, "Truth and Forgetting in Guatemal," 154.

— Chapter 5 —

The Crucified People

State Oppression in El Salvador

"You can tell them, if they succeed in killing me, that I pardon them, and I bless those who may carry out the killing"

—Archbishop Óscar Arnulfo Romero

El Salvador was the name given to the city and future nation, by the Spanish conquistador Pedro de Alvarado, in honour of Jesus, the Savior of the World. Mirroring the life and death of Jesus, many people in this country, especially the poor and indigenous population, have been cruelly treated and have died under the weight of colonial exploitation, social injustice, and despotic rule. These victims, who lived in poverty and were massacred in death, are the "crucified people." Ignacio Ellacuría taught that "[t]his crucified people are the historical continuation of the servant of Yahweh, whom the sin of the world continues to deprive of any human features, which the powers of this world continue stripping of everything, wresting his life from him as long as he lives."[1]

Constituting the majority in the Third Word, the crucified people are deprived of the basic necessities of life. Their suffering unmasks unjust socio-economic structures that cause deprivations and poverty, which are the consequences of human failures. Jon Sobrino writes, "In this crucified people Christ acquires a body in history and that the crucified people embody

---

1. Quoted in Sobrino, "Our World: Cruelty and Compassion," 18. For a comprehensive study of the violence and its agents, see Americas Watch Committee, *El Salvador's Decade of Terror*. See also Lucia, "The Anthropological Function of Dialogue in Political Reconciliation Processes," 125–41.

Christ in history as crucified."[2] The crucified people—poor, dispossessed, and marginalized—embody the presence of Christ, crucified in our midst. In El Salvador, caught between murderous military regimes and the guerrillas, they were also victims of political violence and revolts.

Conflicts and violence have afflicted El Salvadorans throughout their history. From 1980 to 1992, during the civil war between the Farabundo Marti Front for National Liberation (FMLN) and the Salvadoran army, more than 75,000 people died, 8,000 disappeared, and over one million went into exile. These twelve years of violence included the 1980 assassination of Archbishop Óscar Romero, the murder of four American churchwomen in the same year, and the 1989 massacre of six Jesuits and their housekeeper and daughter at Central American University (UCA).

This chapter examines the life and teaching of Archbishop Óscar Romero as the voice of the crucified people, the mission of the Church in El Salvador and its role in the promotion of pardon and peace. In a nation torn by conflict and violence, Romero preached forgiveness and reconciliation, convinced that peace can only exist when there is justice and truth. Thus, his death inspired the Church to redefine its understanding of martyrdom in modern times. To appreciate the profound witness of Romero as a martyr, it is necessary to have some basic understanding of El Salvador's tragic history and the root causes of its conflict.

Land of Inequality

The division of land has dominated El Salvador since the sixteenth century when the Spaniards occupied the territory. Like most countries in Central America, El Salvador has huge plantations that grow commodities such as cocoa, indigo, and coffee for export. These plantations were first owned by the Spanish and later transferred to Salvadorans of European ancestry. The natives, especially the indigenous people, who comprised 95 percent of the population, were left with almost nothing. Thus, they had to work on these plantations for very low wages.

In El Salvador today, 4 percent of the people own 60 percent of the land while the rest of the population living in rural areas are dispossessed. In the late 1800s, fourteen families (*Las Catorce*) controlled the land in El Salvador. When peasants, as part of the indigenous population, demanded better living conditions and revolted in 1932, the government responded with

2. Sobrino, *Jesus the Liberator*, 255.

violence, killing approximately 30,000 people, or 4 percent of the population, within a week. This event is known as *La Matanza* (The Massacre). Following this genocide, the authorities began to abolish traces of indigenous culture, language, clothing, and music.[3] The surviving natives were forced to adopt customs of the *mestizos* or *Ladinos*, people of mixed indigenous and European ancestry. As a result of *La Matanza*, El Salvador today does not have a significant indigenous population. The revolt and subsequent massacre changed the face of El Salvadoran society and initiated cycles of peasant rebellion and military repression.

After *La Matanza*, a series of military dictatorships controlled El Salvador and ensured that the unequal socio-economic structures remained intact for the next forty years. Criticism of and organized opposition to the alliance between the military and landowners were quickly and mercilessly suppressed. In 1960, the Christian Democratic Party (PDC), which adopted a moderate but critical policy towards the establishment was formed.[4] Though it had substantial support from the people, it could not achieve political power in a system controlled by powerful conservative forces supported by the military.

In the 1970s, American corporations such as General Foods, Procter and Gamble, ESSO, Westinghouse, Kimberly-Clark, and Texas Instruments began operation in the country, taking advantage of the low wages and minimal worker-protection laws.[5] Only these companies and the oligarchs in the country benefited from the investments, thus widening the gap between the rich and the poor. Subsequently, for more than thirty years after *La Matanza*, the life of the average peasant in El Salvador had not improved. Due to unfair land distribution and social inequity, their lives became worse. Most people in the country had limited access to basic necessities such as water, decent housing, health care, education, and gainful employment.

---

3. Violence is very much part of El Salvador's history: during the first fifty years of Spanish conquest, the Indian population in El Salvador was reduced from 500,000 to 75,000 through massacres and illness. "History of El Salvador," *Teaching Central America*.

4. Peterson, *Martyrdom and the Politics of Religion*, 28.

5. "History of El Salvador," *Teaching Central America*.

Be a Patriot. Kill a Priest

In the 1970s, groups of teachers, students, workers, priests, and religious brothers and sisters began to organize themselves and demand a more equitable sharing of wealth and resources in the nation. In the rural areas, peasants organized themselves and demanded fairer wages, land distribution, and better living conditions. The main peasant groups, led by Catholic activists, were the Christian Peasants' Federation (FECCAS) and the Union of Farmworkers (UTC). Fighting for social justice, they established bases for Christian communities and other pastoral and educational programs. Quite a few priests and sisters actively encouraged their flock to participate in these popular movements.

Progressive candidates were elected as presidents in 1972 and 1977, but they were unfairly disqualified by the regimes. Government-backed right-wing death squads began to assassinate opposition activists and community and church leaders. These death squads consisted of heavily armed soldiers, police, and National Guardsmen in civilian clothes. Some of them were members of ORDEN, a paramilitary group founded by National Guardsmen and the notorious White Warriors' Union. One of their slogans was "Be a Patriot. Kill a Priest," an assignment that they carried out frequently. These death squads sought to repress activists, divide the opposition, and create a "culture of fear" by their random killings.[6]

The Farabundo Marti Front for National Liberation (FMLN), consisting of students, teachers, factory and farm workers, and ex-government officials, was established in 1980 to fight against the government by armed resistance. It was named after a militant attorney who led Salvadoran peasants during the 1920s and was killed *in La Mantanza*. The FMLN wanted to establish a democratic government that was inclusive and willing to accept the co-operation of different political organizations. It demanded that perpetrators involved in kidnapping and murder be prosecuted and convicted before they would lay down their arms. In addition, the FMLN advocated land reform and a mixed economy.

Sadly, increased resistance from the FMLN followed by intensified state repression led to a full-fledged civil war. The El Salvadoran military was determined to eliminate the FMLN's sphere of influence with large-scale bombing, resulting in the displacement of a quarter of the nation's population. The civil war divided the country geographically into three

---

6. Peterson, *Martyrdom and the Politics of Religion*, 63, 33.

different kinds of territory: government-controlled, mostly in the cities; conflict zones, where the FLMN and the government army fought for control; and "liberated zones," in the mountains and coastal areas, controlled by the FLMN.[7]

The United States government considered the FMLN a "terrorist organization" because it was financially supported by the Soviet Union and had close connections to the socialist governments in Cuba and Nicaragua. In spite of documented gross human rights abuses, including the killing of American citizens, the Reagan and Bush administrations supported the government of El Salvador throughout the 1980s in the hope of eliminating the "communist" FMLN.[8] Between 1980 and 1990, the Salvadoran government received over four billion dollars in US aid, military training, and advice, which enabled the army to launch a brutal counterinsurgency war in the rural areas controlled by the FLMN. Aerial bombings and mortar attacks in the 1980s killed more civilians than the guerillas.[9] Archbishop Óscar Romero wrote to former president Jimmy Carter, pleading with him to stop supporting the murderous regime in his country.

Nonetheless, with around 13,000 regular fighters in addition to some 40,000 part-time militia members mostly in the rural areas, the FMLN had developed into a formidable force. Widely supported by the civilian population and with good military strategy, the FMLN were able to maintain a stalemate with the government. Though small in numbers and with inferior arms, the guerillas were highly motivated compared to the government forces.

On November 11, 1989, the FMLN launched a nationwide assault and held the capital city, San Salvador, for weeks. Determined to crush the insurgency at all costs, the government ordered aerial bombing of urban areas and arrested scores of activists. Entering the campus of Central American University (UCA), the military killed six Jesuit priests, leading intellectuals in El Salvador who were vocal critics of the government, and their two housekeepers.

The 1989 offensive proved to be a turning point in the history of El Salvador. The killing of the Jesuits and their two helpers at UCA sparked off international outrage and prompted the US government to support peaceful

---

7. Peterson, *Martyrdom and the Politics of Religion*, 36.

8. The Reagan and Bush administrations called the military regime in El Salvador the "good guys." See "Truth or Consequences in El Salvador," 3.

9. Peterson, *Martyrdom and the Politics of Religion*, 35–36.

negotiation rather than training of the Salvadoran army. Criticizing the US assistance to the military in El Salvador, Fr. A. O'Hare SJ, President of Fordham University in 1989, asked this question, "Can we hand weapons to butchers and remain unstained by the blood of their innocent victims?"[10] The killing of the Jesuits reveals the Catholic Church's deep involvement in the struggle for justice and peace on behalf of the poor in the nation. It was also evident in the brutal murder of Óscar Romero, which made a deep impact on the people and on the Jesuits who worked at UCA at that time.

Óscar Arnulfo Romero

Born on August 15, 1917, in Ciudad Barrios, El Salvador, Óscar Romero came from a humble family. Since his parents could not afford to send him to school after the age of twelve, he worked as an apprentice carpenter. Determined to become a priest, Romero entered the seminary at the age of fourteen and was ordained in 1942 when he was twenty-five years old. Realizing the power of transistor radio, he attempted to reach out to the peasant farmers by broadcasting his Sunday homilies through radio stations. In 1970, he was made the Auxiliary Bishop in San Salvador, and in 1974, the Bishop of Santiago de Maria.

A traditionalist, Romero supported the hierarchy and conformity to church teachings. He was against political activism that challenged the government. In fact, when news came from Rome that Romero had been chosen to succeed Archbishop Chávez, the government of El Salvador and the oligarchy were very pleased. They believed that Romero, being a conservative, would not threaten the status quo. Most clergy in the archdiocese, however, were disappointed; they thought that Romero was keener to maintain good relations with the government than to serve the needs of the people. They were mistaken. Soon Romero proved his mettle by championing the rights of the poor and downtrodden. It was not a sudden change, but a gradual transformation as he began to notice the social reality in El Salvador.

After being the Bishop of Santiago de Maria for two years, Romero soon understood that the social injustice existing in society was the root cause of many of the evils in society. For example, he witnessed children dying because their parents were too poor to seek medical help. Using the resources in his diocese, Romero began to help the poor. Over time, he

---

10. "Is Justice Still a Long-way Off for Jesuit Martyrs in El Salvador?" 3.

realized that charity was not enough. To dismantle unjust economic and social structures, there must be a conversion of hearts. Convinced that the Spirit was speaking through the suffering of the people, he defended activist priests fighting for the rights of the poor. When Rutilio Grande, a Jesuit working for the poor in rural areas, was murdered in 1977, he realized he had to take sides but also be prepared to forgive.

At the funeral mass for Fr. Rutilio Grande and his two companions, Romero preached that the Church, inspired by love, is able to reject hatred: "We want to tell you, murderous brothers, that we love you and that we ask of God repentance for your hearts, because the Church is not able to hate, it has no enemies. Its only enemies are those who want to declare themselves so. But the Church loves them: 'Father forgive them, they know not what they do.'"[11] Later, Romero acknowledged it was the assassination of Rutilio Grande, his personal friend, that motivated him to put into practice the teachings of Vatican II and Medellín, calling for solidarity with the poor, marginalized, and dispossessed.

Though devastated by the brutal killing of Grande, Romero harbored no ill will nor hatred, but continued to preach reconciliation: "Let there be no animosity in our heart.... Let this Eucharist, which is a called to reconciliation with God and our brothers and sisters, leave in all hearts the satisfaction that we are Christians.... Let us pray to the Lord for forgiveness and for the due repentance of those who converted a town into a prison and a place of torment."[12] As a man against violence, Romero believed that those who live by the sword will die by the sword. He pleaded for repentance from the perpetrators so that God's mercy and kindness would fall upon them like the rain and they would all become brothers and sisters.

Romero continued to witness more atrocities committed by the military when he became the Archbishop of El Salvador in 1977. Confronting President Carlos Humberto of El Salvador regarding human rights violations, he became the "voice of the voiceless," one who offered his people faith and hope for a better life.[13] He defended progressive priests, religious sisters, and lay persons who dared to denounce the atrocities of the authorities. Visiting churches in his archdiocese, especially those harassed by the military in rural areas such as Chalatenango and Aguilares, Romero also made a passionate plea for the rights of his people to protest. During

---

11. Quoted in Brockman, *Romero: A Life*, 10.
12. Quoted in Brockman, *Romero: A Life*, 63.
13. "Oscar Romero Bio." *Caritas Australia*.

Sunday homilies in the cathedral, he denounced the brutality of the army and greed of the government as well as the oligarchy, those who controlled most of the country's natural resources.

An outspoken vocal critic of the violent activities of right-wing groups, as well as the leftist guerillas, Romero began to raise global awareness with reports of murder, torture, and kidnapping that were rampant throughout the country. Addressing soldiers and policemen, Romero cried: "I beg you, I implore you, I order you . . . in the name of God, stop the repression!"[14] Unfortunately, his pleading fell on deaf ears. Yet he never gave up working towards peace and reconciliation in his country. He avoided partisan political positions and advised his priests to do the same. Viewing the country's division and the Church's involvement in the unrest as social rather than ideological, Romero held that the conflict was not between the Church and the state, but between the state and the people. The Church stood with the people because the people are with the Church.[15]

In order to restore trust and confidence between the Church and the state, Romero was prepared to dialogue with the government. He wanted the authorities in El Salvador to account for the disappearance of persons, to end torture and arbitrary arrests, and provide due process for priests who were expelled.[16] In setting the conditions for a successful dialogue with the authorities, Romero wanted all sides to be present and all violence to cease, especially government repression of civilians. The subject for dialogue was the call to dismantle unjust structures that promote violence. Terrorists and those who supported violence would lay down their arms if they have a sincere desire for dialogue. Romero emphasized the critical importance of protecting the freedom of expression through various labor organizations—these would be the signs of the presence of democracy in El Salvador.

Romero's outspoken defense of the poor and victims of violence made him a target of violence. In the face of threats to his life, he declared his willingness to sacrifice for the "redemption and resurrection" of El Salvador.[17] Ironically, the President of El Salvador offered protection by providing Romero with security guards and an armored car. Romero politely rejected this offer of protection, and wrote to the government in 1979: "I

14. "Oscar Romero Bio," *Caritas Australia*.
15. Peterson, *Martyrdom and the Politics of Religion*, 62.
16. Brockman, *Romero: A Life*, 84.
17. "St. Óscar Romero," *Encyclopedia Britannica*.

wouldn't accept that protection, because I wanted to run the same risks that the people are running; it would be a pastoral anti-testimony if I were very secure, while my people are so insecure."[18] Instead, Romero took the opportunity to ask the president for protection for the people, especially at military checkpoints and roadblocks.

Like most people, Romero was afraid of violent death, but he never neglected his duty and responsibility in accompanying his flock when they were in danger. Neither did he seek protection for his priests. He said: "How sad it would be, in a country where such horrible murders are being committed, if there were no priests among the victims! A murdered priest is a testimonial of a church incarnate in the problems of the people."[19] Persecution produces Christian hope for the Church.

Two weeks before his death, Romero had already forgiven his killers: "If they kill me, I will rise again in the people of El Salvador. . . . You can tell them, if they succeed in killing me, that I pardon them, and I bless those who may carry out the killing. But I wish that they could realize that they are wasting their time. A bishop will die, but the Church of God—the people—will never die."[20] Just before his death, Romero uttered these prophetic words: "Those who surrender to the service of the poor through love of Christ will live like the grain of wheat that dies. . . . The harvest comes because of the grain that dies."[21] On March 24, 1980, while celebrating Mass in the chapel of Divine Providence Hospital, Óscar Romero was gunned down by an assassin belonging to a right-wing death squad.

In spite of prevailing violence, tens of thousands of mourners attended Romero's funeral, transforming the service into one of the biggest demonstrations the country had ever witnessed. Romero lives on in the lives and memories of his people, especially among poor, whom he identified himself with. Even before his beatification, the people considered Romero a martyr.

Violence against the Church

Repression of peasant movements and popular organizations leading to the killing of thousands of the natives has taken place in Latin America

---

18. Quoted in Peterson, *Martyrdom and the Politics of Religion*, 62.
19. McDermott, "In the Footsteps of Martyrs," 19.
20. Closkey and Hogan, "Introduction," 5.
21. "Oscar Romero Bio," *Caritas Australia*.

since colonial days. But persecution of the Church is a recent phenomenon, given the fact that Roman Catholicism was the dominant religion in the continent. This attack on the Church coincided with the Church's teaching on the preferential option for the poor in the 1960s and the establishment of base Christian communities.[22] As a result, thousands of Catholic activists, clerics, religious, and lay persons, were imprisoned, tortured, and murdered by the military for their involvement in fighting for justice and equitable distribution of land. Between 1971 and 1990, more than forty religious sisters and priests and one archbishop were killed. Most of these murders took place in El Salvador.

Archbishop Óscar Romero and the other activists were assassinated not for their faith but for denouncing the government and the elites in El Salvador, who were responsible for running a country that systematically exploited the poor for their own advantage. Romero said, "Our church is persecuted precisely for its preferential option for the poor and for trying to incarnate itself in the interest of the poor."[23] The victims were mostly the poor and those who defended them. The attack on the clergy led to widespread persecution of the Christian community.

The conservative establishment in El Salvador, including many bishops, insisted that the attack was committed in retaliation for Romero's political involvement. They blamed left-wing Catholics for getting involved in politics and thus incurring the wrath of the government and the military. Romero, they maintained, should not have been involved in politics but confined himself to the spiritual care of his flock. In fact, even sympathetic citizens in El Salvador interpreted the attack on the Church as politically motivated. The oligarchy, colluding with the government and the military, sought to crush all opposition, be it secular or religious. The growth of base Christian communities, led by the clergy and lay leaders, became a threat to the established order. Hence, some were brutally killed by death squads not because they were Catholics but because they threatened the wealth and privileges of the elites. As such, can these Catholics, priests and laity, who were massacred because they stood by the side of the oppressed and downtrodden, be regarded as martyrs in the Church or of the Church?

---

22. Peterson, *Martyrdom and the Politics of Religion*, 63. For a review on works written about the violence in El Salvador, see Brockett, "El Salvador: The Long Journey from Violence to Reconciliation (Book Review)," 174–87.

23. Quoted in Peterson, *Martyrdom and the Politics of Religion*, 62.

Martyrdom

In the classical sense, a martyr is a person who dies for the faith, such as Justin Martyr, Perpetua, and Felicity. The early church suffered much persecution at the hands of authorities in the Roman Empire and countless people died for their Christian faith. The period of martyrs ended with the Edict of Toleration issued by Emperor Constantine in Milan in 313 AD. The lives of martyrs paralleled the life of Jesus who died on the cross. Thus, the early Christians revered the martyrs as exemplary witnesses of their faith. Like Jesus, the proto-martyr, they died a gruesome death at the hands of those motivated by hatred of the faith (*odium fidei*).

In the twentieth century, in Latin America, many Christians who fought for justice died at the hands of their fellow Christians because of differences in political ideology. Can these be regarded as martyrs in the Catholic tradition? Óscar Romero and Rutilio Grande were killed by death squads in El Salvador—are they Christian martyrs or victims of political assassinations? In a broad sense, they were martyrs who died struggling for justice on behalf of the poor against a ruthless military regime. Even though they might be baptized Catholics, those leaders who ordered the killings and those who carried out the orders were anything but Christian. Victims of repression in Latin America have inspired the Church to expand and re-define the meaning of Christian martyrdom.

In the light of the situation in Latin America, Karl Rahner argued that someone who dies fighting for a cause related to his/her Christian conviction can be regarded as a martyr, provided the death is not directly sought. Of course, not everybody who dies fighting on the Christian or Catholic side in a religious war should be considered a martyr. In Rahner's opinion, however, someone like Romero, who died while fighting for justice in society due to his profound Christian conviction, should be considered one. Himself in favor of a legitimate political theology, Rahner called upon the Church to be aware of its responsibility to promote justice and peace in society.[24]

John Paul II had in fact broadened the term "martyr" in his 1995 encyclical, *Ut Unum Sint*: "In a theocentric vision, we Christians already have a common Martyrology. This also includes the martyrs of our own century, more numerous than one might think, and it shows how, at a profound

---

24. Rahner, "Dimensions of Martyrdom," 10.

level, God preserves communion among the baptized in the supreme demand of faith, manifested in the sacrifice of life itself."[25]

These martyrs include religious (priests, brothers, and sisters), who were killed during the Spanish Civil War and in concentration camps in Germany, for instance. In Latin America, there were many who died as Christians protesting against the atrocities of military dictatorship. Faithful to the gospel and to Church teaching on the preferential option for the poor, they stood for social justice and peace.

In his Apostolic Letter *Novo Millennio Ineunte* (2001), John Paul II wrote: "May the shining example of the many witnesses to the faith whom we have remembered during the Jubilee sustain and guide us in this confident, enterprising, and creative sense of mission."[26] We used to associate martyrs with the early Church, but John Paul II reminded us that in our own time we have many witnesses who in different ways were able to live the gospel fully to the point of sacrificing their lives so that others may live. A good example is the Polish Franciscan, Maximilian Kolbe, killed by the Nazis in 1941; his death inspired the Church to expand its conception of martyrdom. Kolbe was killed not directly for his faith but for a political cause. Yet, in 1982, Pope John Paul II canonized Kolbe as a "martyr of charity."[27]

Romero himself had taught that those who died fighting for justice are "martyrs": "For me, who are the true martyrs in the popular sense? . . . They are real people who have gone to the dangerous limits, where the White Warrior Union threatens them, where warnings can be sent to people and they end up being killed, as Christ was killed."[28] Romero, in fact, was popularly venerated as a martyr and saint just after his death in 1980. Many people came to his tomb to pray and to lay flowers at the Cathedral of the Holy Savior in San Salvador. He was declared a martyr by Pope Francis on February 3, 2015 and canonized as a saint on October 14, 2018.

The situation in Latin America is problematic in declaring someone a martyr because there are Christians killing Christians. There could be a Catholic bishop killed by soldiers ordered by their lieutenant or general, perhaps with the permission of the president of the country, *all of whom* were supposedly baptized Catholics! Thomas Aquinas taught that

---

25. John Paul II, *Ut Unum Sint*, On Commitment to Ecumenism, no. 84.

26. John Paul II, *Novo Millennio Ineunte*, no. 41.

27. "St. Maximilian Kolbe, 'Martyr of Charity': Feast Day, Aug. 14," *Catholic News Herald*.

28. Quoted in Sobrino, "Our World," 18.

a martyr is simply a Christian killed by enemies trying to destroy the Catholic faith. Liberation theologians expand the definition of martyrdom to those who, motivated by their faith, died while defending the poor against the injustice of the state, because such martyrdom in Latin America occurs frequently.

Leonardo Boff, a Brazilian theologian, views Jesus as the proto-martyr and emphasizes that it is not the suffering and death that makes a martyr but the "cause."[29] The Gospel of Matthew teaches: "Blessed are those who are persecuted for righteousness' sake, for theirs is the kingdom of heaven" (Matt 5:10); "you will be brought before governors and kings for my sake, as a testimony to them and to the Gentiles" (Matt 10:18). Stressing the politically subversive nature of Christianity, Boff holds that Christians were killed because they threatened the political-religious foundation of the Empire and its leaders. Stretching the concept of martyrdom, Boff thus asserts that modern-day martyrs die for their faith like Christians in earlier times: "Not a few Christians . . . because of the Gospel, make a preferential option for the poor, for their liberation, for the defence of their rights. In the name of this option they stand up and denounce the exercise of domination and all forms of social dehumanisation. They may be persecuted, arrested, tortured, and killed. They, too, are martyrs in the strict sense of the word."[30] With this supposition, martyrs thus can include those Christians who died for their faith in their effort to defend their brothers and sisters from injustice and exploitation.

Jon Sobrino writes that in our time, the situation in Latin America has resulted in Christians who died violently not "on account of their witness to faith but because of the compassion that stems from their faith."[31] They are "Jesus martyrs" who suffered violent death like the Savior. Strictly speaking, they are not those "who die *for* Christ" but "those who die *like* Jesus *for the cause of Jesus*"; they are "martyrs *in* the church but not martyrs *of* the church."[32] These martyrs find their configuration in the life and death of Jesus. They were killed not because of hatred for their faith but, rather, hatred for their involvement with the lives of the poor and dispossessed, which they carried out in mercy and compassion for God's people.

---

29. Boff, "Martyrdom," 13.
30. Boff, "Martyrdom," 13.
31. Sobrino, "Our World," 17.
32. Sobrino, "Our World," 19.

These Christians include bishops, priests, sisters, lay workers, peasants, students, lawyers, and journalists. In one way or another, they exposed the unjust structures in society that have caused the suffering and death of many poor people. They are compassionate individuals who fought against the social, economic, and political elites who were determined to maintain their wealth and privileges at the expense of the poor.

The reality of El Salvador had prompted Romero to preach the significance of Rutilio Grande's death: "What does the church offer in this universal fight for the liberation from all this misery?"[33] The liberation that the Church offers is exemplified by the ministry of Rutilio, working for and with the poor in solidarity against injustice and exploitation. Rutilio died because he was faithful to the social doctrine of the Church. Deeply saddened by Rutilio's death, Romero made a personal plea to the perpetrators: "I want to tell you, criminal brothers, who already are in ex-communion with the church, and are listening on the radio, . . . I want to tell you, criminal brothers, that we love you and we ask God for forgiveness for your hearts, because the love of the church is not capable of hating, it does not have enemies. The love of the Lord inspired the action of Rutilio Grande."[34]

Romero thanked the Society of Jesus for sending men like Rutilio Grande to El Salvador and "illuminating so many on the roads to Aguilares."[35] The roads to Auguilares symbolize the El Salvadoran way of the cross, where suffering and death for justice, peace, and righteousness will lead to the resurrection. Rutilio Grande was the first Salvadoran priest to be killed in the 1970s for political reasons. But he was regarded by many in the country as a martyr for justice.

Willing to sacrifice his life for his fellow Salvadorans, Romero has taught that martyrdom is a grace of God. If his enemies succeeded in killing him, he would pardon them so that they would know they were wasting their time—a bishop will die but the people of God, the Church, will never perish. The many martyrs in El Salvador manifest that the Church is persecuted for its fidelity to the teaching of Jesus Christ. This sad state of affairs—persecution and martyrdom—is also a glorious witness to the faith of the people in the nation which has the Savior himself as its patron.

During that same year when Romero was murdered, Maryknoll Sisters Maura Clarke and Ita Ford, Maryknoll lay missionary Jean Donovan

---

33. Quoted in Thiede, *Remembering Oscar Romero and the Martyrs of El Salvador*, 41.
34. Quoted in Thiede, *Remembering Oscar Romero and the Martyrs of El Salvador*, 42.
35. Quoted in Thiede, *Remembering Oscar Romero and the Martyrs of El Salvador*, 42.

and Ursuline Sister Dorothy Kazel, all from the United States, were raped, tortured, and killed on December 2, 1980. And yet, the United States continued to support the military government in El Salvador throughout the 1980s. On December 11, 1981, an armed battalion executed more than 800 civilians in a village called El Mozote—this event is now referred to as the El Mozote Massacre.[36]

A right-wing Arena Party led by Roberto D'Aubuisson came into power in the 1989 election. In that year, six Jesuit priests and their housekeepers were killed by the army on the campus of Central American University (UCA). The death of these priests, nuns, and lay people forms a tiny fraction compared to the over 80,000 Salvadorans killed by the government-backed death squads since 1979.[37] Their victims were people working in religious and secular organizations who were demanding land reform and better working conditions for the poor. We can consider these victims "anonymous martyrs" because they died fighting for the kingdom of God.

Mission of the Church

The Church's mission in El Salvador is to proclaim the kingdom of God, which is the reign of peace, justice, and truth. The bishops' task is to make this proclamation a reality so that the political, social, and economic situation in El Salvador conforms to God's plan. This involves dismantling the unjust social structure that promoted a "false humanism of profit, social position, power, and privilege and giving dignity and the means of decent existence to those who are forgotten and excluded."[38] Although the Church has the task of announcing the good news to all people, it must demonstrate clearly that the gospel is most especially for the poor and dispossessed, the marginalized and the exploited.

---

36. "History of El Salvador," *Teaching Central America*. US complicity in the horrors that afflicted Latin America has often been overlooked. The military officers who ordered the assassination of Óscar Romero and others were trained in the United States. Secretary of State Henry Kissinger assured Admiral Cesar Augusto Guzzetti of Argentina, who was directing the "Dirty War" that "I have an old-fashioned view that friends ought to be supported. What is not understood is that you have a civil war. We read about human rights, but not the context. The quicker you succeed, the better." With no objection from the Americans, between 9,000 and 30,000 people were killed or disappeared during the next couple of years. "Holding Ourselves Accountable," 28.

37. "History of El Salvador," *Teaching Central America*.

38. Quoted in Brockman, *Romero: A Life*, 7–8.

Following the guidelines of Vatican II (1962 to 1965) and the Medellín Conference held in Colombia (1968), the Church in El Salvador identified itself with the poor and dispossessed. It gave preference to the poor and marginalized, who are the majority of Salvadorans. Critics, however, accused the Church of preaching hatred, promoting class struggle, and meddling in politics, which should not be its concern. This was complicated by the fact that some bishops supported the establishment and refused to co-operate with Romero.

Begging pardon for the Church, Romero considered this disunity in the hierarchy as the "most visible sin."[39] He wanted the Church to be united by taking sides with the poor and downtrodden: "an invitation to all, regardless of class, to accept and take up the cause of the poor as though accepting and taking up their own cause, the cause of Christ himself."[40] He called for a conversion of all Christians, rich and poor alike, and a preferential option for the poor regarding the Church's mission.

In his second pastoral letter (1977), Romero highlighted the Church as the body of Christ in history. He was aware that this letter would displease and disturb many people because they were told to change and to be converted. This change was clearly difficult for the rich and powerful who were accustomed to so-called Catholic tradition where the Church confined itself to the spiritual sphere. But now the Church has to be conscious of its presence in the world and its duty to speak out against injustice, poverty, and suffering of people—the call for conversion of "hearts and structures."[41]

The rich and powerful did not have a problem with conversion of "hearts," but were very concerned with the conversion of "structures," which threatened their privileged position and the status quo. This conversion of structures included changing the economic and social frameworks in Salvadoran society and calling for a more equitable sharing of resources. Steeped in self-interest and traditionalism, critics attacked Romero. The rich and powerful, the oligarchs, did not want the kind of change in the Church that would threaten their affluent lifestyle.

Romero, however, wanted to protect the outcasts, the *campesinos* (peasant farmers), slum dwellers, exploited laborers, and prisoners who were exploited by the government and military that were supported by the oligarchy. Denouncing social, cultural, economic, and political structures

39. Brockman, *Romero: A Life*, 189.
40. Brockman, *Romero: A Life*, 189.
41. Brockman, *Romero: A Life*, 81.

that dehumanized and destroyed families, the Church was not inspired by hatred or resentment against the rich, but "seeks conversion of hearts and salvation of all."[42] Because the Church denounced unjust structures in society, it was accused of betraying the gospel, preaching hatred, embracing Marxism, and meddling in politics.

Records, however, have shown that the Church in El Salvador promoted love and forgiveness. Romero emphasized that the Church rejected Marxism as an atheistic philosophy, but also denounced capitalism for its excessive materialism. Not wishing to be identified with any political ideology, the Church's main concern is the faith of the people. Acknowledging that some actions of the bishops and priests have political effects, Romero emphasized that the Church does not employ the mechanisms of political organizations to accomplish its pastoral work. Rejecting privileges, the Church wants to be faithful to the teaching of Christ by denouncing injustice and rejecting violence.

Justice and Peace

Romero was also convinced that peace and non-violence could only be achieved when there is justice. In other words, violence is a product of unjust economic and social structures in society, which the bishops at Medellín characterized as institutional violence. This institutionalized or legalized violence comes in the form of economic exploitation, political domination, or violation of human rights by the military. The fact is that "violence starts with the structures of violence."[43]

In El Salvador, when people started to organize themselves to dismantle those structures of violence, the elites would retaliate with increased violence with the help of the government-backed military. The wealthy class would do all they could to stop any revolutionary change that threatened their life-style—the "privileged few repressed the ones seeking change, so this violence of oppression became a violence of repression."[44] The oppressed believed the only way to bring about change was through the violence of revolution. But Ignacio Ellacuría insisted that the solution is to struggle against the first violence so as to prevent the

---

42. Quoted in Brockman, *Romero: A Life*, 82.
43. Gumbleton, "If You Want Peace, Work for Justice," 38.
44. Gumbleton, "If You Want Peace, Work for Justice," 38.

violence of repression and revolutionary violence through negotiation, dialogue, and reconciliation.

While the Church permits a "legitimate defense" as a means to uphold human rights, it fervently promotes non-violence. This is based on the teaching of the Gospels—turning the other cheek to an attacker. Not regarded as a passive response, this turning the other cheek to the aggressor requires moral strength and the conviction that peace is more powerful than violence. Unfortunately, in El Salvador there existed fanatical groups who believed in "divinizing violence as the only source of justice."[45] Be that as it may, violence is not going to stop if there is vast economic disparity between the rich and the poor. There is no justice and peace if widespread poverty prevails.

John Paul II was the first pontiff to highlight how our social mechanisms can lead to poverty, which is the thrust of his teaching on structural sin: "social, economic, and political structures, which are frequently agents of violence and injustice."[46] This means no peace, no justice. Today, we have 20 percent of the world's people living in abject poverty, 60 percent in some degree of poverty, and the remaining 20 percent enjoying 87 percent of the earth's resources and wealth. This happens not because those living in the northern hemisphere are smarter or work harder than the poor people in other parts of the planet. It is because they have manipulated the economic order, the structures and systems, solely to their advantage and benefit.

According to Gustavo Gutiérrez, poverty is the result of how we have organized our society, not only the way we distribute our resources, but the way we think and classify racial, cultural, and gender issues. Poverty has many aspects, including economic, cultural, racial, social, and gender-related. We now understand that poverty is not destined; it is man-made, a misfortune produced by injustice, which can be avoided. Theologically speaking, the root of poverty is injustice, which is the refusal to love. The core of our Christian faith is love, and thus refusal to love is sin.[47]

Back in 1967, Pope Paul VI wrote an encyclical letter entitled *Populorum Progressio* (On the Development of Peoples) where he lamented that "in certain regions a privileged minority enjoys the refinements of life, while the rest of the inhabitants, impoverished and disunited, 'are deprived of almost all possibility of acting on their own initiative and responsibility,

---

45. Brockman, *Romero: A Life*, 143–44.
46. Christiansen, "Catholic Peacemaking, 1991–2005," 21–28.
47. Gutiérrez, "Liberation Theology for the Twenty-First Century," 50.

and often subsist in living and working conditions unworthy of the human person."[48] Most wealthy faithful do not see structural injustice, nor do they feel obligated to reach out to those who are in need.

In 1971, Pope Paul VI called a Synod of Bishops and produced a document entitled *Justice in the World*. This synod was of historical importance as it put the Church squarely on the side of those who fight against injustice, on the side of the poor, oppressed, and voiceless. The Synod placed the theme of social justice and concern into the center of the Church's life. The document acknowledges the concept of structural or institutionalized injustice in society. Liberation in Christ includes all aspects of life and not merely inner spiritual transformation. Education is not just learning traditional values but "conscientization and criticism of structures, standards and values obtaining in various societies" and "social reform has been firmly included as an essential element of the pastoral ministry at all levels."[49]

Peace Accords of 1992

The Peace Accords signed in Chapultepec, Mexico, on January 16, 1992 between the government of El Salvador and the FMLN ended twelve years of civil war. The state agreed to uphold the rule of law, implement land distribution, protect human rights, and transfer power to a civilian government. The FMLN agreed to disarm itself and became a legal political party whose members can stand for election. The military was reduced in size, and the National Police and death squads were dismantled. The Accords established the National Civilian Police (PNC), of which 30 percent of the members were from the FMLN. With compensation, the combatants from both sides were assisted to transition into civilian life. Finally, the Accords mark the end of an era of atrocities, economic exploitation, and political repression by the state.

In spite of its limitations and shortcomings, the international community regarded the Salvadoran Accords as one of the most successful peace agreements in the world. In March 1999, President Bill Clinton said that in such a short period of time, "a battlefield of ideology has been transformed into a marketplace of ideas. Decades of struggle have brought a victory to democracy ... no nation has traveled a greater distance to overcome deeper

---

48. Paul VI, *Populorum Progressio*, no. 9.

49. "Critical Comments Selected by Gerald Darring, 1971 Synod of Bishops, Justice in the World," *JustMeCatholicFaith*.

wounds."[50] In fact, El Salvador has made great progress towards reconciliation even though it continues to struggle for peace in the nation. On the whole, the Peace Accords can be regarded as a success because it ended the civil war and prevented further bloodshed and violence. Furthermore, the Accords helped to dismantle the political structure of military domination, thus paving the way for a peaceful transition to a democratic society.

Salvadoran Truth Commission

The Accords authorized the UN-backed Salvadoran Truth Commission (STC) to investigate human rights violations and uncover the truth of what had happened during the civil conflict. The STC received over 22,000 reports of human rights violations, murders, disappearances, and tortures. The military and state police committed 95 percent of the crimes and 5 percent was attributed to the FMLN. President Mauricio Funes formally asked the forgiveness of the Salvadoran people for the atrocities and human rights violation committed by the state during the civil war.[51]

Jon Sobrino called the STC report, which was entitled *From Madness to Hope: The Twelve-Year War in El Salvador*, "the most important official document in the country's recent history . . . a symbol of truth, subversion and liberation."[52] Sobrino hoped that the reporting of the truth would help to set people free so that they could move on with their lives. Not surprisingly, the military authorities accused the findings of the STC report of being "unfair, incomplete, illegal, unethical, biased, and insolent."[53]

---

50. Quoted in Estrada, "Grassroots Peacemaking," 74. American withdrawal of support from the government of El Salvador hastened the peace process. But the US had little credibility to be a peacemaker given its long-standing support of the El Salvadoran army in the past. It was the United Nations that played a significant role in the peace process. Regarding the demobilization of combatants from both the military and the guerillas, see Barany, "Building National Armies after Civil War," 225–30.

51. "President of El Salvador Asks for Forgiveness," *El Salvador Perspective*. For an indictment against the US government and more details of the atrocities, see Engler, "Truth and Fantasy."

52. Quoted in Pope, "The Convergence of Forgiveness and Justice," 814. See Brockett, "El Salvador: The Long Journey from Violence to Reconciliation (Book Review)," 174–86.

53. Estrada, "Grassroots Peacemaking," 440. Regarding the limited success of the Salvadoran Truth Commission's efforts at reconciliation, see Herrera and Nelson, "Salvadoran Reconciliation," 24–30.

In fact, three days after the publication of the report, President Alfredo Cristiani criticized the Truth Commission for not providing a framework for national reconciliation. The president insisted that the people in El Salvador must "forgive and forget" about the painful past. He wanted "to erase, eliminate and forget everything in the past" and proposed a "general and absolute" amnesty for all the perpetrators of violence and atrocities during the civil war.[54] Emphasizing that the country must move forward, Cristiani urged the people to support this sweeping amnesty in the interests of peace and national reconciliation. To avoid prosecution of its own members and out of the desire to have a democratic government, the leaders of FMLN also agreed to a general amnesty law.

A blanket amnesty law was hastily passed in 1993, ignoring the recommendations of the Truth Commission that legal action must be taken against perpetrators who committed crimes. This means that victims who survived and their families could not get any compensation or even ask for judicial investigation. Even worse, the thousands who were killed could not get any justice. So the question remains: can there be forgiveness and reconciliation without any justice?

Justice and Forgiveness

Stephen Pope, a moral theologian, examines the relationship between justice and forgiveness with three different positions: forgiveness means the forgoing of justice; justice means renouncing forgiveness; forgiveness and justice complement each other.[55] The strongest support for adopting the first position of forgiving and forgetting is that it is forward-looking and allows for the building of a democratic future for El Salvador. It helps people come to terms with what happened in the past and protects ex-combatants from the guerillas and the army from prosecution. From the theological perspective, Christians from both sides of the conflict ought to forgive and forget about the evil committed in the past so that the citizens can start a new life. In this case, it does not matter whether the perpetrators felt remorse or repentance because vengeance or punishment belongs to God (Rom 12:19).

The second position calls for justice instead of forgiveness. Because of the extent of atrocities and killings, many victims who survived have said,

54. Pope, "The Convergence of Forgiveness and Justice," 815.
55. Pope, "The Convergence of Forgiveness and Justice," 817–18.

"We're not going to forgive. We're not going to forget. We're going to carry on with our fight."[56] They demand that justice must come first before any attempt to forgive. We have no right to forgive on behalf of the victims who are dead. This refusal to forgive also stems from the duty to protect the dignity and honor of the victims. The families and those who suffered at the hands of the military and death squads have the right to feel anger, resentment, and outrage. Besides, there must be some compensation and redress for the surviving victims if national reconciliation is to be achieved. Accountability is necessary for social stability—there is no peace without justice.

Forgiveness cannot be a substitute for justice. The prophets in the Old Testament insisted on justice for the oppressed and punishment for evildoers. True forgiveness does not mean forgiving without demanding repentance from the perpetrator. Confession and repentance is *always* to be sought. However, even if it is not given, the victim may still be able to offer forgiveness unconditionally. This liberates victims from the power of the offender. Yet, in such a case, the offender receives no benefit from the forgiveness offered. No reconciliation is achievable. Forgiveness offered only benefits the offender if met with repentance so as to receive it.

Further, the government has no right to pardon its own criminal agents on behalf of the victims, many of whom are already dead. The Gospels teaches us that "if another disciple sins, you must rebuke the offender, and if there is repentance, you must forgive" (Luke 17:3b). The perpetrators of human rights violations must acknowledge their guilt before they can receive any official pardon. Justice must be meted out before we can pardon perpetrators. This brings us to the third position: justice and forgiveness placed in complementary relation.

Pardon for Truth

The soldiers and officers who killed the six Jesuits plus their housekeeper and her daughter at UCA in 1989 were given "pardon for truth" when they publicly acknowledged their guilt.[57] Willing to pardon those who were convicted in a fair trial, the Jesuits in El Salvador have emphasized "justice and not revenge":

---

56. Quoted in Pope, "The Convergence of Forgiveness and Justice," 820.
57. Quoted in Pope, "The Convergence of Forgiveness and Justice," 824.

> The reasons that motivate us are the following: Derived from the very first given Christian forgiveness, we conditioned a legal pardon in the Jesuit case on a process of truth and justice. We believe that with respect to these two persons [i.e., Benavides and Mendoza], truth and justice have been sufficiently established and what remains is legal pardon, which we will request in the next few days. . . . [W]e have never harbored hate toward these people, and we have extended Christian forgiveness to them from the beginning.[58]

Since the killers were brought to trial and confessed their crimes, forgiveness in this case does not undermine accountability and truthfulness. Here we witness truth setting forth in motion the application of justice and the offer of pardon in the legal sense and forgiveness in the Christian sense. The late John Paul II too said: "Forgiveness, far from excluding the search for truth, demands it. . . . There is no contradiction between forgiveness and justice, . . . forgiveness does not eliminate nor diminish the demand to repair, which is the work of doing justice."[59] Forgiveness requires the search for truth. The evil committed must be acknowledged and corrected as much as possible. Truth-telling opens the door for genuine forgiveness and justice.[60] However, forgiveness must be given the first priority, because God's love is unconditional.

Perhaps it is relatively easy for the Jesuits to forgive the murderers of their confrères and to work for social justice and peace. It is their duty and vocation as members of the Society of Jesus. But for the surviving victims and their families, and combatants from both sides of the conflict, it is not that simple. Even after the signing of the Peace Accords, many people in El Salvador had little trust and confidence in their government leaders who continued to protect their own self-interest in the name of peace and reconciliation.

Question of Reconciliation

Many Salvadorans rejected reconciliation initiated by the state because they equated it with "forgive and forget." A Truth and Reconciliation

---

58. Quoted in Pope, "The Convergence of Forgiveness and Justice," 825.
59. Quoted in Pope, "The Convergence of Forgiveness and Justice," 826.
60. See John Paul II, "Message of His Holiness Pope John Paul II, for the Celebration of the XXX World Day of Peace," no. 5.

Commission made up of members of the political establishment tends to overlook the question of social injustice and economic disparities. In fact, the Salvadoran Truth Commission (STC) was comprised of foreigners, who, though highly qualified and respected, had little understanding and experience of the local context characterized by poverty and military repression. The STC failed to promote reconciliation because qualified local Salvadorans who had a stake in the country were not invited to participate in the Peace Accords. An ad hoc Commission made up of moderate and respected Salvadorans was later established to investigate military atrocities and abuses. This proved to be more effective in addressing human rights abuses by the military.[61]

Research by Ruth Estrada, an anthropologist of social activism, showed that a grassroots movement that promotes reconciliation at the community level is more realistic. This movement tackles issue of socio-economic disparities and allows individuals to process their own physical and psychological wounds. Not associated officially with any institution, this "grassroots peacemaking" movement would allow ex-combatants to initiate their own practices of peaceful co-existence with their former enemies, such as supporting each other in providing for economic and healthcare needs. Grassroots peacemaking is more effective than state-sanctioned reconciliation because it enables the parties from both sides to fight social injustice and other forms of domination, rather than to fight against each other.[62] Members taking part in grassroots peacemaking can develop a political consciousness not based on ideology but on ways to survive and forge a new life for their families. Due to its widespread influence, the Catholic Church can be an effective instrument to promote such peacemaking and unity in society through a more equitable distribution of resources.

The Church's Role in *Re-conciliation*

As a sign and instrument of reconciliation, the Church must co-operate with God's work of redemption in reconciling human beings to one another. At the same time, the Church, the people of God, are both victims and perpetrators of injustice. The process of reconciliation can take place only when perpetrators confess their crimes, express contrition, and perform penance.

---

61. Guardado, "Outsiders in El Salvador," 449. See also Ekern, "The Modernizing Bias of Human Rights," 219–41.

62. Estrada, "Grassroots Peacemaking," 80.

Although the Church cannot be involved in partisan politics, it must side with the poor in promoting social justice and peace.

In a society where there are profound economic disparities and social inequity, "reconciliation" may not be an appropriate term to describe the healing process.[63] Reconciliation presupposes that there was once a harmonious relationship that was broken and now is the time for a restoration of broken friendship. But as we have seen, the poor have been exploited and many executed by the ruling party in collusion with the military for many decades. The division between the political and economic elites of European ancestry and the *campesinos* are deep-rooted. Ruth Estrada narrates an occasion when Roberto, a former captain in the Salvadoran Army's Atlacatl Battalion, shared a meal in a restaurant with Diego, a former combatant of the FMLN. Diego said:

> Reconciliation doesn't exist. Having former army and guerrilla combatants sitting together is not reconciliation. Reconciliation would be if these combatants were friends before the war, then during war became enemies, and in the postwar era became friends once again. There needs to be a rupture and repair [in order for a relationship to be understood as reconciliation]. What I have with Roberto is another thing—a newly formed, caring friendship.[64]

The majority of the poor people in El Salvador never had a harmonious relationship with members of wealthy families—how could they have had when there were such big economic disparities? The same can be said of the guerillas and the military, the *camposinos* (peasant farmers) and shareholders of multi-national corporations or owners of huge plantations. Political tensions and social conflicts have always been in El Salvador since colonial times. The civil war in El Salvador simply prolonged and enlarged the rupture that was embedded in the structures of society.

Stephen Pope suggests using the word "conciliation" (from *conciliatus* in Latin) to describe the process of uniting, winning over, or assembling the people in El Salvador. He writes, "Conciliation is gained by acts that mollify, settle differences, and create good will. Perhaps the use of terminology here also indicates something important about social priorities."[65] *Re-conciliation* is not appropriate because it suggests returning to the

---

63. Pope, "The Convergence of Forgiveness and Justice," 834.
64. Quoted in Estrada, "Grassroots Peacemaking," 79.
65. Pope, "The Convergence of Forgiveness and Justice," 835.

status quo, which the rich and the powerful had sought to maintain at all cost before the civil war.

The situation of the poor in El Salvador has not improved much and in some cases, the people are worse off than before the Peace Accords.[66] Thus, Stephen Pope says that conciliation reminds us of the social and economic challenges facing the people of God. The Church has an important function and responsibility to facilitate conciliation, which will lead the people to establish mutual trust and respect, and promote genuine communication, justice, and peace in Salvadoran society. As an embodiment of reconciliation, the Church must help the people to discover the truth that leads to justice and forgiveness.

Romero had said that if he were killed, his blood would be "the seed of freedom and the signal that hope will soon be a reality."[67] In other words, a better world is possible in El Salvador.

---

66. See Silber, "Mothers/Fighters/Citizens," 561–87.

67. Quoted in Peterson and Peterson, "Martyrdom, Sacrifice, and Political Memory in El Salvador," 511. See also Howard, "A Wounded Church."

— Chapter 6 —

From Denunciation to Dialogue

Division in the Catholic Church in China

The Vatican has always opposed the atheistic philosophy of Marxism. When China became a communist nation in 1949, conflicts and difficulties in Sino-Vatican relations threatened the lives and faith of millions of Chinese Catholics. Persecution of religious believers reached its height during the Cultural Revolution (1966–76), followed by a more open policy of religious freedom during the time of paramount leader Deng Xiaoping. Of late, due to the rapid expansion of Christianity, often perceived as a threat by the Chinese Communist Party (CCP), a crackdown on churches has begun to intensify. This chapter shows how the Vatican has taken steps to initiate reconciliation and dialogue with the Chinese authorities, culminating in the historical yet also controversial Provisional Agreement of September 22, 2018.

To appreciate the undertakings leading to the Provisional Agreement, this chapter attempts to trace the tortuous history of Sino-Vatican relations from denunciation of communism by the Church in the nineteenth and early twentieth centuries to the efforts by recent Pontiffs such as John Paul II, Benedict XVI, and Francis to seek dialogue with the Chinese government. The desire to engage with the Chinese authorities is very much in line with Pope Francis' policy of accommodation and adaptation.

Like all communist countries, China embarked on a policy of eradicating religion on October 1, 1949, when Mao Zedong established the People's Republic of China. Yet in spite of restrictions, religion continues to flourish. The Chinese government decided to allow religion to exist under its control through patriotic associations. Through these associations,

Chinese authorities attempted to establish an independent Catholic Church. An effective way to establish an independent church is for the government to nominate its own bishops, selecting candidates who are compliant to state policy.

The Catholic Church in China is multi-faceted and continuously changing, but this always occurs according to the dictates of the Chinese Communist Party. It is a pluralistic church with members living in tension and anxiety. Wounded and disunited through periodic persecutions and crackdowns, the Chinese Church, especially its underground movement, has suffered immensely. In spite of all these setbacks, or ironically perhaps because of these persecutions, the Church has been flourishing and moving forward. Guided by the Holy Spirit, the Church has witnessed an increase in members through baptism and an increase in priestly and religious vocations. Foreign priests and members of religious orders who have visited Catholics in China are very inspired by their faith and living testimonies.

The main concern of Pope Francis and his predecessors has always been the unity of the Church. Pope John Paul II in his three speeches to the Catholic Church in China in 1981 (Manila), 1989 (Seoul), and 1990 (Rome) made no distinction between members of the underground and official movements. He addressed the Catholics in China as one community. It is wrong to label them as "official church" and "underground church" because there is only *one* Church—the Church of Jesus Christ. However, in reality, as Cardinal John Tong points out, divisions and infighting exist due to government policies and mistakes from the past.[1] The CCP has not succeeded in destroying the Catholic Church, but it has succeeded very well in dividing it. The spirit of reconciliation and forgiveness is much needed to heal the wounds of the past and the present for the Church to be united as one.

However, inner healing is difficult to achieve because of deep division between the official church and the underground movement, which involves memories and emotions born from years of bitter sufferings. Only the Chinese themselves can undertake such process of healing of the wounds and division. Healing involves the purification of memory, forgiveness, and being willing to move beyond one's own viewpoints, as Pope Benedict XVI has emphasized; hence reconciliation between Rome and Beijing can be a starting

---

1. Tong, "The Church from 1949 to 1990," 26. This chapter is a synopsis of the author's book *Sino-Vatican Relations: From Denunciation to Dialogue* which examines role of the Church in facilitating dialogue, reconciliation, and forgiveness.

point. There are obstacles to be overcome, but these deal with emotional issues rather than theological or canonical principles.[2]

From the West we hear constant complaints about the repressive measures of the Chinese government in dealing with the Church. Yet often people forget that monarchies in Europe were no less coercive and manipulative in their relationship with the Church throughout history. However, while the Church was more accommodative to communism in Eastern Europe, it generally adopted a hardline policy towards China. As a result, those who suffered most were the local Chinese Catholics who kept the faith and were loyal to the Pope in spite of threats of imprisonment, torture, and death. When the Church finally understood that communism is here to stay in China, it began to change its position from denunciation to dialogue with the Chinese government, culminating in the provisional agreement regarding the appointment of bishops.

Threats to Unity

In October 1949, the Red Army under Chairman Mao Zedong finally drove the ruling Nationalist forces out of the vast hinterland and into the China Sea. Mao was the new de facto ruler, with as much absolute power as the old dynastic emperors. But unlike his predecessors, he was determined to control not just the lives of his subjects, but also the inner recesses of their minds.

Catholics faced a grim, unenviable choice: to be loyal to the Pope in the Vatican or to the new Chairman in Beijing. There was no comfortable compromise of rendering to Caesar the things of the world and to God the things of the spirit. Mao and his lieutenants saw the entire issue of loyalty in black and red—every citizen was either one tint or the other, with no shade of pink or grey. Loyalty had to be *total*. Former government officials, businessmen, foreign residents, and even petty tradesmen were all black, hence enemies of the people as represented by the Chinese Communist Party. Even blacker than these folks were the landlords, underworld gangs, prostitutes, and followers of foreign religions. All had to undergo "class struggle" and be transformed into patriotic citizens of the state.

The Catholic Church was identified as a particularly virulent threat to the Party for a number of reasons. Foremost and most vividly remembered was that it formed part of the colonial train of invaders from the

---

2. King, "A Schismatic Church?—A Canonical Evaluation," 98.

late nineteenth century to the Second World War that controlled large swathes of China's economy in the rich maritime provinces. Missionaries from Europe and America came to China under the protection of Western gunboats, and their local converts were regarded as cultural turncoats who, for the sake of a bowl of rice, were willing to forsake the gods of their fathers for a strange, bearded deity of Middle Eastern origin. Worse, these converts—Catholics or Protestants—were seen as joining the white man in the continual humiliation of the Chinese population.

In 1900 and 1901, hot-headed Chinese youths, armed with only a broadsword and a yellow paper charm pasted on their vests, rose in rebellion against the Western forces in Beijing, Shanghai, and other so-called treaty ports. These are lands where Westerners controlled the customs, post, port dues, railway, road tolls, and other rich sources of revenues. Calling themselves the Righteous Boxers, they believed Chinese boxing or kungfu was sufficient to protect them from Western bullets and cannon balls. They attacked missionaries, pastors, priests, and converts, and burned church compounds. The Western powers responded by sending in their own troops armed with Gatling machine guns and Henry Martini rifles, and massacred the Boxers. Survivors were captured, stripped, and executed. Scenes of the Righteous Boxers kneeling in public squares and being beheaded, under the sneering gaze of white men as military judges, scorched the Chinese public memory.

To the youth of China, alive in a bitter sea, the other most workable political solution they could find was Marxism. Mao, born in 1893, was too young to understand the events of 1900 and 1901, but he was greatly influenced by the Xinhai Revolution that overthrew the dynastic regime in 1911 and the May Fourth Movement of 1919 that sought to eradicate foreign influence once and for all in China. Mao's military triumph in October 1949 heralded a new order in the old empire. No longer would the country and its people remain the economic slaves of the West and its cultural and spiritual institutions; the Chinese would rise up to challenge Western hegemony and, hopefully, sweep it aside. "*The East is Red*" was the war cry of Red China, and all organizations and institutions that were still white had to become crimsoned or be destroyed.

The Chinese government regarded and still regards the Catholic Church, with its headquarters in faraway Rome, as an important threat that must be dealt with as sternly as possible. This hostile attitude towards Catholicism is deep-rooted, made worse no doubt by memory of the Vatican's strong anti-communist stance as early as the 1930s when the Red Army was at its weakest and the threat of extinction imminent. As a result, the loyalty of Chinese Catholics is called into question and Sino-Vatican relations have become an emotional patriotic issue, not a serene religious one.

After a decade of collectivism, economic mismanagement, and widespread famine, the CCP decided in 1959 that the Church must be destroyed: "When the political struggle and the forces of production have reached a high rate in the development of their forces, then it will become possible to destroy the Catholic Church. This is the objective we aim to reach and it is for this that we struggle."[3] The Party's goal was clear, and so was the goal of quite a few Catholic priests and laity who would fight for survival at all cost. Ironically, the CCP mirrors the Catholic Church in its emphasis on a hierarchical structure, strict obedience to policies, and loyalty of its members.

Anti-Communism

As early as 1846, Pope Pius IX condemned communism as the "infamous doctrine" that will destroy society if adopted. Pope Leo XIII described socialism as "the deadly plague that is creeping into the very fibre of human society and leading it on to the verge of destruction."[4] The strongest condemnation of communism, however, came from Pope Pius XI in 1937 in his encyclical *Divini Redemptoris*. The Pontiff accused communism of "upsetting the social order and ... undermining the very foundations of Christian civilization." A "pseudo-ideal," such doctrine leaves "no room for the idea of God."[5]

It is important, however, to make a distinction between communism as ideology and as the ethos of a political party, and between activists and sympathizers. If the Church had been thoughtful in appreciating such distinctions, perhaps it could have accommodated itself to the realities in China when the CCP came to power.

The government (Party and government are interchangeable) regarded Catholics as suspect because of their primary allegiance to the Pope, who represented a competing ideology from abroad and a sidelining of the nation's sovereignty. Even after every foreign missionary had left China, Rome insisted on having complete control over the Catholic

---

3. Quoted in Mariani, *Church Militant*, 5.
4. Leo XIII, *Quod Apostolici Muneris*.
5. Pius XI, *Divini Redemptoris*.

Church and demanded loyalty from the locals, which is in accordance with Church teaching. The CCP felt that Chinese sovereignty was under threat when Catholics in China pledged allegiance to the Roman Pontiff, an act the CCP interpreted as "unpatriotic."[6]

When dealing with local Catholics, the government emphasizes patriotism; this is not limited just to a sense of nationalism, but includes support for government policies and the leadership of the CCP. Religious leaders are obliged to teach their members to be good citizens by upholding socialist principles as dictated by the government. Loyalty to the nation must take precedence over everything else. The CCP demands absolute obedience from its citizens, ironically, much like the Catholic Church demanding obedience to the teaching of the Magisterium: "The Communist regime mirrored the Catholic Church in its obsession with hierarchy. . . . Radiated through layers and layers of bureaucracy, this central authority created subordinate microcosms of itself at different levels."[7]

The CCP had liberated China from the yoke of colonialism and imperialism; naturally, it also wanted the Church to be liberated from such bondage. The restoration of sovereignty and national pride had to be carried out in all aspects of Chinese society, including its religious life. The attempt to establish an independent church was a purely political move on the part of the Chinese government without any consideration of the theological implications.

Cupimus Imprimis (1952)

The Vatican responded on January 18, 1952, when Pope Pius XII issued the apostolic letter *Cupimus Imprimis* addressed to all Catholics and communist cadres in China concerning the persecution of their Church. This letter expressed the Pope's great admiration and love for the Chinese and his sadness in learning that the Church had been accused of being an enemy to the nation. Pope Pius XII emphasized the Church's role in spreading the love of Jesus Christ through service to the people, especially the poor and needy. He also stressed the Church's inclusive love for all of humankind, with no distinction or discrimination.

Further, the Pontiff stated that foreign missionaries in China are not agents of imperialist powers. The Church has no political motive but only

---

6. Chan, *Towards a Contextual Ecclesiology*, 51.
7. Madsen, *China's Catholics*, 34.

the desire to spread the gospel and, for this purpose, it was the intention of the Holy See to establish a hierarchy of native Chinese priests in China. The contributions of religious sisters in education and healthcare were highlighted in this apostolic letter as evidence of the Church's mission in spreading the love of God.[8] Catholics in China were exhorted to be brave and to be faithful to the Church. The letter ends with the assurance that the Catholic Church, though attacked, will never be defeated.

Ad Sinarum Gentes (1954)

In October 1954, Pope Pius XII published the encyclical *Ad Sinarum Gentem* (To the People of China). While defending past missionary efforts and condemning the idea of establishing an independent or national church, the Pontiff once again expressed his desire for a truly Chinese church governed by native clergy.

This encyclical was, in effect, critical of the communist regime and supported those who resisted the government's effort to establish a national church. This further offended the Chinese authorities, which led to more arrests and the persecution of Catholics. In September 1955, Bishop Ignatius Gong Pinmei of Shanghai was arrested, together with a large number of religious sisters and brothers. Gong was one of the strongest critics of the communist government and its policy of setting up an independent church that was cut off from Rome. In 1958, Bishop Dominic Tang Yee-ming (Deng Yiming) of Guangzhou was also arrested and imprisoned.

"Tempest in a Tea Cup"

Accused of "counter-revolutionary activities," Bishop Dominic Tang of Canton (Guangzhou) spent twenty-two years in prison, eventually being released on June 8, 1980.[9] These "activities" included support for the outlawed Legion of Mary and for Pius XII's condemnation of the three autonomies movement in China. After his release, Bishop Tang went to Rome where he was received in a private audience by Pope John Paul II on April 30, 1981. The Holy Father had great esteem for Bishop Tang, seeing him as a good representative for the Church as well as for China. In other words, the Vatican thought Bishop

---

8. Pius XII, *Cupimus Imprimis*.
9. Lazzarotto, *The Catholic Church in Post-Mao China*, 47.

Tang would be an ideal person to initiate dialogue between Beijing and the Vatican. Those who knew Dominic Tang were impressed by his character, his sincere love for China and for the Church. In spite of his poor health, he possessed an extraordinarily optimistic outlook and he never complained about the ill treatment he received in prison.

John Paul II promoted Bishop Dominic Tang to the "metropolitan See of Canton (Guangzhou)" as archbishop. Before this promotion, Tang had been the apostolic administrator. Unfortunately, the promotion of Tang by John Paul II sparked a protest from Bishop Michael Yang Gaojian, who accused the Vatican of not respecting the sovereignty of the Catholic Church in China. He denounced Tang's promotion as "illegal."[10] By accepting this promotion, Tang had violated the principle of independence of the Chinese Church. Bishop Yang was speaking on behalf of the Chinese Catholic Patriotic Association, the Administrative National Commission of the Catholic Church and the Chinese Catholic Bishops' Conference of which he was vice president.

The Vatican, thinking that the elevation of Tang would be welcomed by all, was obviously confused by such a vehement statement from Bishop Yang. In fact, it was reported that Beijing authorities had been consulted before Tang's appointment. Perhaps the official church felt insulted because it was not consulted or even informed. They accused Rome of interfering in China's affairs and Tang's acceptance was seen as a private move behind the back of the official church, going against the principle of independence and self-administration of the Chinese Catholic Church.

Returning to Hong Kong on June 22, 1981, Tang told a press conference that his appointment as archbishop of Canton (Guangzhou) was just an administrative procedure according to ecclesiastical practice, part of the Holy See's effort to set up a local hierarchy in China. In fact, Tang had been made responsible for the diocese of Canton (Guangzhou) on October 1, 1950, long before his arrest. However, he had not been called "archbishop" because the title was retained by a retired French bishop, Antoine Fourquet, who had by then returned to Paris. By making Tang archbishop of Canton (Guangzhou), Pope John Paul II was "simply normalizing" his title and seeking to improve the relationship between the Church and China.[11]

A letter to all the clergy and faithful throughout China was sent out on July 18, 1981, signed by the three executive committees of the official

10. Lazzarotto, *The Catholic Church in Post-Mao China*, 133.
11. Lazzarotto, *The Catholic Church in Post-Mao China*, 138

church. Condemning the appointment of Bishop Tang as archbishop as illegal, the letter issued a strong protest against the Vatican for not respecting the autonomy of the Chinese Church. It accused Rome of creating chaos within the Chinese Church and leading people to sin. More importantly, it insisted on the right of the clergy and faithful to select their own bishops. It emphasized the fact that a bishop has great influence on the welfare of the nation and on the political and religious life of the Church. "No government can allow anyone to usurp Church power to the harm of our country."[12] Mentioned in this letter are several countries with which the Vatican has signed special treaties regarding the nomination of bishops: sometimes the Holy See proposes a candidate and sometimes the Vatican consults the civil authorities concerned. However, in the case of Bishop Tang, the Vatican had not made any effort to consult the local church.

In retaliation for the appointment of Bishop Tang, the official church in China consecrated five newly appointed bishops in Beijing for the dioceses of Nanjing, Suzhou, Shenyang, Gansu province, and Shaanxi province. The ceremony was conducted in Latin by Bishop Joseph Zong Huaide, national president of the Chinese Catholic Patriotic Association, with the assistance of four other bishops, in the Cathedral of the Immaculate Conception, Beijing.[13] As a counter-blow to the Vatican, the Chinese Catholic Patriotic Association was demonstrating its determination to run an independent church.

In a complex political situation such as Sino-Vatican relations, the best of intentions might not reap the best outcomes. By promoting Tang to be archbishop of Guangzhou, the Vatican thought that its relationship with China would improve, but the opposite happened. The intention of the Holy See was good, but it acted too hastily and blatantly without consulting the official church, which felt humiliated and as if it had "lost face." Tang's readiness to accept the promotion revealed his lack of political awareness and the sensitivity of his former captors. The government released him because they thought he had repented of his past "crimes." Tang did not consult them when he was promoted, thus neglecting to "give face" to the authorities. Rome might have informed Beijing, but this was not enough for the church in China. The appointment of Dominic Tang as archbishop is a normal ecclesiastical matter and many in the West wondered why there was such a "tempest in a teacup"

---

12. Lazzarotto, *The Catholic Church in Post-Mao China*, 140
13. Lazzarotto, *The Catholic Church in Post-Mao China*, 140–41.

over it.[14] But they forgot that traditional Chinese teacups are actually small and fragile, easily displaced and broken.

Chinese Catholic Patriotic Association

One must not overlook that there were also Catholics who were in favor of an independent church that strictly observed patriotism and love for the nation, instead of the Three Autonomies: self-governing, self-supporting, and self-propagating. For this group, the formation of the "Patriotic Association" seemed to be acceptable because of its emphasis on loving one's country.

Members of the Chinese Catholic Patriotic Association (CCPA), established in 1957 with Shenyang Archbishop P'i Sou-shih (Pi Soushi) as its president, denounced the Vatican because it refused to recognize the newly appointed bishop in Shanghai to replace Bishop Ignatius Gong Pinmei. The Chinese government insisted on electing and ordaining bishops without seeking Rome's approval, in spite of opposition by some of the bishops within the CCPA. Since 1957, new priests from the CCPA had been chosen as bishops to fill in episcopal vacancies. In 1958, thirteen more "patriotic" bishops in six Chinese dioceses were ordained without approval from Rome.[15] Some argued that the refusal of the Vatican to replace those expelled led to the formation of the Patriotic Association and the illicit ordination of Chinese bishops.

The CCPA was set up as an instrument for the Communist Party to assert control over the church in China, replacing Vatican rule with a new structure. This was nothing new, as similar associations were established in other communist countries. The CCPA wanted to show that China had got rid of foreign missionaries and Western imperialism, and was determined to establish an independent church, one that can be Catholic and patriotic at the same time.

The CCPA is a separate organization from the Vatican, but at the same time, also a parallel organization, because it does not change the doctrine of the Church while helping Catholics to be more patriotic. In fact, it could be viewed as a bridge between the Church and the government. At a National Congress of the CCPA in 1957, Bishop Louis Li Po-yu (Li Boyu) of Zhouzhi of Shaanxi province stressed that the CCPA is an organization of Catholics who love their country and also their religion. Despite not being part

---

14. Lazzarotto, *The Catholic Church in Post-Mao China*, 150.
15. Tong, "The Church from 1949 to 1990," 14.

of the universal Church, members must obey the directives of the Pope in religious and ecclesiastical matters; at the same time, they also work towards the reconstruction of their country, alongside non-Catholic citizens. Priests and faithful were told to participate fully in the socialist construction of the nation, such as patriotic movements to foster peace, to encourage patriotic studies, and to help the government to implement religious policy.[16]

Regarding relations with Rome, the CCPA wants to preserve the spirit of the Holy Catholic Church. As just mentioned, it has no problem obeying the Pope regarding religious doctrines and ecclesiastical rules. Nonetheless, the CCPA expressed regret that the Vatican had been hostile towards the Chinese church when the Congregation of Propaganda did not recognize Fr. Chang Shih-lang (Zhang Shilang) as the legitimate vicar capitular of the Diocese of Shanghai. The Vatican had its own preference, which the CCPA posited as interference in the internal affairs of the Chinese church. The Catholic Church in China desires independence, freedom, and autonomy, but will obey the Pope's teaching on faith and morals.[17] However, given the Vatican's anti-communist stand and its historical ties with imperialism, the CCPA can maintain only strictly *religious* bonds with Rome.

In spite of the fact that the CCPA had promised to follow the ecclesiastical regulations of Rome, it actually violated them when it appointed and consecrated its own bishops without Holy See approval. The first episcopal elections took place in Hankou and Wuchang from March 18 to March 19, 1958, when Dong Guangqing and Yuan Wenhua were respectively elected bishops of the two cities. Rome reacted by threatening excommunication of the two priests and the consecrators should they proceed with the ordination.

According to Pope Pius XII's encyclical letter in 1958, *Ad Apostolorum Principis* (The Pope Speaks), excommunication would automatically be incurred with *illegal* ordination. Since 1962, forty-two more bishops throughout China were *illegally* ordained. Nonetheless, Rome did not explicitly mention excommunication when these actually took place. During the reign of Pius XII only one explicit excommunication was issued, and that was to Li Wei-kuang (Li Weiguang) in 1955. Pope Pius XII died in October 1958 and was replaced by Pope John XXIII.

While one may condemn the unauthorised ordination of bishops in China as threatening the unity of the Church and the notion of catholicity,

16. Barry, "The Formation of the Chinese Catholic Patriotic Association," 122–23.
17. Barry, "The Formation of the Chinese Catholic Patriotic Association," 122–23.

one also needs to appreciate the dilemma of the local Catholics who have to bear the result of past mistakes of the Church associated with imperialism and anti-communism. At the end of 1957, there were no more foreign bishops in China and only thirty or so local bishops. Six left their dioceses and others were in prison, leaving about a hundred vacant sees and no responsible person in charge.

Another negative part of history was that many of the foreign missionaries, who were later expelled, had been arrogant, leaving a bad impression that cast a shadow over the Church. The local Catholics were left to fend for themselves, perceived as traitors by some countrymen. Chinese church adminstrators, on the other hand, were struggling to preserve the church from disappearing and had to deal with hard dilemmas, such as whether or not to join the Patriotic Association. Unfortunately, at that time, Rome did not provide any well thought-through guidelines to protect the welfare of the Catholics. They only wrote letters condemning communism and the illegal ordination of bishops.

Many of the early church leaders joined the Patriotic Association as the only strategy to preserve the Catholic Church in China. It was a question of survival. They loved and supported the new China and wanted to contribute to the social reconstruction of the nation. At the same time, they wanted to dissociate themselves from the Church that was closely associated with imperialism and had humiliated China in the past, but they desired to obey the Pope in religious and ecclesiastical matters. These church leaders had always insisted that the CCPA is not a church but a bridge between Church and government.[18] Thus the overriding motive for Catholics to join the CCPA was their love for the motherland as well as their love for the Church—patriotism and faithfulness.

Although there is development of doctrine, as observed by John Henry Newman, the Catholic Church's teaching has always remained constant and consistent—*semper idem*. Policies of Pontiffs, however, do change as historical circumstances change. The fierce anti-communist stance of Pope Pius XI and Pope Pius XII has given way to the more conciliatory policies of Pope John XXIII—the Church has moved from denunciation to dialogue. Pius XII thought it was impossible to have a dialogue with Marxists because Christianity and Marxism have no common language. John XXIII made a distinction between a philosophy and the policies and programs that were drawn from that philosophy. His

---

18. Barry, "The Formation of the Chinese Catholic Patriotic Association," 127.

focus was on the practical good that Marxists were attempting to do for the people rather than on their ideology.[19]

Marxism is indeed a godless ideology that preaches class struggle between the proletariat and the bourgeoisie, something unacceptable to Christians. But Marxism also upholds social justice and care for the poor and oppressed, which the gospel prioritizes as well. The theology of liberation is a good example of how Christian teaching can incorporate positive elements in Marxism for effective evangelization. If we examine the Church's social teaching of the last forty years, it is debatable that Catholicism is the incontestable enemy of socialism in China.

It should also be noted that the administration of the Church has changed over the years. For example, in other Asian countries, National Bishops' Conferences have been established that grant the local church a certain independence and autonomy. In a similar way, the Chinese government's attitude towards religion has also undergone some changes in those years—nothing is static.

This author believes that Rome should admit that Pope Pius XII erred by not recognizing the local election and consecration of Chinese bishops in 1958. The decentralization of the Church has taken place in many countries and it would have been better if Pius XII, rather than condemning outright, had left the matter regarding the ordination of bishops to the Chinese Church leaders to negotiate with their own government. There are references one could draw from if one looks back in time.

While the appointment of bishops is a contentious subject, history has shown that it was not always a Roman decision. The dispute began with the "lay investiture controversy" in the eleventh century between the Holy Roman Emperor Henry IV (1050–1108) and Pope Gregory VII (d. 1085). The "Padroado" gave the kings of Portugal, in the sixteenth century and subsequent centuries, the right to appoint bishops to all the episcopal sees in the Far East, including China. If the Pontiffs in the past had been so accommodating to European monarchs and leaders, why did twentieth-century popes take such a rigid and uncompromising position towards the leaders in China? With these historical cases as a backdrop, Pius XII's encyclical, *Ad Apostolorum Principis*, addressed to China in the late 1950s, seems somewhat harsh and unsympathetic. The accusation by Chinese authorities that the Catholic Church was associated with Western imperialism was not entirely misplaced.

---

19. See John XXIII, *Pacem in Terris*, no. 158.

Ad Apostolorum Principis (1958)

Nothing is static. Rome responded to the illicit ordination of bishops with an encyclical by Pope Pius XII issued on June 29, 1958, *Ad Apostolorum Principis* (*At the Tomb of the Leader of the Apostles*). The encyclical directly condemns the ideology and the religious policy of the CCPA: "For under an appearance of patriotism, which in reality is just a fraud, this association aims primarily at making Catholics gradually embrace the tenets of atheistic materialism, by which God Himself is denied and religious principles are rejected."[20] It implies that under the guise of patriotism, the CCPA violates human rights, dignity, and freedom. The encyclical encourages Catholics to love their country, but they must obey God, rather than men, even at the risk of persecution.

In this letter, Pius XII also condemns the illicit ordination of bishops and reprimands those who dare to accept episcopal consecration in spite of warning from the Vatican. Accepting such ordination would be an offense against the discipline and unity of the Church and "is completely at variance with the teachings and principles on which rests the right order of the society divinely instituted by Jesus Christ our Lord."[21] The right to appoint bishops is the exclusive right of the Apostolic See, which has the mandate to judge if a person is suitable for the dignity and burden of the episcopacy. Only the Roman Pontiff has the complete freedom to nominate bishops. This suggests that the government can participate in the nomination of bishops, but ultimately it is the Holy See that has the final say.

Sadly, this encyclical only encouraged the Chinese authorities to crack down on Catholics who were loyal to Rome. Programs of indoctrination and meetings to deal with them were set up. They were asked to denounce the Vatican and discuss the advantage of having an independent church. On July 25, 1951, "Catholic Reform Committees" were set up by the Religious Affairs Bureau to control parishes and to lay the foundation of a national Catholic Church. The government told Catholics that it was their patriotic duty to accept these badly needed "reforms" for their Church. But many Catholics rejected this movement to establish an independent church cut off from Rome.[22] The underground church and related movements were born out of this rejection.

---

20. Pius XII, *Ad Apostolorum Principis*, no. 11.
21. Pius XII, *Ad Apostolorum Principis*, no. 37.
22. Tong, "The Church from 1949 to 1990," 11.

The Underground Movement

The underground Catholic church is made up of bishops, priests, and faithful who remained loyal to the Pope and refused to join the Chinese Catholic Patriotic Association. Further events led to the development of this underground movement. During the Cultural Revolution, all places of worship were destroyed. Although there were no public religious activities, Christians kept their faith alive by praying at home secretly. After the Cultural Revolution, most priests returned to their ministries in 1978 and 1979. The CCPA also resurfaced and kept a tight lid on the development of the Catholic Church. Some priests chose to stay in prison rather than join the officially sanctioned church. Some appealed to Rome for more bishops and priests to cater to the sacramental needs of the faithful. Rome gave approval for bishops to name and ordain their successors, which led to many ordinations of priests and bishops. Most of these clerics were poorly trained and had limited pastoral experience. In some places, several bishops were ordained for the same diocese, which led to conflicts, and the common good was sacrificed in the interest of clannishness.[23]

In fact, the Vatican had issued an order entitled *Facultates et privilegia sacerdotibus fidelibusque in territoria sinarum degentibus consessa his perdurantibus circumstantis* (Faculties and Privileges Granted to Clergy and Faithful who Reside in China under Difficult Circumstances) that gave Catholic priests flexibility in managing their pastoral work. These special faculties should only be applied under certain stipulated conditions. Needless to say, such an order created tensions within the Church: one party followed Rome's faculties and the other followed the government's religious policies.

The official church stresses independence and the need for the Church to integrate with Chinese society and support the modernization of China. The underground movement, in contrast, stresses the unity of the Church under the authority of the Pope. To understand the underground church in China, it is necessary to perceive the disparate elements in a complex situation that is always changing. To speak of an underground church implies a division in the Church of China, which the religious and civil authorities would rather avoid. In fact, officials from the CCPA accused Rome of attempting to divide the Church in China by authorizing the ordination of underground bishops. In principle, there is

---

23. Charbonnier, "The 'Underground' Church," 57.

only one Catholic Church, faithful on the whole, but with an "official face" and a "concealed one."[24] Nonetheless, the conflicts and rivalries between the official church and the underground movement are real and they wound the body of Christ grievously.

Apart from the official church and the clandestine movement, the majority of Catholics in China belong to an intermediate group who practice their religion openly and are loyal to the Pope. The Patriotic Association is not present everywhere in China. Sometimes Catholics are able to work with civil authorities and are given some freedom to worship and organize their religious activities openly. In some villages, Catholics reject the priests from the official church and prefer to seek out underground clergy. In a number of provinces, some bishops were ordained secretly but obtained approval from the Chinese authorities to exercise their pastoral ministries. There were also bishops who were ordained illicitly but later obtained approval from Rome.[25] Concurrently there are official bishops secretly approved by Rome and underground bishops recognized by the government, creating rivalry and persecutions whereby each diocese claims its own right.

The division and conflict between the underground church and official church is deep and bitter. Underground church leaders preach loyalty to the Pope but often overlook the fundamental truth of Christian teaching, which is love and forgiveness. Fr. Jean Charbonnier, MEP, a sinologist, points out that the root cause of this bitter division between the two faces of the Church is "class struggle and revolutionary activism."[26] Catholics who support the Three-Self Movement are asked to denounce fellow Catholics. The escalation of troubling activities calls for an urgent need for mediation and reconciliation.

For reconciliation to take place, it is necessary to remove the threat of excommunication. Although there has been a breach of communion between China and the Church in Rome, it is not a total breach that would lead to a schismatic church.[27] Pope John Paul II called for prayers for China and spoke of ties with the Holy See as an indispensable condition for belonging to the universal Church. In virtue of this catholicity or universality, each part of the Church should contribute its own gifts to all for the common good. Division needs to be healed; differences can enrich unity. In spite of the many

---

24. Charbonnier, "The 'Underground' Church," 53.
25. Charbonnier, "The 'Underground' Church," 55.
26. Charbonnier, "The 'Underground' Church," 65.
27. King, " A Schismatic Church?—A Canonical Evaluation," 96.

obstacles, the author believes that as long as both parties are willing to communicate, there is hope for dialogue and reconciliation, and that the Chinese can be loyal followers of both the papacy and the CCP.

Letter of Pope Benedict XVI (2007)

One of the main goals of Pope Benedict's papacy was reconciliation with the Church in China. This is obvious in his letter of May 27, 2007, addressed to the bishops, priests, religious, and laity in China. In this letter, Benedict took a conciliatory attitude towards the official church while emphasizing the importance of communion with the Holy See. While he strongly upheld the importance of the Petrine Office, Benedict was also sympathetic to the plight and dilemma of Chinese Catholics. Aware of the widespread persecution of Christians in China and the misunderstanding and hostility of the authorities towards the Church, Benedict expressed his admiration for the Chinese faithful, who were shining examples of Christian witnessing. As Supreme Pontiff, his main desire was "to confirm the faith of Chinese Catholics and favour their unity with the means proper to the Church."[28]

Gone were the days when the Holy See indiscriminately condemned communist nations; Benedict was now seeking friendship and cooperation with China. Nonetheless, the burden of history, past misunderstandings, and conflicts weighed heavily on both the Church and the Chinese government. Not seeking any privilege, Benedict told the Chinese authorities that he was keen to establish a relationship based on mutual respect and deeper understanding: "Let China rest assured that the Catholic Church sincerely proposes to offer, once again, humble and disinterested service in the areas of her competence, for the good of Chinese Catholics and for the good of all the inhabitants of the country."[29]

Benedict assured the Chinese authorities that the Church by nature of its vocation is not identified with any political system. This means that the political sphere and the ecclesiastical sphere are independent of each other—both are called to serve the welfare of people in different ways and

---

28. Benedict XVI, Letter of the Holy Father Pope Benedict XVI to the Bishops, Priests, Consecrated Persons and Lay Faithful of the Catholic Church in the People's Republic of China, no. 4.

29. Benedict XVI, Letter of the Holy Father Pope Benedict XVI to the Bishops, Priests, Consecrated Persons and Lay Faithful of the Catholic Church in the People's Republic of China, no. 4.

they should cooperate with each other. This assurance by Benedict is a far cry from the days when the Church was identified closely with imperialist powers. He held that the Church cannot replace the political order or the state. A just society can be established only through the efforts of the state, and the Church can help in the promotion of justice and the common good. Catholics are taught to be good citizens and the state must respect their religious freedom. The state should not attempt to divide the Church. Pope Benedict XVI wrote, "In the Catholic Church which is in China, the universal Church is present, the Church of Christ, which in the Creed we acknowledge to be *one, holy, catholic and apostolic*, that is to say, the universal community of the Lord's disciples."[30] The Church in China is bound by a profound unity with the rest of the churches throughout the world as all Catholics share in one common baptism, Eucharist, and episcopate. The episcopate is united under the Roman Pontiff as successor of Peter, in apostolic succession. The Chinese Church continues to be faithful to the teachings of the apostles handed down through the ages.

Reflection

In this conciliatory letter of 2007, Benedict XVI revoked "all the faculties previously granted in order to address particular necessities that emerged in truly difficult times."[31] These "faculties" refer to dispensations given to allow the underground church to ordain priests and appoint bishops. This revocation was given as a gesture of reconciliation with the official church and the Chinese authorities. Official seminaries have better facilities for the formation of priests compared with the underground seminaries, which operate on a master-apprentice system. In revoking the faculties given to the underground church, the Vatican was depriving the underground movement of its power while at the same time regularizing the official church.[32]

---

30. Benedict XVI, Letter of the Holy Father Pope Benedict XVI to the Bishops, Priests, Consecrated Persons and Lay Faithful of the Catholic Church in the People's Republic of China, no. 5.

31. Benedict XVI, Letter of the Holy Father Pope Benedict XVI to the Bishops, Priests, Consecrated Persons and Lay Faithful of the Catholic Church in the People's Republic of China, no. 18.

32. Moody, "The Catholic Church in China Today," 411.

It does seem that the Vatican was anxious to regularize its relationship with the Chinese Church, thus following the path of least resistance to allow the official church more freedom to act on its own. This is in line with post-Vatican II ecclesiology that favors an alliance between Church and state. Peter Moody, a professor of political science, warns that the Leninist negotiation strategy is to obtain concessions without offering any in return.[33] This suggests that Pope Benedict's letter can be regarded by the CCP as a blank endorsement of what was previously illicit, such as the appointment of bishops without Vatican approval. Chinese authorities tend to insist strongly on principles when negotiating with foreigners, but once an agreement is finalized, the Chinese tend to be flexible or ambiguous on executing specific issues.

The main aim of Benedict's letter was to forge reconciliation between the underground church and the official church, which presupposes an accommodation between the universal Church and the Chinese government. The official church in China has embraced Vatican II's teaching on inculturation and greater local autonomy as a rationale for its adherence to the demands of the Chinese government.

Since its foundation, Christianity has always sought to accommodate itself to the political and social reality in which it was planted. Although Christianity had a Jewish origin, it adapted successfully to the Hellenistic-Roman milieu in its early days. Its religious practices and doctrinal expressions were influenced by the cultures of Greece and Rome. In spite of their diverse expressions, Christian truths, however, transcend culture. One of the themes of Vatican II was inculturation—adapting Christian truths to particular cultures—which resulted in using the vernacular and other cultural expressions in its liturgy.

This policy of inculturation naturally leads to the desire for greater ecclesiastical autonomy in worship and pastoral practices. This desire for greater autonomy is related to pastoral concern that the Church should engage with the modern secular world instead of closing in upon itself in a Church-versus-the-world mentality.[34]

Keen to normalize the position of the Church, some Catholics have regarded the underground church as an obstacle to moving forward. Much as they admire the underground church for their fidelity to the Pope, they see the underground Christians as self-righteous and intolerant of those

---

33. Moody, "The Catholic Church in China Today," 412.
34. Moody, "The Catholic Church in China Today," 404.

who joined the official church. The underground church is unwilling to cooperate with the civil authorities and condemns Christians who do so. Their strong faith allows them to face persecution, but in peaceful times, they are incapable of seeing anything beyond their own sufferings and hardships, and of moving to a more positive view that would allow them to play a constructive role in modern Chinese society.

The letter of Pope Benedict offered many concessions to the official church in the hope that the Chinese authorities would reciprocate. While the Pope was firm on certain basic principles of Catholicism, such as papal authority, he left room for accommodation and compromise on particular matters to be worked out between the local church and the relevant Chinese authorities. There was no alternative to forging a united Church. Benedict's goal in the letter is unity based on apostolic succession symbolized by the Pope and the bishops under his authority.

The Church has a long history of accommodation to different political realities. In fact, many governments in the West, through concordats, were able to participate in episcopal selection. For many, this is a fair price to pay for greater religious freedom; but for the underground Catholics in China, it is seen as giving in to the CCP. The reality is that some accommodation from both sides of the divide could go a long way to heal the division between Catholics.

Recent Developments

Official negotiations between Beijing and Rome began in June 2015 with a meeting of respective representatives in Rome—a first since 2010. Both the Vatican and China expressed their hopes for sincere dialogue. A second round of talks was held in Beijing. Cardinal Parolin confirmed the event was part of the efforts towards normalization. The third round of negotiations between representatives of the Secretariat of Vatican State and the Chinese Foreign Ministry was held in Rome. This session was regarded as a "breakthrough in Sino-Vatican relations"—both parties agreed on the ordination of three episcopal candidates.[35] During the fourth round of talks, the Vatican proposed to set up a committee to sort out difficult issues. That both sides, Beijing and the Vatican, are keen to keep the channels of communication open is revealed by the frequency of discussions.

---

35. Ticozzi, *The Never Ending March*, 167.

The Holy See is concerned that Catholics in China can live their faith in a positive way and contribute to the welfare of Chinese society. Its main purpose is to foster reconciliation between the official and the underground communities. China is also keen to enter into dialogue with the Vatican to show its openness to the world as one of the key players in international relations. For the first time, Beijing has accepted the role of the Holy See in the appointment of bishops. The Bishops' Conference of the Catholic Church in China (BCCCC) will propose names of the candidates for approval by Rome. Further, there are two more main issues to be solved: the official recognition of the underground bishops by the Chinese authorities and the pardon of the eight illegitimate ones by the Holy See.

Besides the pardoning of illegitimate bishops, the Holy See has gone out of its way to ask Bishop Zhuang Jianjian of Shantou to retire so that the excommunicated bishop, Huang Bingzhang, a member of China's National People's Congress, could take his place. The Holy See has also asked Bishop Vincent Guo Xijin of Mindong to become auxiliary to the illegitimate Bishop Zhan Xilu. Requesting two legitimate bishops to give up their positions to two *illegitimate* ones naturally created strong outcry and criticism, especially from members of the underground movement, who have suffered so much for their fidelity to the Holy Father. They see the Vatican's decision as an act of gross betrayal. Rome hoped that the endorsement of illegitimate bishops would unite the two faces of the Catholic Church, the official and underground communities. Unfortunately, it has served only to divide them further.

Power and Legitimacy

The imperial state cult of China might have been destroyed by communism, but the Party is still preoccupied with state power and legitimacy supported by a particular ideology. Chinese authorities are still "using religion to police and regulate religion, just as the imperial state had done for more than two millennia."[36] Arguably there was never a period in the history of China, before or after the communist revolution in 1949, when the government allowed total free expression and religious freedom, except during the "Let a Hundred Flowers Bloom" campaign in 1956 (which turned out to be a trap to identify critics of Chairman Mao). The central government has always subscribed to a form of state religion or ideology,

---

36. Yu, *State and Religion in China*, 145.

be it an imperial cult or Marxism. For more than two thousand years, "the core ideological convictions shaping and buttressing imperial governance also direct correlatively the purpose and process to regulate, control, and exploit all rivalling religious traditions whenever it is deemed feasible and beneficial to the state."[37] The state always has the upper hand in its effort to control and regulate religion because it makes sure that only "patriotic" citizens serve as religious leaders.

The Chinese government will continue to limit the degree of religious freedom as it did in ancient times under the Confucian ruling class. Like the Confucian elite, the Chinese Communist Party has no need of religion in principle. In the interest of self-protection of state religion or ideology, anything foreign or heterodox must be supervised, controlled, or suppressed. A strong Chinese state is unlikely to tolerate a religion independent of its control. In view of this, the Church has either to comply or contest. In the early twentieth century, the Holy See backed by Western gunboats could afford to denounce communism when China was poor and backward. No longer.

Except for being a moral and spiritual force in international relations, the Vatican today has nothing concrete to offer to China. It has no army, no aircraft carriers, no marketable products (maybe some antiquarian books), and no research institutes to transfer knowledge of unique value for China. However, for the Church to engage in dialogue with China is its most valued political capital as China is anxious to portray itself as a global leader supported by countries in need of her guidance and aid.

Provisional Agreement

Among the most significant results of dialogue was the signing of a provisional agreement with the People's Republic of China on September 22, 2018, whereby Pope Francis lifted the excommunication of seven bishops. As mentioned earlier, these seven were ordained with government approval but without the Vatican's consent. The Vatican made it clear that the aim of the provisional agreement is a pastoral one. This agreement was also the fruit of a long and careful negotiation with an option to review its implementation. As this agreement concerns the nomination of bishops, it is of great importance for the life of the Church and opens up further opportunities for further cooperation. The Vatican's Secretary of State, Cardinal

---

37. Yu, *State and Religion in China*, 3.

Pietro Parolin, asserted that the agreement is of special significance for the Catholic Church in China in terms of dialogue between the Holy See and the Chinese authorities.

Pope Francis is aware that Catholics are a "small flock" in China, living in precarious times. Some have endured suffering because of their fidelity to the Pontiff and they feel that the Holy See has abandoned them. There are others who are hoping for a better future where the Church can flourish. The Pontiff expresses his admiration for the Catholics in China, and for their gift of fidelity and trust in God in adverse and difficult circumstances. Their sufferings and pain are part of the "spiritual treasury" of the Chinese Church and of all God's children.[38]

The negotiations between the Holy See and the Chinese authorities were initiated by Pope John Paul II and continued by Pope Benedict XVI. For the Vatican, the purpose of agreement is solely to attain the Church's spiritual and pastoral objectives: to preach the good news and "to establish and preserve the full and visible unity of the Catholic community in China."[39] This unity of the Church is related to the issue of the appointment of bishops, which in recent times has been marked with conflict, pain, and tension. The bishop is the guardian of unity and the authenticity of the faith; thus, episcopal appointment is a contentious issue when the state intervenes.

The underground church emerged as a reaction against government-appointed bishops, a space that is beyond the competence of the state. It is a clandestine Catholic community, which is not a normal part of Church life. Francis knows that many Catholics wish to live their faith in full communion with the Pope as a source of unity of the entire Church. He has received "numerous concrete signs and testimonies" from them, including illicit bishops, of their desire for communion in the Church.[40]

From his personal contacts and correspondence with Chinese bishops and clergy, Cardinal Fernando Filoni, Prefect of the Congregation for the Evangelization of Peoples, is very much aware of their desire to return to a sense of "normality" within the Church.[41] In other words, these

---

38. Francis, "Message of Pope Francis to the Catholics of China and to the Universal Church," 68.

39. Francis, "Message of Pope Francis to the Catholics of China and to the Universal Church," 69.

40. Francis, "Message of Pope Francis to the Catholics of China and to the Universal Church," 70.

41. Filoni, "Holy See-China Provisional Agreement of 'Historical Significance.'"

Catholic leaders are hoping for reconciliation between the official and underground communities.

Pope Benedict XVI said that an underground movement is justified when necessary for the protection of lives and the defense of the faith in difficult times. This happens when there are attempts by civil authorities to impose ideologies that are incompatible with Catholic teaching and against one's conscience. However, he said, times have changed and we need to move forward and seek "the purification of memory" between the various conflicting parties.[42] This can take place only with the unity of the bishops, the participation of Catholic laity and clergy, and dialogue between the Holy See and the Chinese government. Cardinal Filoni said, "We cannot stay still in a world that, from many perspectives, is running at a supersonic pace, yet, at the same time, experiences the urgent need to rediscover the spiritual and human values that give firm hope to people's lives and create a more cohesive society."[43]

After reflection and prayer, and with the welfare of the Chinese Church at heart, Pope Francis decided to grant reconciliation to the remaining seven "official" bishops, who were ordained without papal approval, and readmit them to full ecclesial communion. He also demanded of them to express concretely their restored unity with the universal Church and to remain faithful in spite of difficulties. Francis sees these seven bishops as prodigal sons who have returned to their father. No law can prevent God from embracing a repentant son who returns to him to start a new life. The decision to recognize the seven bishops was made with the purpose of healing the wounds of the past, restoring full communion among all Chinese Catholics and renewing their commitment to proclaim the gospel.

It is the hope of Pope Francis that the provisional agreement will help to provide the Catholic community with good shepherds. The entire Church in China is called upon to seek good candidates for the important ministry of bishop. It is not a question of seeking capable functionaries to deal with religious issues, but of finding good shepherds, committed to the service of God's people. Francis reminds us that the agreement is only an "instrument," hence incapable of solving all problems. It is useless unless

---

42. Benedict XV, "Letter of the Holy Father Pope Benedict XVI to the Bishops, Priests, Consecrated Persons and Lay Faithful of the Catholic Church in the People's Republic of China," 6.

43. Filoni, "Holy See-China Provisional Agreement of 'Historical Significance.'"

we are committed to changing our attitude and conduct so they conform more closely to the vision of the Church.

Calling upon the Church in China to be united so as to overcome the divisions of the past, which caused so much suffering, the Pope emphasizes that all Christians "must offer gestures of reconciliation and communion."[44] He also reminds Chinese Catholics to love and serve their country diligently and to the best of their ability. As Catholics, they are expected to have greater commitment to promoting the common good and harmony in society. They must help to build and to bear witness to the kingdom of God. At times, this requires of them constructive criticism, but not sterile opposition, for the purpose of establishing a more humane and just society.

Bishops, priests, and consecrated persons are called upon to leave past conflicts and self-interest behind. They must work towards reconciliation and unity in the Church. Francis invites the leaders of China to continue engaging in dialogue with the Church. The Pope also calls upon young Chinese Catholics to cooperate in building the future of their nation with the talents and gifts God has given them. The Holy See sincerely wants to establish friendship with the Chinese people. The present contact between Rome and Beijing has proved to be useful for overcoming differences and for starting a new chapter in Sino-Vatican relations.

At the local level, honest dialogue through impartial listening is required to overcome conflicts between civil and ecclesiastical leaders. In order to ensure that pastoral activities are carried out properly, there must be direct cooperation between local authorities and ecclesiastical authorities. Pope Francis insists the Church is not seeking any privilege, but rather, to establish a relationship based on mutual respect and understanding through dialogue with the civil authorities.

Many Christians are concerned about Pope Francis' kind gesture towards the official church for fear it would eventually force the underground bishops and priests to join the Chinese Catholic Patriotic Association. Registration with the government involves the signing of a statement supporting the independent administration of the Church in China. Peter Barry believes that it would be a great force for peace and reconciliation on both sides if the Chinese government were to refrain from forcing the underground clergy to join the CCPA or to sign the statement supporting the independence of the Chinese Church. The underground clergy should

---

44. Francis, "Message of Pope Francis to the Catholics of China and to the Universal Church," 72.

be given time and freedom to choose their own route and be reassured that the government has trust in them. This would create a more relaxed atmosphere where both sides of the Church could enter into dialogue, work out their differences, and build a closer relationship. Pastoral needs should take precedence over political considerations. We must trust in the Holy Spirit to heal the wounds of the past and to bring peace and unity to the Chinese Catholic community.[45]

The Pontiff understands that we cannot think of world peace without considering the new role that China wants to play in the international arena. He speaks of being "politically constructive" in international relations because he understands that the world's most populous nation and second largest economy after the United States is a power to reckon with.

Such rapid economic progress, though, has not eliminated the spiritual quest of the people. Unlike the West, where secularism has reduced church attendance to the minimum, we are witnessing a religious revival in China, a phenomenon that alarms the Communist Party. Determined to control and contain religion, President Xi Jinping spoke of the "sinicization" of religion in 2016.[46] Xi urged believers to keep their basic faith and core doctrines, and to extract those religious teachings that are beneficial to social harmony and are compatible with socialist principles.

What should the Catholic Church do now? To challenge the Chinese Communist Party is foolhardy, to say the least. The challenge is for the Church to redefine its relations with the CCP, not necessarily by always agreeing with its political values, but by finding ways and means to cooperate, to accommodate, and to build a more humane and equitable society. The Church must work with the government to find ways to continue its pastoral mission.

There are divisions, tensions, and conflicts between the so-called patriotic, official church and the underground Catholic communities, which involve long-lasting bitter memories that cannot be ignored. Both have suffered grievously, but to move forward, one cannot remain bound forever to the past. By the grace of God, through forgiveness and the purification of memories, suffering can bear fruit for reconciliation. The two communities must not allow hatred and injuries from the past to block them from

---

45. Barry, "The Church in China Facing Severe Political Pressure," 65–66.
46. "Sinicization of China Church: The Plan in Full."

proclaiming the gospel. Cardinal Parolin has said, "Certainly, there are many wounds still open. To heal them we need the balm of mercy."[47]

Let the Healing Fountain Start . . .

In spite of its many wounds and scars, the Catholic Church in China is not schismatic because the division did not amount to total breach from the Holy See. It is more of a political problem than a doctrinal deviation. There is hope that healing, forgiving, and reconciling between different parties can take place in spite of obstacles.

Mistrust still exists between the underground movement and the Chinese government-sanctioned open church. But there are signs that bitter accusations and criticism have given way to mutual respect and desire for cooperation and reconciliation. The dividing line between the "two churches" appears to be narrowing. Fidelity to the Holy See is not a big issue now as the Pontiff had legitimized most the bishops from the official church and new ones have been ordained with Vatican approval.

For the new generation of clergy, sisters, and the faithful, born in the new millennium, the division does not make sense. Besides, the new China, a key player in global affairs, is anxious to show the world that its citizens enjoy freedom of religious belief. Acting as a bridge between the two sides of the church, the late Pope John Paul II urged the faithful to love, understand, forgive, and reconcile with one another.

The Church in China today also needs to forgive the mistakes of foreign missionaries in the nineteenth century who supported the European imperialist powers to gain privileges for themselves. The Church ought to acknowledge and confess its guilt-stained past so that the healing process can begin. We cannot return to the past to remedy the mistakes, but we can prevent further wounds from occurring.

It is not easy to separate Christianization from colonization of the nation, when European powers pursued imperialistic conquest with contempt for Chinese customs and traditions. Chinese Christians are only too willing to offer forgiveness if the Church in the West acknowledges their wrongdoings.

Local Chinese Christians also appreciate the selfless love of some foreign missionaries and the good work they had done in the fields of education, healthcare, and the promotion of women's rights. The dark side of European

---

47. Spadaro, "The Agreement between China and the Holy See," 7.

imperialism can be dispelled by the good work of many exceptional missions. Thus, the past can be a gift paving the path of hope for the future.

> *In the deserts of the heart*
> *Let the healing fountain start,*
> *In the prison of his days*
> *Teach the free man how to praise.*[48]

Ultimately, our hope lies in the assurance given by the Lord himself: "And I say to thee: That thou art Peter; and upon this rock I will build my church, and the gates of hell shall not prevail against it" (Matt 16:18). Jesus is, of course, referring to Peter's earlier confession of and testimony to Christ as the rock of faith that is able to resist everything that the forces of evil throw against it.

Do we, today, have this rock of faith?

---

48. From the poem, "In Memory of W. B. Yeats," by W. H. Auden.

Epilogue

In this work, we have explored the theme of forgiveness and reconciliation by considering examples from different countries and different eras, premised on the belief that to forgive is not to forget. This is especially relevant and critical as we examine forgiveness in different political contexts, in countries that have experienced civil war, genocide, and religious persecution: *the past is never past*. The root cause of conflict and violence in society is often the result of unjust political and social structures that protect the rich minority at the expense of the poor majority. There can be no peace, let alone forgiveness, without justice. However, there is always hope that a better world is possible. This utopian vision can be realized if we all play our part in promoting peace and forgiveness, relying not only on our individual efforts but on the power of the Holy Spirit. In some cases, forgiveness is humanly impossible, but "for God all things are possible" (Matt 19:26).

The Provisional Agreement of September 22, 2018, recently extended for two more years, for example, gives us hope that the years of mistrust and conflict between the Vatican and Beijing might come to an end. The purpose of this Agreement is to heal the division between the underground movement and the official church in China. Hong Kong, though part of China, has a high degree of autonomy with its own executive, legislative, and independent judicial powers guaranteed by the Basic Law (1997). This autonomy also bestows on the city the power to self-govern, limited election rights, and a legal system, which is very different from mainland China. In this Epilogue, I have focused on Hong Kong to illustrate and pull the threads together, for at this moment it is experiencing political tension layered upon the current health crisis caused by the corona virus.

China's recent approval of a proposal to impose a new national security law in Hong Kong has exacerbated the winter of discontent by further fueling fear among the people who are worried about additional encroachment into their freedom. Carrie Lam, the Chief Executive of Hong Kong, has attempted, without success, to assure citizens that their rights and freedoms will not be curtailed because this legislation specifically targets extremists, that small minority of dissidents bent upon destroying the city through violence and terrorism. Lam believes this proposed legislation will protect national security and safeguard economic stability in the city. However, many are not convinced. China's decision to go ahead with the new legislation sparked off mass protests after weeks of relative peace while the territory observed partial lockdown and social distancing rules.

There is widespread fear that the national security law will seriously erode Hong Kong's autonomy and freedom, the essence of what makes this city so prosperous and vibrant. Many Hongkongers believe that by imposing this new law, China would be breaching its obligations under the Sino-British Joint Declaration (1984), which established the territory's "one country, two systems" structure. The proposal of this national security law serves only to widen the existing division in society.

This proposal also further aggravates the conflicts and tensions between the blue and yellow camps, which symbolize two different attitudes towards the Hong Kong Special Administrative Region (HKSAR) government. Blue represents those who support the establishment and yellow represents demonstrators with grievances against China, the Hong Kong government and its police force in particular. The original clash took place in February 2019, when the Hong Kong government proposed an extradition bill. What began as a peaceful demonstration in support of having the bill withdrawn evolved into a broader pro-democracy movement with five demands: i. not to have the protests categorized as a "riot"; ii. amnesty for arrested protesters; iii. an independent inquiry into alleged police brutality; iv. immediate implementation of universal suffrage; v. withdrawal of the extradition bill.

There were such serious accusations of police brutality that some people called for the prosecution of police officers who allegedly used excessive force to stop the demonstrators. However, one of the five official demands included "amnesty for arrested protesters." Therefore, if protesters are to be forgiven, should not the police who were accused of misconduct also be

EPILOGUE

forgiven? This particular demand brings us to the issue of political forgiveness and reconciliation in the context of Hong Kong.

Forgiveness in the Chinese community is often more about social obligation and the need to maintain peace and harmony than about religious conviction. The word forgiveness is usually translated as *kuan shu* (寬恕) or *rao shu* (饒恕) or taken to mean pardon. The word 恕 (*shu*) appears in Confucian philosophy suggesting "reciprocity" or "putting yourself in someone else's shoes." In *The Analects*, *shu* is associated with the silver rule: "What you do not want done to yourself, do not do to others" (15:24). Thus, if you do not want to be "unforgiven," then you should refrain from being "unforgiving" to others. The etymology of the character 恕 (*shu*) is a combination of 如 and 心 meaning that the pardon is from the kindness of the heart. This implies empathy and compassion for others. Confucius also insisted that we "recompense injury with justice, and recompense kindness with kindness" (*The Analects* 14:34).[1] We can forgive without renouncing justice: forgiveness and justice can be complementary.

It is possible to govern a society by employing pardon as well as punishment. In Hong Kong there exists an Independent Police Complaints Council (IPCC) to deal with issues such as police brutality. It was responsible for investigating the alleged excessive use of force by the police during the anti-extradition protests. However, the protesters demanded a committee totally separate from the IPCC but were ignored. Last month, the IPCC published its investigation results which were overshadowed by the debates on the National Security Law taking place at that time. Hopefully, eventually the truth will set us free. Police officers should be punished if found guilty. This being so, there should not be a blanket amnesty for protesters or rioters who perpetrated violence and vandalism, destroyed property, and caused grievous harm to others. In Hong Kong, people have the right to demonstrate peacefully, to remind the government to uphold the Basic Law that guarantees the city's autonomy and to safeguard their freedom. Manipulated by foreign powers and extremists within the territory, peaceful protests have degenerated into violent confrontation between demonstrators and the security forces. We have witnessed aggression committed by both sides. Many of the demonstrators are young people who have a stake in this city. They are fighting for a better world.

---

1. See Lai Pan-chiu, "Political Forgiveness: A Contextual and Multidisciplinary Exploration of Reinhold Niebuhr."

Good government, according to Confucius, rules not by physical force but by moral power. He advocated the family structure as the model for society as a whole. Hence, a ruler was regarded as a parent to the people. Carrie Lam apparently adopted this metaphor when she compared her relationship with the demonstrators to that of a mother and child. In a TV interview broadcast on June 12, 2019, Lam said that if she gave into the whims and fancies of her son, she would spoil him and regret giving him what he wanted. Later in life, the son would blame her for not teaching him how to distinguish right from wrong. Regrettably, this analogy did not work. Eventually, yielding to the overwhelming opposition, Lam withdrew the extradition bill, but only after much damage had already been done to property and public services. Perhaps we should say Lam acted wisely, for the common good and welfare of society, in that she finally gave into one of the demonstrators' five demands. Better late than never.

Although forgiveness usually occurs at the inter-personal level it can also be applied in a political context. Confucianism views political forgiveness as an aspect of statecraft or as a strategy for survival. Archbishop Desmond Tutu says that there is no future without forgiveness in South Africa. Forgiveness in this context may not be based on love for our enemies as taught by Jesus but may well be grounded in the determination to move on rather than be paralyzed by the past. Political forgiveness is desirable for our own survival. It is considered necessary if we are to fulfill our basic human need to live in a harmonious society or, if not harmonious, at least one in which we can peacefully co-exist with others, even those who may have historically been our enemies.

Cultural norms and religious beliefs can facilitate forgiveness. South Africans have the advantage of *ubuntu*, which allows victims to see the common humanity they share with their oppressors. By acknowledging its own failures and shortcomings, the Church can promote forgiveness through the sacrament of penance, confession, and reconciliation. A "wounded healer," the Church is not a hotel for saints, it is a hospital for sinners, according to St. Augustine.

Hong Kong is a city with a predominantly Chinese population steeped in Confucian values, so the people understand the importance of having a stable and harmonious society in which to raise families and to conduct business, the mainstay of the economy. Quite a few leaders in Hong Kong from both sides of the divide are devout Christians or have been educated in Christian or Catholic schools. They understand the importance of forgiveness and reconciliation, especially when the protesters are young people with high ideals and aspirations. Although China is hell-bent on punishing the protesters who have broken laws and desecrated the Chinese flag, Hong Kong with its own judicial system could choose a different path by tempering justice with mercy:

> The quality of mercy is not strained.
> It droppeth as the gentle rain from heaven
> Upon the place beneath. It is twice blessed:
> It blesseth him that gives and him that takes.
> 'Tis mightiest in the mightiest. It becomes
> The thronèd monarch better than his crown.
> His scepter shows the force of temporal power,
> The attribute to awe and majesty
> Wherein doth sit the dread and fear of kings,
> But mercy is above this sceptered sway.
> It is enthronèd in the hearts of kings.
> It is an attribute to God himself.
>
> —William Shakespeare, *The Merchant of Venice*

Bibliography

Adorno, Theodor W. "The Meaning of Working through the Past." In *Critical Models: Interventions and Catchwords*, translated by Henry W. Pickford, 89–104. New York: Columbia University Press, 1998.

"Afri-Forum and Another v Malema and Others." *Southern African Legal Information Institute* (SAFLII). http://www.saflii.org/za/cases/ZAEQC/2011/2.html.

Americas Watch Committee. *El Salvador's Decade of Terror: Human Rights since the Assassination of Archbishop Romero*. Human Rights Watch Books. New Haven: Yale University Press, 1991.

Amstutz, Mark R. *The Healing of Nations: The Promise and Limits of Political Forgiveness*. Lanham, MD: Rowman & Littlefield, 2005.

"Apartheid." In *Encyclopædia Britannica*. https://www.britannica.com/topic/apartheid.

Aquino, María Pilar, Kevin F. Burke, and Robert Anthony Lassalle-Klein, eds. *Love That Produces Hope: The Thought of Ignacio Ellacuría*. Collegeville, MN: Michael Glazier, 2006.

Arendt, Hannah. *The Human Condition*. 2nd ed. Chicago: University of Chicago Press, 1958.

Auden, W. H. "In Memory of W. B. Yeats." https://poets.org/poem/memory-w-b-yeats.

Barany, Zoltan. "Building National Armies after Civil War: Lessons from Bosnia, El Salvador, and Lebanon." *Political Science Quarterly* 129.2 (2014) 225–30.

Barry, Peter. "The Church in China Facing Severe Political Pressure." *Tripod* 38.188 (Spring 2018). http://hsstudyc.org.hk/en/tripod_en/en_tripod_188_01.html.

———. "The Formation of the Chinese Catholic Patriotic Association." *Ching Feng* 24.2 (June 1981) 119–41.

Barth, Karl. *Church Dogmatics, Volume 1, Part 2—The Doctrine of the Word of God*. Edinburgh: T. & T. Clark, 1957.

———. *Church Dogmatics: Volume 2—The Doctrine of God*. Translated by T. H. L. Parker et al. 1934. Reprint, Edinburgh: T. & T. Clark, 1964.

Bash, Anthony. *Forgiveness and Christian Ethics*. New Studies in Christian Ethics. Cambridge: Cambridge University Press, 2007.

BIBLIOGRAPHY

Battle, Michael. "The Effects of Christian Mission on Political Change in South Africa: A Case Study—Archbishop Desmond Tutu." *Sewanee Theological Review* 40.4 (1997) 467–85.

———. "A Theology of Community: The Ubuntu Theology of Desmond Tutu." *Interpretation* 54.2 (2000) 173–82.

Baum, Gregory. "Middle-Class Religion in America." *Concilium* 125 (December 1979) 15–23.

Benedict XVI. Letter of the Holy Father Pope Benedict XVI to the Bishops, Priests, Consecrated Persons and Lay Faithful of the Catholic Church in the People's Republic of China. https://w2.vatican.va/content/benedict-xvi/en/letters/2007/documents/hf_ben-xvi_let_20070527_china.pdf.

Beintker, Michael. "Remembering Guilt as a Social Project: Some Reflections on the Challenge of Working through the Past." *Studies in Christian Ethics* 24.2 (2011) 210–31.

Berryman, Phillip. "The Challenge of the Poor Majority." In *Towards a Society that Serves Its People: The Intellectual Contribution of El Salvador's Murdered Jesuits*, edited by John J. Hassett and Hugh Lacey. 171–76. Washington, DC: Georgetown University Press, 1991.

Biggar, Nigel. "Forgiving Enemies in Ireland." *Journal of Religious Ethics* 36.4 (2008) 559–79.

Boff, Leonardo. "Martyrdom: An Attempt at Systematic Reflection." *Concilium* 163 (1983) 12–17.

Bole, William, et al. *Forgiveness in International Politics: An Alternative Road to Peace.* Washington, DC: United States Conference of Catholic Bishops, 2004.

Boraine, Alex. *A Country Unmasked.* Oxford: Oxford University Press, 2001.

Brett, Roddy. "Peace without Social Reconciliation? Understanding the Trial of Generals Ríos Montt and Rodriguez Sánchez in the Wake of Guatemala's Genocide." *Journal of Genocide Research* 18.2/3 (2016) 285–303.

Brockett, Charles D. "El Salvador: The Long Journey from Violence to Reconciliation (Book Review)." *Latin American Research Review* 29.3 (1994) 174–87.

Brockman, James R. *Romero: A Life.* Maryknoll, NY: Orbis, 1989.

Burgerman, Susan D. "Building the Peace by Mandating Reform: United Nations-Mediated Human Rights Agreements in El Salvador and Guatemala." *Latin American Perspectives* 27.3 (2000) 63–87.

Burke, Kevin F., and Robert Anthony Lassalle-Klein. *Love That Produces Hope: The Thought of Ignacio Ellacuría.* Collegeville, MN: Liturgical, 2006.

Calder, Bruce J. "The Role of the Catholic Church and Other Religious Institutions in the Guatemalan Peace Process, 1980–1996." *Journal of Church and State* 43.4 (2001) 773–97.

Castillo, José M. "Utopia Set Aside." *Concilium* 5 (December 2004) 35–41.

Chan, Kim-Kwong. *Towards a Contextual Ecclesiology: The Catholic Church in the People's Republic of China (1979–1983): Its Life and Theological Implications.* Hong Kong: Phototech System, 1987.

Charbonnier, Jean. "The 'Underground' Church." In *The Catholic Church in Modern China: Perspectives*, edited by Edmond Tang and Jean-Paul Wiest, 52–70. Maryknoll, NY: Orbis, 1993.

Christiansen, Drew. "Catholic Peacemaking, 1991–2005: The Legacy of Pope John Paul II." *Review of Faith & International Affairs* 4.2 (2006) 21–28.

BIBLIOGRAPHY

Closkey, Pilar Hogan, and John P. Hogan. "Introduction: Romero's Vision and the City Parish-Urban Ministry and Urban Planning." In *Romero's Legacy: The Call to Peace and Justice*, edited by Pilar Hogan Closkey and John P. Hogan, 1–14. Lanham, MD: Rowman & Littlefield, 2007.

Commission for Religious Relations with the Jews. *We Remember: A Reflection on the Shoah.* http://www.vatican.va/roman_curia/pontifical_councils/chrstuni/documents/rc_pc_chrstuni_doc_16031998_shoah_en.html

Council on Foreign Relations. "The Northern Ireland Peace Process." https://www.cfr.org/backgrounder/northern-ireland-peace-process.

"Critical Comments Selected by Gerald Darring, 1971 Synod of Bishops, Justice in the World." *JustMeCatholic Faith.* https://justmecatholicfaith.wordpress.com/2012/08/19/1971-synod-of-bishops-justice-in-the-world-2/.

De Gruchy, John. "Giving Account." *The Christian Century* 114.36 (1997) 1180–82.

Declaration on the Relation of the Church to Non-Christian Religions. *Nostra Aetate*, proclaimed by His Holiness, Pope Paul VI, on October 28, 1965. http://www.vatican.va/archive/hist_councils/ii_vatican_council/documents/vat-ii_decl_19651028_nostra-aetate_en.html.

Derrida, Jacques. *On Cosmopolitanism and Forgiveness.* Translated by Mark Dooley and Michael Hughes. London: Routledge, 2001.

Dierckxsens, Wim. "The End of Neo-Liberalism, Unsustainable Capitalism, and the Need for a New Utopia." *Concilium* 5 (December 2004) 15–26.

Dixon, Maria A. "The Words Get in the Way: The Paradox of Reconciliation." *Liturgy* 23.4 (2009) 3–9.

Dobkowski, Michael N. "Forgiveness and Repentance in Judaism after the Shoah." *Ultimate Reality and Meaning* 27.2 (2004) 94–107.

Downie, R. S. "Forgiveness." *The Philosophical Quarterly* 15.59 (1965) 128–34.

Doyle, Kate. "Monsignor Juan José Gerardi: A Martyr for Truth." *Americas.* https://www.americasquarterly.org/monsignor-juan-jose-gerardi-a-martyr-for-truth.

Egan, Kevin. "Understanding Forgiveness." *The Furrow* 67.7–8 (2016) 387–95.

Ekern, Stener. "The Modernizing Bias of Human Rights: Stories of Mass Killings and Genocide in Central America." *Journal of Genocide Research* 12.3–4 (2010) 219–41.

Ellacuría, Ignacio. *Freedom Made Flesh: The Mission of Christ and His Church.* Translated by John Drury. Maryknoll, NY: Orbis, 1976.

Elliott, Laurence. "Religion and Sectarianism in Ulster: Interpreting the Northern Ireland Troubles." *Religion Compass* 7.3 (2013) 93–101.

Engler, Mark. "Truth and Fantasy." *New Internationalist.* December 1, 2005. https://newint.org/features/2005/12/01/powerpolitics.

Estrada, Ruth Elizabeth Velasquez. "Grassroots Peacemaking: The Paradox of Reconciliation in El Salvador." *Social Justice* 41.3 (2015) 69–86.

Falconer, Alan D. "Healing the Violence: Christians in Community." *Mid-Stream* 35.2 (1996) 163–76.

Fanon, Frantz. *The Wretched of the Earth.* New York: Grove, 1968.

Fetscher, Iring. "The 'Bourgeoisie' (*Bürgertum*, Middle Class): On the Historical and Political Semantics of the Term." *Concilium* 125 (December 1979) 3–14.

Filoni, Fernando. "Holy See-China Provisional Agreement of 'Historical Significance.'" *Vatican News*, February 2, 2019. https://www.vaticannews.va/en/vatican-city/news/2019-02/cardinal-filoni-on-holy-see-agreement-for-chinese-bishops.html.

BIBLIOGRAPHY

Finn, Stephen M. "Truth without Reconciliation? The Question of Guilt and Forgiveness in Simon Wiesenthal's *The Sunflower* and Bernhard Schlink's *The Reader*." *South African Journal of Philosophy* 20.34 (2001) 308–19.

Francis. "Message of Pope Francis to the Catholics of China and to the Universal Church." *Tripod* 38.191 (2018) 67–76.

Friedlander, Albert H. "Judaism and the Concept of Forgiving." *Christian Jewish Relations* 19.1 (1986) 6–13.

Frundt, Henry J. "Guatemala in Search of Democracy." *Journal of Interamerican Studies and World Affairs* 32.3 (1990) 25–74.

Garrard, Eve. "Forgiveness and the Holocaust." *Ethical Theory and Moral Practice* 5.2 (2002) 147–65.

Geffré, Claude. "The God of Jesus and the Possibilities of History." *Concilium* 5 (December 2004) 69–76.

Gotkowitz, Laura. *Histories of Race and Racism: The Andes and Mesoamerica from Colonial Times to the Present.* Durham, NC: Duke University Press, 2012.

Guardado, Ana G. "Outsiders in El Salvador: The Role of an International Truth Commission in a National Transition." *Berkeley La Raza Law Journal* 22 (2012) 433–57.

"Guatemala." *Encyclopædia Britannica.* https://www.britannica.com/place/Guatemala.

Guatemala Human Rights Commission. *Assassination of Bishop Gerardi.* https://www.ghrc-usa.org/our-work/important-cases/assassination-of-bishop-gerardi/

Guatemalan National Revolutionary Unity (URNG). *Global Security.* https://www.globalsecurity.org/military/world/para/urng.htm.

Gumbleton, Thomas J. "If You Want Peace, Work for Justice." In *Romero's Legacy: The Call to Peace and Justice*, edited by Pilar Hogan Closkey and John P. Hogan, 35–44. Lanham, MD: Rowman & Littlefield, 2007.

Gutiérrez, Gustavo. "Liberation Theology for the Twenty-First Century." In *Romero's Legacy: The Call to Peace and Justice*, edited by Pilar Hogan Closkey and John P. Hogan, 45–60. Lanham, MD: Rowman & Littlefield, 2007.

Handy, Jim. "Anxiety and Dread: State and Community in Modern Guatemala." *Canadian Journal of History* 26.1 (1991) 43–65.

Harms, Patricia. "God Doesn't Like the Revolution." *Frontiers* 32.2 (2011) 111–39, 170.

Hart, Julie. "Grassroots Peacebuilding in Post-Civil War Guatemala: Three Models of Hope." *Mennonite Life (Online)* 60.1 (March 2005). https://mla.bethelks.edu/ml-archive/2005Mar/hart.php.

Hassett, John, and Hugh Lacey, eds. *Towards a Society That Serves Its People: The Intellectual Contribution of El Salvador's Murdered Jesuits.* Washington, DC: Georgetown University Press, 1991.

Hatcher, Rachel. "Truth and Forgetting in Guatemala: An Examination of Memoria Del Silencio and Nunca Más." *Canadian Journal of Latin American and Caribbean Studies* 34.67 (2009) 139–60.

Haws, Charles G. "Suffering, Hope and Forgiveness: The Ubuntu Theology of Desmond Tutu." *Scottish Journal of Theology* 62.4 (2009) 477–89.

Hernández Sandoval, Bonar L. *Guatemala's Catholic Revolution: A History of Religious and Social Reform, 1920–1968.* Notre Dame, IN: University of Notre Dame Press, 2018.

———. "Reforming Catholicism: Papal Power in Guatemala during the 1920s and 1930s." *The Americas* 71.2 (2014) 255–80.

Herrera, M. Chris, and Michael G. Nelson. "Salvadoran Reconciliation." *Military Review* 88.4 (2008) 24–30.

"History of El Salvador." *Teaching Central America: A Project of Teaching for Change.* https://www.teachingcentralamerica.org/history-of-el-salvador.

"Holding Ourselves Accountable." Latin America. Editorial. *National Catholic Reporter* 40.39 (2004) 28.

Howard, Richard. "A Wounded Church." *Commonweal* 119.9 (1992) 13–16.

"Irish Republican Army." *Encyclopaedia Britannica.* https://www.britannica.com/topic/Irish-Republican-Army.

"Is Justice Still a Long-way Off for Jesuit Martyrs in El Salvador?" *America* 222.6 (2020) 1–3.

Isaacs, Anita. "At War with the Past? The Politics of Truth Seeking in Guatemala." *International Journal of Transitional Justice* 4.2 (2010) 251–74.

———. "Truth and the Challenge of Reconciliation in Guatemala." *Reconciliation(s): Transitional Justice in Postconflict Societies*, edited by Joanna R. Quinn, 117–46. Montreal: McGill-Queen's University Press, 2009.

Jasper, David. "Retrieving a Theological Sense of Being Human." *Literature and Theology* 29.2 (2015) 125–37.

John XXIII. *Pacem in Terris*. Encyclical of Pope John XXIII on Establishing Universal Peace in Truth, Justice, Charity, and Liberty. April 11, 1963. http://w2.vatican.va/content/john-xxiii/en/encyclicals/documents/hf_j-xxiii_enc_11041963_pacem.html.

John Paul II. Apostolic Journey to Ireland. *Holy Mass in Drogheda, Homily of His Holiness John Paul II.* Saturday, September 29, 1979. http://www.vatican.va/content/john-paul-ii/en/homilies/1979/documents/hf_jp-ii_hom_19790929_irlanda-dublino-drogheda.html.

———. "Message of His Holiness Pope John Paul II, for the Celebration of the XXX World Day of Peace." http://www.vatican.va/content/john-paul-ii/en/messages/peace/documents/hf_jp-ii_mes_08121996_xxx-world-day-for-peace.html.

———. *Novo Millennio Ineunte.* http://www.vatican.va/content/john-paul-ii/en/apost_letters/2001/documents/hf_jp-ii_apl_20010106_novo-millennio-ineunte.html.

———. *Ut Unum Sint.* On Commitment to Ecumenism. http://www.vatican.va/content/john-paul-ii/en/encyclicals/documents/hf_jp-ii_enc_25051995_ut-unum-sint.html.

Jonas, Susanne. "Can Peace Bring Democracy or Social Justice? The Case of Guatemala." *Social Justice* 25.4 (1998) 40–74.

Jones, L. "Stumped by Repentance." *Christianity Today* 42.12 (1998) 94–97.

King, Geoffrey. "A Schismatic Church? A Canonical Evaluation." In *The Catholic Church in Modern China: Perspectives*, edited by Edmond Tang and Jean-Paul Wiest, 81–102. Maryknoll, NY: Orbis, 1993.

Klenicki, Leon. "Can Jews Forgive after the Holocaust? Historical Experience, Reckoning of the Soul and Reconciliation." *Ecumenical Trends* 31.11 (2002) 161–65.

Klerk, B. J. "Nelson Mandela and Desmond Tutu: Living Icons of Reconciliation." *Ecumenical Review* 55.4 (2003) 322–34.

Kolnai, Aurel. "Forgiveness." *Proceedings of the Aristotelian Society* 74 (1973) 91–106.

Krog, Antjie. "The Young Wind Once Was a Man." *International Journal of Public Theology* 8.4 (2014) 373–92.

BIBLIOGRAPHY

Lai, Pan-chiu. "Political Forgiveness: A Contextual and Multidisciplinary Exploration of Reinhold Niebuhr." Conference paper presented at the International Symposium on "Human Nature, Justice, and Society: Reinhold Niebuhr in the Chinese Context" at The Chinese University of Hong Kong on December 12, 2019.

Lazzarotto, Angelo S. *The Catholic Church in Post-Mao China*. Hong Kong: Holy Spirit Centre, 1982.

Leer-Salvesen, Paul. "Reconciliation without Violence." *Studia Theologica—Nordic Journal of Theology* 63.2 (2009) 162–77.

Lennon, Brian, SJ. "Forgiving: A Doubting Thomas." In *Forgiving & Remembering in Northern Ireland: Approaches to Conflict Resolution*, edited by Graham Spencer, 21–40. New York: Continuum, 2011.

Leo XIII. *Quod Apostolici Muneris*. Encyclical of Pope Leo XIII on Socialism promulgated on 28 December 1878. http://www.ewtn.com/library/ENCYC/L13APOST.htm.

Lephakga, Tshepo. "Radical Reconciliation: The TRC Should Have Allowed Zacchaeus to Testify?" *HTS Teologiese Studies/Theological Studies* 72.1 (2016) 1–10.

Lewis, Bernard. *Semites and Anti-Semites: An Inquiry into Conflict and Prejudice*. New York: Norton, 1986.

Lucia, José. "The Anthropological Function of Dialogue in Political Reconciliation Processes: Ethical Analysis of Ignacio Ellacuría's Thought on the 25th Anniversary of His Death (1989–2014)." *Ramon Llull Journal of Applied Ethics* 5 (2014) 125–41.

Madsen, Richard. *China's Catholics: Tragedy and Hope in an Emerging Civil Society*. Comparative Studies in Religion and Society 12. Berkeley: University of California Press, 1998.

Makransky, John. "Confronting the 'Sin' out of Love for the 'Sinner': Fierce Compassion as a Force for Social Change." *Buddhist-Christian Studies* 36 (2016) 87–96.

Maluleke, Tinyiko. "Desmond Tutu's Earliest Notions and Visions of Church, Humanity, and Society." *The Ecumenical Review* 67.4 (2015) 572–90.

Mariani, Paul P. *Church Militant: Bishop Kung and Catholic Resistance in Communist Shanghai*. Cambridge, MA: Harvard University Press, 2011.

Marsden, John. "The Political Theology of Johannes Baptist Metz." *Heythrop Journal* 53.3 (2012) 440–52.

McDermott, Robert T. "In the Footsteps of Martyrs: Lessons from Central America." In *Romero's Legacy: The Call to Peace and Justice*, edited by Pilar Hogan Closkey and John P. Hogan, 15–24. Lanham, MD: Rowman & Littlefield, 2007.

McFadyen, Alistair I. *Forgiveness and Truth: Explorations in Contemporary Theology*. London: T. & T. Clark, 2001.

McGarry, John, and Brendan O'Leary. *Explaining Northern Ireland: Broken Images*. Oxford: Blackwell, 1995.

McKeever, Martin, C.Ss.R. *One Man, One God: The Peace Ministry of Fr Alec Reid C.Ss.R.* Dublin: Redemptorist Communications, 2017.

McLernon, Frances, et al. "Views on Forgiveness in Northern Ireland." *Peace Review* 14.3 (2002) 285–90.

Menchú, Rigoberta. *Crossing Borders*. Translated and edited by Ann Wright. New York: Verso, 1998.

———. *I, Rigoberta Menchú: An Indian Woman in Guatemala*. Edited and Introduced by Elisabeth Burgos-Debray. Translated by Ann Wright. London: Verso, 1984.

Metz, Johann Baptist. *The Emergent Church: The Future of Christianity in a Postbourgeois World*. Translated by Peter Mann. London: SCM, 1981.

———. *Faith in History and Society: Toward a Practical Fundamental Theology*. Translated by David Smith. New York: Seabury, 1980.

———. *Theology of the World*. London: Herder and Herder, 1969.

———. "Toward a Christianity of Political Compassion." In *Love That Produces Hope: The Thought of Ignacio Ellacuría*, edited by Kevin F. Burke and Robert Lasalle-Klein, 250–53. Collegeville, MN: Liturgical, 2006.

Metz, Johannes Baptist, et al. *Martyrdom Today*. Concilium: Religion in the Eighties 163. Edinburgh: T. & T. Clark, 1983.

Miller, Hubert J. "Conservative and Liberal Concordats in Nineteenth-Century Guatemala: Who Won?" *Journal of Church & State* 33.1 (1991) 115–30.

Millett, Richard. "Guatemala's Painful Progress." *Current History* 85.515 (1986) 413–16.

———. "Limited Hopes and Fears in Guatemala." *Current History* 90.554 (1991) 125–28.

Mong, Ambrose. *A Better World Is Possible: An Exploration of Western and Eastern Utopian Visions*. Cambridge: James Clarke, 2018.

———. *Sino-Vatican Relations: From Denunciation to Dialogue*. Cambridge: James Clarke, 2019.

Moody, Peter R. "The Catholic Church in China Today: The Limitations of Autonomy and Enculturation." *Journal of Church and State* 55.3 (2013) 403–31.

Nietzsche, Friedrich Wilhelm, et al. *"On the Genealogy of Morality" and Other Writings*. Cambridge: Cambridge University Press, 2011.

Nostra Aetate. Declaration on the Relation of the Church to Non-Christian Religions. Proclaimed by His Holiness, Pope Paul VI, on October 28, 1965. http://www.vatican.va/archive/hist_councils/ii_vatican_council/documents/vat-ii_decl_19651028_nostra-aetate_en.html.

Oettler, Anika. "Encounters with History: Dealing with the 'Present Past' in Guatemala." *European Review of Latin American and Caribbean Studies / Revista Europea de Estudios Latinoamericanos y Del Caribe* 81 (2006) 3–19.

Oglesby, Elizabeth. "Educating Citizens in Postwar Guatemala: Historical Memory, Genocide, and the Culture of Peace." *Radical History Review* 97 (2007) 77–98.

Okure, Teresa, et al. *Rethinking Martyrdom*. Concilium 2003/1. London: SCM, 2003.

Olson, Krisjon. "Waging Peace: A New Generation of Ixiles Confronts the Debts of War in Guatemala." *Journal of Genocide Research* 18.2/3 (2016) 343–59.

O'Neill, Kevin Lewis. "Writing Guatemala's Genocide: Truth and Reconciliation Commission Reports and Christianity." *Journal of Genocide Research* 7.3 (2005) 331–49.

"Oscar Romero Bio." *Caritas Australia*. http://www.caritas.org.au/docs/primary-school-resources/oscar-romero-biography.docx.

Pallister, Kevin. "Why No Mayan Party? Indigenous Movements and National Politics in Guatemala." *Latin American Politics and Society* 55.3 (2013) 117–38.

Pastoral Constitution on the Church in the Modern World. *Gaudium et Spes*. http://www.vatican.va/archive/hist_councils/ii_vatican_council/documents/vat-ii_cons_19651207_gaudium-et-spes_en.html.n.1.

Paul VI. *Populorum Progressio*. Encyclical of Pope Paul IV on the Development of Peoples. http://www.vatican.va/content/paul-vi/en/encyclicals/documents/hf_p-vi_enc_26031967_populorum.html.

Peterson, Anna Lisa. *Martyrdom and the Politics of Religion: Progressive Catholicism in El Salvador's Civil War*. Albany, NY: State University of New York Press, 1997.

BIBLIOGRAPHY

Peterson, Anna L., and Brandt G. Peterson. "Martyrdom, Sacrifice, and Political Memory in El Salvador." *Social Research* 75.2 (2008) 511–42.

Petras, James, and Henry Veltmeyer. *Imperialism and Capitalism in the Twenty-First Century: A System in Crisis.* Farnham, UK: Ashgate, 2013.

Piketty, Thomas. *Capital in the Twenty-First Century.* Cambridge, MA: Belknap, 2014.

Pius XI. *Divini Redemptoris.* Encyclical of Pope Pius XI on Atheistic Communism. http://www.vatican.va/content/pius-xi/en/encyclicals/documents/hf_p-xi_enc_19370319_divini-redemptoris.html.

Pius XII. *Ad Apostolorum Principis.* Encyclical of Pope Pius XII on Communism and the Church in China. http://w2.vatican.va/content/pius-xii/en/encyclicals/documents/hf_p-xii_enc_29061958_ad-apostolorum-principis.html.

———. *Cupimus Imprimis.* Sobre la situación en China (Regarding the Situation in China). Apostolic Letter of Pope Pius XII. January 18, 1952. http://www.mercaba.org/PIO%20XII/cupimus_imprimis.htm.

Pope, Stephen. "The Convergence of Forgiveness and Justice: Lessons from El Salvador." *Theological Studies* 64.4 (2003) 812–35.

"The Possibility of Forgiveness: An Interview with Duncan Morrow." In *Forgiving & Remembering in Northern Ireland Approaches to Conflict Resolution,* edited by Graham Spencer, 253–70. New York: Continuum, 2011.

"President of El Salvador Asks for Forgiveness." *El Salvador Perspective.* January 17, 2010. http://www.elsalvadorperspectives.com/2010/01/president-of-el-salvador-asks-for.html.

Preti, Alessandro. "Guatemala: Violence in Peacetime—A Critical Analysis of the Armed Conflict and the Peace Process." *Disasters* 26.2 (2002) 99–119.

Rahner, Karl. "Dimensions of Martyrdom: A Plea for the Broadening of a Classical Concept." *Concilium* 163 (1983) 9–11.

"Reflections on Judicial Views of *Ubuntu.*" *Southern African Legal Information Institute* (SAFLII). http://www.saflii.org/cgi-bin/disp.pl?file=za/journals/PER/2013/67.html&query=%20ubuntu.

Reilly, Charles A. *Peace-building and Development in Guatemala and Northern Ireland.* New York: Palgrave MacMillan, 2008.

Rubenstein, Richard L. *After Auschwitz: History, Theology, and Contemporary Judaism.* 2nd ed. Johns Hopkins Jewish Studies. Baltimore: Johns Hopkins University Press, 1992.

Samson, C. Mathews. "From War to Reconciliation: Guatemalan Evangelicals and the Transition to Democracy, 1982–2001." In *Evangelical Christianity and Democracy in Latin America,* edited by Paul Freston, 63–93. New York; Oxford: Oxford University Press, 2008.

Schirmer, Jennifer. "The Guatemalan Politico-Military Project: Legacies for a Violent Peace?" *Latin American Perspectives* 26.2 (1999) 92–107.

Schrijver, Georges de. "The Distinctive Contribution of Ignacio Ellacuría to a Praxis of Liberation." *Louvain Studies* 25.4 (2000) 312–35.

Scott, Peter, and William T. Cavanaugh. "Introduction." In *The Blackwell Companion to Political Theology,* edited by Peter Scott and William Cavanaugh, 1–3. Oxford: Blackwell, 2004.

Seils, Paul F. "Reconciliation in Guatemala: The Role of Intelligent Justice." *Race & Class* 44.1 (2002) 33–59.

Shriver, Donald W., Jr. *An Ethic for Enemies: Forgiveness in Politics.* Oxford: Oxford University Press, 1998.
Silber, Irina Carlota. "Mothers/Fighters/Citizens: Violence and Disillusionment in Post-War El Salvador." *Gender & History* 16.3 (2004) 561–87.
"Sinicization of China Church: The Plan in Full." *UCAnews.* July 31, 2018. https://www.ucanews.com/news/sinicization-of-china-church-the-plan-in-full/82931.
Sinner, Rudolf von. "Religion and Power: Toward the Political Sustainability of the World." *Concilium* 5 (December 2004) 96–105.
Smith, Carol A. "The Militarization of Civil Society in Guatemala: Economic Reorganization as a Continuation of War." *Latin American Perspectives* 17.4 (1990) 8–41.
Smyth, Geraldine, OP. "Respecting Boundaries and Bonds." In Explorations in Reconciliation: New Directions in Theology, edited by David Tombs and Joseph Liechty, 137–56. Aldershot, UK: Ashgate, 2006.
Sobrino, Jon. "Fifty Years for a Future that Is Christian and Human." *Concilium* 1 (2016) 67–82.
———. *Jesus the Liberator: A Historical Theological Reading of Jesus of Nazareth.* London: Burns & Oates, 1993.
———. "On the Way to Healing: Humanizing 'a Gravely Ill World.'" *America*, October 29, 2014. http://www.americamagazine.org/issue/way-healing.
———. "Our World: Cruelty and Compassion." *Concilium* 1 (2003) 15–23.
———. "Turning Back History." *Concilium* 5 (2004) 125–33.
Social Democratic and Labour Party (SDLP). https://www.sdlp.ie.
Spadaro, Antonio, SJ. "The Agreement between China and the Holy See." *La Civiltà Cattolica*, September 25, 2018. https://laciviltacattolica.com/the-agreement-between-china-and-the-holy-see/.
Spencer, Graham. *Forgiving & Remembering in Northern Ireland: Approaches to Conflict Resolution.* New York: Continuum, 2011.
"St. Maximilian Kolbe, 'Martyr of Charity': Feast Day, Aug. 14." *Catholic News Herald.* May 23, 2016. https://www.catholicnewsherald.com/faith/186-news/faith/faith-aug/103-st-maximilian-kolbe-martyr-of-charity-feast-day-aug-14.
"St. Óscar Romero." *Encyclopedia Britannica.* https://www.britannica.com/biography/Oscar-Arnulfo-Romero.
Stoll, David. *Rigoberta Menchú and the Story of All Poor Guatemalans.* Boulder, CO: Westview, 1999.
Sung, Jung Mo. "Economics and Spirituality: Towards a More Just and Sustainable World." *Concilium* 5 (December 2004) 106–14.
Susin, Luiz Carlos. "Introduction: This World Can Be Different." *Concilium* 5 (December 2004) 7–12.
Tang, Edmond, and Jean-Paul Wiest. *The Catholic Church in Modern China: Perspectives.* Maryknoll, NY: Orbis, 1993.
Thiede, John S. *Remembering Oscar Romero and the Martyrs of El Salvador: A Cloud of Witnesses.* Lanham, MD: Lexington, 2017.
Ticozzi, Sergio, PIME. *The Never Ending March: China's Religious Policy and the Catholic Church.* Hong Kong: Chorabooks, 2018.
Tombs, David. "The Offer of Forgiveness." *Journal of Religious Ethics* 36.4 (2008) 587–93.
Tombs, David, and Joseph Liechty, eds. *Explorations in Reconciliation New Directions in Theology.* Aldershot, UK: Ashgate, 2006.

BIBLIOGRAPHY

Tong, John. "The Church from 1949 to 1990." In *The Catholic Church in Modern China: Perspectives*, edited by Edmond Tang and Jean-Paul Wiest, 7–27. Maryknoll, NY: Orbis, 1993.

Tracy, David. *The Analogical Imagination*. New York: Crossroad, 1981.

"Truth and Fantasy." *New Internationalist*. December 2005. http://search.ebscohost. com. easyaccess2.lib.cuhk.edu.hk/login.aspx?direct=true&db=asn&AN=19414508&site= ehost-live&scope=site.

"Truth or Consequences in El Salvador." Editorial. *America* 168.11 (1993) 3–4.

Tück, Jan-Heiner. "Unforgivable Forgiveness? Jankékévitch, Derrida, and a Hope against All Hope." *Communio* 31.4 (2004) 522–39.

Tutu, Desmond. *No Future without Forgiveness*. New York: Doubleday, 2000.

Tutu, Desmond, et al. *Hope and Suffering: Sermons and Speeches*. London: Fount, 1984.

Vela Castañeda, Manolo E. "Perpetrators: Specialization, Willingness, Group Pressure and Incentives; Lessons from the Guatemalan Acts of Genocide." *Journal of Genocide Research* 18.2/3 (2016) 225–44.

Villa-Vicencio, Charles. *A Theology of Reconstruction: Nation-Building and Human Rights*. London: Cambridge University Press, 1992.

Vorster, Nico. "Reformed Theology and 'Decolonised' Identity: Finding a Grammar for Peaceful Coexistence." *HTS Teologiese Studies* 74.4 (2018) 1–9.

Vosloo, Robert. "Difficult Forgiveness? Engaging Paul Ricoeur on Public Forgiveness within the Context of Social Change in South Africa." *International Journal of Public Theology* 9.3 (2015) 360–78.

We Remember: A Reflection on the Shoah, edited by Commission for Religious Relations with the Jews. http://www.vatican.va/roman _curia/pontifical_ councils/chrstuni/ documents/rc_pc_chrstuni_doc_16031998_shoah_en.html.

Wee, Paul A. "The Role of the Lutheran World Federation in the Guatemala Peace Process." *Lutheran Forum* 45.1 (2011) 49–54.

Weld, Kirsten A. "Dignifying the Guerrillero, Not the Assassin: Rewriting a History of Criminal Subversion in Postwar Guatemala." *Radical History Review* 2012.113 (2012) 35–54.

Wells, Ronald A. "Facing Truth." *The Christian Century* 123.13 (2006) 27–30.

———. *People Behind the Peace: Community and Reconciliation in Northern Ireland*. Grand Rapids: Eerdmans, 1999.

Wiesenthal, Simon. *The Sunflower: On the Possibilities and Limits of Forgiveness*. New York: Shocken, 1997.

Wilfred, Felix. "Searching for David's Sling: Tapping the Local Resources of Hope." *Concilium* 5 (December 2004) 85–95.

Worthington, Everett L. *Handbook of Forgiveness*. London: Routledge, 2005.

Yancey, Philip. "Holocaust & Ethnic Cleansing: Can Forgiveness Overcome the Horror?" *Christianity Today* 37.9 (August 16, 1993) 24–28.

Yu, Anthony C. *State and Religion in China: Historical and Textual Perspectives*. Chicago: Open Court, 2005.

Index

accomodation, 71, 115, 133–34
Ad Apostolorum Principis, 125, 127–28, 156
Adams, Gerry, 60
adaptation, 115
Adorno, Theodor W., 11–13, 149,
African philosophy, xix, 23, 39
Afrikaners, 31
albatross, 32
altruistic, 10, 34
amnesia, 29
anger, xv, xvii, xviii, 5, 7, 34, 43, 65, 70, 86, 110
animistic spirituality, 71
anti-Semitism, 12, 15–16, 18, 29–30
apartheid, vii, ix, 5, 22–24, 26–31, 34–36, 40–41, 149
Arendt, Hannah, 61, 149
atheistic, 16, 105, 115, 128, 156
atrocities, xvi, xx, 1, 4–6, 8–9, 11, 16, 26, 28, 31, 36, 38, 42, 57, 63, 65–66, 79–80, 82–83, 85–86, 95, 100, 107–9, 112,
Auschwitz, 13, 15, 156
authority, 8–9, 31, 35, 51, 55, 59–60, 75, 120, 129, 134
autonomy, xi, 123, 125, 127, 133, 143–45

Bantu, 23, 24, 32, 39
Barth, Karl, 149

Basic Law, xi, 143, 145
"Be a Patriot. Kill a Priest", 92
beatification, 97
Belfast, 48, 60, 63–64
Benedict XVI, Pope, xx, 115–16, 131–32, 137–38, 150
Bible, 17, 38, 40–41
Biggar, Nigel, 48, 63–64, 150
Boff,, Leonardo, 101, 150
Botha, P.W., 26–28

Cape Colony, 23
capitalism, 75, 105, 151, 156
Carey, George, 56
carnage, 29, 47
Catholicism, 13, 53, 58, 68, 98, 118, 127, 134, 152, 155
cheap grace, xvii, 5
Chinese Catholic Patriotic Association, 122–126, 129, 139, 149
Christianity, xvi, xvii, xviii, xix, 6, 13, 15–17, 19, 39–40, 42, 52, 58, 61, 68, 80, 101, 115, 126, 133, 153–56, 158
church, vii, ix, xii, xx, 5, 13–18, 22, 31, 40, 47–48, 51–52, 54–57, 59, 63, 65–69, 72, 75, 77–83, 85–88, 90, 92, 94–107, 112–43, 146, 149–58

INDEX

civil war, vii, xv, xx, 66, 68–69, 73, 75, 81–82, 86, 90, 92, 100, 103, 107–9, 113–14, 143, 149, 152, 155
colonialism, 40, 53, 120,
communication, 25, 50, 55, 59, 114, 134,
communion, 100, 102, 130–31, 137–39
communism, 26, 75, 86, 115, 117, 119, 126, 135–36, 156,
"communitarian logic" , 39
compañero, 72
compartmentalization, 26
compassion, 4–8, 10–11, 17, 19–20, 30, 32–33, 39, 50–51, 58, 63–65, 72, 89, 101, 145, 154, 155, 157
compensation, 43, 107, 109–10
conciliation, 33, 112–14
conduct, 32–33, 139, 146
conscience, 5, 15, 54, 84, 138
conscientization, 107
consensus, 48, 52, 69, 78
conversion, 6, 95, 104–5
Crossing Borders, xx, 66, 69–74, 154
crucified people, vii, 89–90,
Cupimus Imprimis, 120–21, 156

Dalai Lama, 5, 6
Daly, Cahal, 56–57
D'Aubuisson, Roberto, 103
De Klerk, F.W., 35
deceit, xvii, 14, 19
democracy, 23, 41, 53, 62, 72, 75–78, 87, 96, 107, 144, 152–53, 156
Derrida, Jacques, xvi, 151, 158
despotism, 23, 41
deviation, 141
dignity, 10, 15, 30, 33, 38, 41, 63, 72, 103, 110, 128
discrimination, 16, 23–24, 41, 45–46, 53, 71, 73, 120
Divini Redemptoris, 119
Dutch Reformed Church, 31, 40

El Salvador, vii, xx, 67, 89–91, 93–99, 102–14, 149–53, 156–58
Ellacuría, Ignacio, xx, 89, 105, 149–51, 154–56
England, 46–47

Esquipulas II, 77,
evil, xvi, 2, 5, 7, 9, 11–13, 17, 19, 26, 28, 37–38, 40–41, 43, 49, 63, 71, 88, 109, 111, 142
excommunication, 125, 130, 136
exploitation, xvi, 25, 29, 42, 70, 73, 89, 101–2, 105, 107
Extradition Bill, xi, 144, 146

failures, 31, 40, 49, 59, 89, 146
Fanon, Frantz, 25, 40–41, 151
Faulhaber, Cardinal, 15
forgiveness, vii, ix, xii, xv-xx, 1–12, 17–24, 26, 29–40, 42–44, 46, 56–65, 81–88, 90, 95, 102, 105, 108–11, 113–14, 116, 130, 140–41, 143, 145–47, 149–52, 154, 156–58
Francis, Pope, xx, 100, 115–16, 136–39, 152
freedom, 19, 30, 41, 47, 82, 96, 114–15, 125, 128, 130, 132–36, 140–41, 144–45, 151
French Revolution, 54
Freud, Sigmund, 12

Geffré, Claude, 48, 53
Gerardi, José, 66, 84–87, 151–52
ghetto, 3
Good Friday Agreement (GFA), 59–60, 63–64
grace, xvii, 5, 42, 64, 80, 84, 102, 140
Grande, Rutilio, 95, 99, 102
Guatemala, vii, xx, 66–87, 150, 152–58
Gutiérrez, Gustavo, 106, 152

harmony, xi, 33–34, 38, 73, 87, 139–40, 145
health, xvii-xviii, 60, 81, 91, 122, 143
Hobbes, Thomas, xi, xii
Holocaust, vii, ix, 1, 3–4, 8–14, 17–18, 20, 29–32, 43, 152–53, 158
Holy Spirit, 48–49, 51, 116, 140, 143, 154
Hong Kong, ix, xi-xii, xx, 122, 143–47, 150, 154, 157
human rights, xvi, xx, 10, 27–28, 30, 36, 38, 41, 69, 71–73, 75–76, 78,

INDEX

82–86, 93, 95, 103, 105–8, 110, 112, 128, 149–52, 158
humanity, xvi-xvii, xix, 1–2, 4, 8, 10–13, 17–18, 22–23, 29, 32–34, 37–38, 41–42, 45, 62, 65, 72, 82, 85, 88, 146, 154
hypocrisy, xvi-xvii

Rigoberta Menchú, xx, 66–67, 69–71, 73–74, 84, 154, 157
illicit ordination, 124, 128, 130
imperialism, 120, 124–27, 142, 156
inculturation, 22, 39, 44, 133
independence, 48, 51, 54, 56, 66, 68, 122, 125, 127, 129, 139
indigenous people, xx, 66, 70–71, 73, 76, 79, 86, 90
inequalities, 36, 53
insights, 37, 51
Irish Republic, 53, 60
Irish Republican Army (IRA), 47–48, 54, 153

Jesuits, xx, 90, 93–94, 110, 111, 150, 152
John Paul II, Pope, 13, 16, 52, 81, 99–100, 106, 111, 115–16, 121–22, 130, 137, 141, 150, 153
Jonker, Willie, 31
Judaism, xvi, xviii, 6, 13–15, 17–19, 30, 151–52, 156
judicial system, 36, 73, 147
Jung, Mo Sung, 157
Justice in the World, 107, 151
justice, ix, xv-xvii, xix-xx, 3, 6–7, 11, 17–18, 20, 27–30, 33, 36, 38, 39, 42–44, 50, 52–53, 56, 62, 64, 71–73, 77–79, 81, 83, 85–88, 90, 92, 94, 98–100, 102–3, 105–11, 113–14, 127, 132, 143, 145, 147, 151–54, 156

King, Martin Luther, 37, 45, 73
Kingdom of God, 42, 103, 139
Kolbe, Maximilian, 100, 157

La Matanza, 91
La Violencia, 74

Lam, Carrie, 144, 146
legitimacy, 135
liberation, xx, 39, 41–42, 75, 90, 92, 101–2, 106–8, 127, 152, 156
liturgy, 133, 151
love, xviii, 5, 15–16, 19, 31, 37–38, 42, 46, 66, 95, 97, 102, 105–6, 111, 120–22, 124, 126, 128, 130, 139, 141, 146, 149–50, 154–55
loyalists, xix, 45, 48, 53

Mandela United Football Club, 27
Mandela, Nelson, 5, 22, 25–27, 29, 34–35, 37–38, 41–42, 153
Mandela, Winnie, 26–28, 38
Mao, Zedong, 115, 117–18, 135
market, 69
martyrdom, xx, 90–93, 96–102, 114, 150, 155–56
martyrs, 94, 97–103, 153–54, 157
Marxism, 75, 105, 115, 118, 126–27, 136
materialism, 105, 128
Maya, xx, 66–67, 70–71, 74
Mayan, 67–68, 70–72, 74, 79, 82, 155
mediation, 33, 53, 80, 130
Memoria del Silencio, 82–84
memory, 2, 9, 11, 14, 42, 61–62, 68, 71, 82–83, 85, 114, 116, 118, 138, 142, 149, 155–56
mercy, xviii, 4–5, 18, 20, 29–30, 81, 88, 95, 101, 141, 147
Metz, Johann Baptist, 154–55
Mexico, 67, 70, 107
military, xvii, xx, 26, 29, 47, 54, 66, 69–70, 72–73, 75–79, 82–83, 85–88, 90–95, 97–100, 103–5, 107–8, 110, 112–13, 118, 152–53, 156
Mit brennender Sorge, 15
Mozote Massacre, 103

nation, xix, 22–26, 28–29, 31, 34–38, 43–44, 51–54, 60–61, 66, 68–70, 76, 79, 81, 89–90, 92, 94, 102, 107–8, 115, 120, 123–26, 139–41, 158
National Commission of Reconciliation (CNR), 77, 79, 122

INDEX

National Security Law, ix, xi, 144–45
nationalists, xix, 1, 45, 47, 51, 53–54, 56–57, 59
Nazism, 12, 15–16
New Testament, xviii, 15, 74
Nietzsche, Friedrich Wilhelm, xvii, 155
No Future without Forgiveness, vii, xvi, xix, 22, 26, 29–33, 35–38, 39–40, 42, 87, 146, 158
Nobel Peace Prize, xx, 30, 60, 66, 69–74
Northern Ireland, ix, xix, 45–46, 48–51, 53–56, 58–61, 63–65, 74, 151, 154, 156–58
Nostra Aetate, 13, 16, 151, 155
Novo Millennio Ineunte, 100, 153
nunca más, vii, 66, 68, 82–86, 88, 152
Nuremberg model, 29–30

Old Testament, xviii, 110
oligarchy, 82, 94, 96, 98, 104

pain, ix, xviii, 2, 7, 9, 11, 42–43, 72, 83–84, 86–87, 137
Paisley, Ian, 48, 60
pandemic, ix, xii
pardon, xviii, 11, 18, 29, 56, 89–90, 97, 102, 104, 110–11, 135, 145
Parnell, Charles Stewart, 47
Parolin, Pietro, 134, 137, 141
patrimony, 16
patriotism, 120, 124, 126, 128
Paul VI, Pope, 106–107, 151, 155
Peace Accords, 68–69, 74, 77, 79–82, 87, 107–8, 111–12, 114
peace, vii, ix, x, xii, xv, xix-xx, 2–4, 11, 18, 30, 32, 35–36, 38, 45–52, 55–82, 86–88, 90, 94, 96, 99–100, 102–3, 105–14, 125, 139–40, 143–45, 150–56, 158
penance, 6, 17, 112, 146
Peres, Shimon, 30
perpetrator, xvi, 9–10, 20, 28, 30, 34, 36–37, 39, 42–43, 62–64, 82, 110
phantom, 29
Pius XII, Pope, 16, 120–21, 125–28, 156
political forgiveness, 61–63, 145–46, 149, 154

popular piety, 68
Populorum Progressio, 106–7, 155
poverty, 36, 48, 89, 104, 106, 112
power, vii, xv, 6–8, 10–12, 20, 23, 26, 29, 35, 45–47, 49, 53, 59–60, 68–70, 74–76, 80, 83, 91, 94, 103, 107, 110, 117, 119, 123, 132, 135, 140, 143, 146–47, 152, 157,
praxis, 42, 156
prejudice, 12–13, 46, 48, 50, 154
propaganda, 1, 8, 12, 15, 26, 125
Protestantism, 53, 58, 68
Provisional Agreement, xx, 48, 115, 117, 136–38, 143, 151
purification of memory, 2, 42, 116, 138, 140

racism, 15–16, 67, 71, 73–75, 88, 152
Rahner, Karl, 99, 156
reconciliation, ix, xii, xv-xx, 4, 8–9, 12, 20, 22, 26, 29–31, 33–37, 39–43, 46, 50–51, 56, 58–61, 63–64, 66–67, 70–71, 77, 79–80, 82–90, 95–96, 98, 106, 108–16, 130–33, 135, 138–41, 143, 145–47, 150–58
Red Army, 117, 119
Redemptorist, 45, 48, 154
rehabilitation, 37, 81
Reid, Alec, xix, 45, 48–56, 72, 154
remembrance, xix, 1, 11–12, 42, 63
reparation, 32, 37, 43, 81, 84,
republicanism, 54
resentment, xv, xvii–xviii, 7, 10, 23, 34, 43, 47, 64–65, 105, 110
restoration, xvi, xviii, 30, 44, 83, 113, 120
restorative justice, xvi, 36, 38, 42–43, 62
retributive justice, 20, 33, 36, 38, 43, 62
Righteous Boxers, 118
Robben Island, 35
Rome, 13, 94, 116, 118–19, 121–30, 133–35, 139,
Romero, Óscar Arnulfo, xx, 89–90, 93–100, 102–6, 114, 149–50, 155, 157

Santayana, George, xv, 30
secular, xviii, 4, 16, 42, 79, 83, 98, 103, 133

INDEX

Secularization, xvii
self-interest, xvii, 104, 111, 139
Sermon on the Mount, 20
Shriver, Donald, 61–62, 157,
Sinarum Gentem, 121
Sinn Féin, 48, 51–54, 56, 59–60
Sino-British Joint Declaration (1984), 144
Sino-Vatican relations, 115–16, 119, 123, 134, 139, 155
Smyth, Geraldine, 58, 157
Sobrino, Jon, 89–90, 100–101, 108, 157
solidarity, 20, 38, 95, 102
South Africa, vii, ix, xix, 5, 22–32, 34–36, 38–44, 61, 64, 146, 150, 152, 158
Strasbourg, 16
structures, xix, 58, 81, 89, 91, 95–96, 102, 104–7, 113, 143
Summi Pontificatus, 15
Sunflowers, The, xix, 2–3, 20
synergy, 79

Teshuvah, 17–19
torture, 27, 29, 76, 81, 86, 88, 96, 117
tragedy, 14, 26, 28, 85, 154
Troubles, The, 47, 51, 57–59, 63–64, 74, 151
Truth and Reconciliation Commission (TRC), xvi, 22, 26, 29–31, 35, 39, 64, 111, 155

Tutu, Desmond, 22–23, 25–26, 28–43, 49, 146, 150, 152–53, 158

ubuntu, xix, 22–23, 32–34, 36, 39, 42–43, 146, 150, 152, 156
Unionist, 48–49, 51–52, 56–60
United Nations, xvi, 71, 78, 80, 108, 150
unity, 15, 25, 52, 72–73, 77, 112, 116–17, 125, 128–32, 134, 137–40, 152
Ut Unum Sint, 99–100, 153
utopia, 72, 150, 151

Vatican II, 79, 95, 104, 133
Vengeance, 32, 48, 62–63, 109
Verwoerd, Hendrik, 24
victim, xvi-xvii, 5, 7–10, 28, 36, 42–43, 49, 62–63, 82, 110
victory, 33, 71, 77, 84–85, 107
virtue, xvi-xvii, xix, 5, 19, 23, 43, 63, 130

White Warrior Union, 100
Wiesenthal, Simon, 1–4, 6–11, 158
Wilfred, Felix, 158
wisdom, 39, 74
Wretched of the Earth, The, 25, 41, 151

Yad Vashem, 11, 30

www.ingramcontent.com/pod-product-compliance
Lightning Source LLC
Chambersburg PA
CBHW050809160426
43192CB00010B/1700